Your Official America Online® Guide to Genealogy Online

2nd Edition

Your Official America Online® Guide to Genealogy Online

2nd Edition

by Matthew L. Helm and
April Leigh Helm

AOL Press

Dulles, VA

Your Official America Online® Guide to Genealogy Online, 2nd Edition

Published by

AOL Press

An imprint of IDG Books Worldwide, Inc.

An International Data Group Company

919 E. Hillsdale Blvd., Suite 400

Foster City, CA 94404

www.aol.com (America Online Web site)

Library of Congress Control Number: 00-104770

ISBN: 0-7645-3497-1

Printed in the United States of America

10 9 8 7 6 5 4 3 2 1

2V/QT/QX/QQ/IN

Distributed in the United States by IDG Books Worldwide, Inc. and America Online, Inc.

For general information on IDG Books Worldwide's books in the U.S., please call our Consumer Customer Service department at 800-762-2974. For reseller information, including discounts and premium sales, please call our Reseller Customer Service department at 800-434-3422.

 is a trademark of America Online, Inc.

 is a registered trademark or trademark under exclusive license to IDG Books Worldwide, Inc. from International Data Group, Inc. in the United States and/or other countries.

Welcome to AOL Press™

AOL Press books provide timely guides to getting the most out of your online life. AOL Press was formed as part of the AOL family to create a complete series of official references for using America Online as well as the entire Internet — all designed to help you enjoy a fun, easy, and rewarding online experience.

AOL Press is an exciting partnership between two companies at the forefront of the knowledge and communications revolution — AOL and IDG Books Worldwide, Inc. AOL is committed to quality, ease of use, and value, and IDG Books excels at helping people understand technology.

To meet these high standards, all our books are authored by experts with the full participation of and exhaustive review by AOL's own development, technical, managerial, and marketing staff. Together, AOL and IDG Books have implemented an ambitious publishing program to develop new publications that serve every aspect of your online life.

We hope you enjoy reading this AOL Press title and find it useful. We welcome your feedback at AOL Keyword: **Contact Shop Direct** so we can keep providing information the way you want it.

About the Authors

Matthew L. Helm holds a bachelor's degree in History and a master's degree in Library and Information Science from the University of Illinois at Urbana-Champaign. Before working for FamilyToolbox.net, Matthew worked as a labor relations specialist for the U.S. Department of Education, the Director of Human Resource Information Systems for the University of Illinois (all three campuses), and Director of Online Editorial Content at Ancestry.com. He is the co-author of *Genealogy Online For Dummies,* 2nd Edition, *Family Tree Maker For Dummies, Tracing Your Family Roots Online,* and *Get Your Degree Online.* Matthew is the publisher of the *Journal of Online Genealogy,* past co-managing editor of *Genealogical Computing,* and past Internet columnist for *Ancestry* magazine. He is also a member of the Board of Directors of GENTECH, Inc. (a non-profit organization promoting the use of technology in the field of genealogy), GENTECH Education Manager, and a member of the Association of Professional Genealogists.

April Leigh Helm holds a bachelor's degree in Journalism and a master's degree in Higher Education Administration from the University of Illinois at Urbana-Champaign. Before working for FamilyToolbox.net, April worked as a policy analyst in the Office of Postsecondary Education for the U.S. Department of Education and in various professional and supervisory positions in the financial aid and student employment office at the University of Illinois at Urbana-Champaign. She is the co-author of *Genealogy Online For Dummies,* 2nd Edition, *Family Tree Maker For Dummies, Tracing Your Family Roots Online,* and *Get Your Degree Online.* April is the editor of the *Journal of Online Genealogy* and the past co-managing editor of *Genealogical Computing* magazine. She also serves as the Communications Manager for GENTECH, Inc. (a non-profit organization promoting the use of technology in the field of genealogy), national public relations chair for GENTECH2001, and is a member of the Association of Professional Genealogists.

Credits

Acknowledgments

Our greatest thanks to our daughter, Brynn Kyleakin, for all her "help" while we were writing this book. Without her gracious understanding and patience, there's no way we could've completed this project.

A special thanks to Lisa Swayne who sought us out to write our very first book and has been there for us ever since.

And thanks to Nicole Haims, Kim Darosett, Barry Childs-Helton, Kathy Yankton, and all the folks at IDG Books Worldwide, Inc. and America Online, who envisioned this book and then pushed to get it into print. We appreciate all of their diligence and the long hours they've spent seeing this project through to fruition.

Dedication

For Brynn Kyleakin Helm — the budding twig on our own family tree.

And for all of the online genealogists who make researching via the Internet fun and successful.

Contents at a Glance

Table of Contents

Introduction

Whether you're new to America Online (AOL), to genealogy, or new to both, this book is intended to help you research your family history with the aid of your computer and the Internet. While it focuses largely on the resources available through AOL, it also offers instructions about how to use many non-AOL tools too.

Allow us to give you a sneak peek . . .

What's Inside

This book has six actual parts, although only four are formally titled. The Quick Start (unnumbered but handy) gives you a heads-up on AOL and the search functions of its two main genealogical forums. Then the four official parts present groups of several related chapters, each part covering a major aspect of doing online geneological research on AOL. Lastly, a glossary gives you a place to turn should you encounter a word or term you can't recall or don't understand. Let's look at each part (except the glossary) in a little more detail.

Quick Start

We've provided a Quick Start section to give you a little practice with your computer and AOL. Quick Start explains how AOL works and the two main keywords you need to know for your genealogical research. It also walks you through using the two main genealogical forums on AOL — the Genealogy Forum and the Genealogy/Family History area.

Part I: Beginning Your Journey into the Past

If you're new to researching your genealogy online and offline, make sure you don't skip over this part! It covers the basics of sound research, setting goals, finding resources on AOL, and using various communication tools (including e-mail, message boards, mailing lists, and chat rooms). There's also a chapter that walks you through the process of selecting an ancestor to research online, and then doing so.

Things you can do when you read this part . . .

- ▶ Develop your own research plan
- ▶ Find beginner tips and help on AOL
- ▶ Use e-mail to communicate effectively with others
- ▶ Practice netiquette when posting anything online
- ▶ Post information to a message board, mailing list, or newsgroup
- ▶ Participate in a chat session
- ▶ Select an ancestor to research by name
- ▶ Find various resources online using that ancestor's name

Part II: Gathering and Sharing Online

This section delves into the nitty-gritty, so to speak. It's the part to turn to when you're looking for explanations of record types, as well as how and where to find actual records, indices, or other information about records online. You'll also find useful information about including photographs and other multimedia objects in your genealogy, and find online sources of up-to-date information about issues and events in online genealogy.

Things you can do when you read this part . . .

- ▶ Search an online database to see what kinds of records are available that pertain to your ancestors
- ▶ Use "You've Got Pictures"
- ▶ Find online newsletters, e-zines, and other sources of news
- ▶ Set up your own News Profiles at AOL

Part III: Storing Your Ancestral Treasures

This part is primarily concerned with using genealogical databases and other computer programs to store, manipulate, and use your genealogical data.

Things you can do when you read this part . . .

▶ Test demonstration programs

▶ Choose a genealogical database

▶ Set up family files in two different genealogical databases

▶ Use photo and graphics software

Part IV: Fun Ways to Share Your History

We always save the best for last, right? This part provides everything you need to know to share your genealogical treasures with other researchers and family members, as well as the rest of the world. It explains what a GEDCOM is, as well as the standard charts and reports that you'll encounter in genealogy and want to produce yourself. There's also information about creating your own Web page or family newsletter containing your genealogical findings and challenges. And we even cover how to plan your family reunion when the time comes that you're ready to meet face-to-face with some of your online researching buddies.

Things you can do upon reading this part . . .

▶ Generate a family tree (Pedigree Chart) using a genealogical database

▶ Create your own Web page on AOL

▶ Publish a family newsletter online

▶ Plan a family reunion

Conventions

Throughout this book, you'll find figures to illustrate sites that we're discussing and icons to help you navigate and find additional information. You'll see six standard icons:

A Tip is a piece of advice or a handy secret that we're offering you.

A Note is just a simple piece of information about which we think you should be aware.

Cross-Reference

A Cross-Reference notifies you of other places in this book where you can get additional information about a subject.

 Definition

Here you'll find an explanation for a term that we're using.

 Find It Online

Find It Online provides the name and URL for an Internet resource discussed or referred to in the text.

 Caution

Caution warns you not to try something or tells you of possible negative consequences.

A re you new to AOL or genealogy — or both? Then you've come to the right place! We want to introduce you to the large genealogical community available at AOL. It is ready, willing, and able to support and help you in your family history endeavors. AOL provides many tools for finding and communicating with other researchers, as well as World Wide Web capabilities so you can surf for information about your family. Now the questions arise: How do you find the genealogical community on AOL? And basically how does it work?

AOL, Members, and Partners

Before we get too far into explaining what you can expect to find on AOL, we need to tell you about the players — those whose names you see throughout this chapter and the rest of the book. Here is a brief list:

▶ **AOL:** We think it's safe to assume that you know that AOL stands for America Online and that you know a little about the service. AOL is the most popular and well-known Internet service provider available. But more importantly, AOL is an on-line community where people can meet and communicate about almost anything.

Definition

An *Internet service provider (ISP)* is an organization that gives people access to the Internet. It can be a company, a school, or another type of organization. Typically, an ISP provides Internet access through dialup services; you use your computer's modem to connect your computer with the ISP's computers and, in turn, connect to the Internet.

Definition

The *Internet* is a collection of computer networks that are connected with backbones (high-speed data lines).

Definition

A *link* (also called a hyperlink) is a bit of text or an object (such as an icon or button) that you can click to jump to another area. You can go to another location in AOL, to another Web site, or to another Internet resource. Links that appear in text usually are a different color.

▶ **Members:** When we refer to *members,* we mean people who subscribe to AOL. Most likely, you're already a member or considering becoming one, and that's why you're reading this book. (If you haven't yet subscribed to AOL, the disk at the back of this book gets you started with a free trial membership.) In your genealogical research, you interact with other members in various forums on AOL, and you may even encounter AOL members in online venues outside of AOL. Most members who are active in the genealogical community are friendly and excited to share information and success stories.

▶ **Partners:** *Partners* are companies or organizations that work with AOL to provide specific information or resources for AOL members. Some of these resources are restricted only to AOL members and are unavailable to other Web surfers and genealogical researchers. Two main partners that you're likely to encounter in the genealogy arena are GenealogyForum.com (also known as the Golden Gate Genealogy Forum) and Ancestry.com (whose parent company is MyFamily.com).

Navigating AOL

You can easily navigate AOL three different ways:

▶ **Buttons and links:** A menu system on the left side of the Welcome screen, shown in Figure Q-1, contains buttons that link to various areas within AOL. Also, in each of the navigation windows (including Welcome), you can find text links that enable you to jump to the referenced sites.

▶ **Keywords:** A *keyword* is a word that acts as a shortcut to an area within AOL or the Web site of an AOL partner. You enter a keyword in the text box on the navigation bar and then click the Go button on the far right of the toolbar to go to the referenced site. Two keywords that we use frequently in this book are **Roots** and **Genealogy**, which lead you to two different genealogical and family history areas. To find out more about keywords, see the sidebar "Discovering Keywords," later in this chapter. Keep reading to find out how you can use these two keywords to get your genealogical search going.

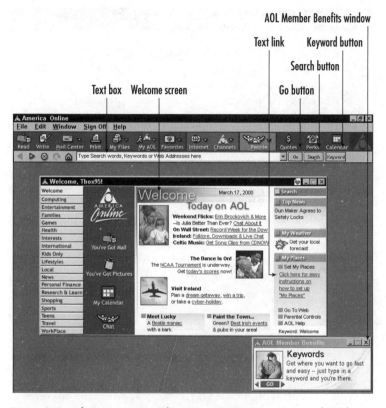

AOL Member Benefits window

Text link   Keyword button

Search button

Text box   Welcome screen   Go button

Figure Q-1. Welcome to America Online! Your computer screen opens to the Welcome screen when you sign on. The details on the screen change often.

▶ **Search:** This is a method of finding every part of AOL that contains your search word or term. You type a search word or term in the text box on the navigation toolbar and then click the Search button to the right of it to execute an AOL search for that word or term. AOL then opens a new window displaying the results of your search, with links to each area that has your search word or term in it.

Cross-Reference

Conducting a general search on AOL typically results in hits that are not specifically related to family research. Instead of having to wade through all the hits to find those of genealogical value, you can search just the genealogy areas on AOL. We examine searching two specific genealogical areas later in this chapter.

Tip

You see a list of AOL keywords by pressing Ctrl+K on your keyboard and clicking the Keyword List button.

Definition

A *keyword* is a shortcut to another area in AOL, a Web site, or another Internet resource.

Note

Click the Go button when the Keywords tip appears in the AOL Member Benefits window (in the lower right of the main AOL screen; see Figure Q-1) to read more about keywords and get additional help on how to use them.

Discovering Keywords

You know you can enter a keyword to jump directly to an AOL area or Web site about a particular topic. But how do you know what the keywords are and where they lead? A special area of AOL identifies all the keywords, and you can access it by following these steps:

1. Sign on to AOL.

2. Type **keyword** in the text box on the navigation toolbar.

3. Click the Go button on the far right of the toolbar. (Or press the Enter key on your keyboard.)

   This brings up the Keyword window. You use the three tabs on the right side of the window — List Most Popular, List Alphabetically, and List by Channel — to see lists of keywords and the forums to which they lead.

4. Click the List Alphabetically tab.

5. Scroll down the list and click the G–GF Keywords link.

6. Scroll down the list to keywords beginning with *gen* to see which words take you to genealogical content on AOL and then click one that interests you.

   AOL then takes you to the area pertaining to genealogy.

Using Keyword: Roots — Learning about the Genealogy Forum

Entering the Keyword: **Roots** takes you to the Genealogy Forum, which is part of the AOL Interests area. GenealogyForum.com provides the content and resources available in the Genealogy Forum. This area is devoted to helping people find genealogical and historical information. It also helps people to prepare, share, and preserve their ancestries for their descendants and future generations.

When you first open the Genealogy Forum window, shown in
Figure Q-2, you see a number of buttons and links that you can
click to go to various parts of the forum. Some of the resources
available through the Genealogy Forum are housed on AOL
servers, whereas other resources are maintained at
GenealogyForum.com. And some of the resources are restricted
to AOL members only. Three of our favorite resources in the
Genealogy Forum are

> ► **Chat rooms for beginners and experienced re-
> searchers:** Here you can discuss research problems
> with others.

> ► **Surname message boards:** Here you can post notes
> about the people you're researching to see if other mem-
> bers are interested in the same family lines as you.

> ► **A monthly newsletter called the Genealogy Forum
> News *(GFNews):*** This newsletter features articles, reg-
> ular columns, bits of comedy, and reports from special
> interest groups.

These are just three of the many resources in this area. The following sections briefly examine all the main buttons in the
Genealogy Forum and the resources to which they lead.

Note

The text box on the navigation toolbar is not case-
sensitive, so you can enter a
keyword with any variety of
upper- and lowercase letters
and get the same results. For
example, entering **roots**,
Roots, **ROOTS**, or **rootS**
brings up the Genealogy
Forum.

Note

You can use the Keywords:
Genealogy Forum, **Gen**,
and **GF** to get to the
Genealogy Forum on AOL,
in addition to the Keyword:
Roots.

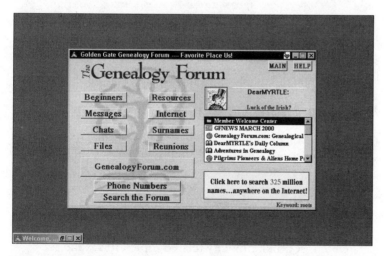

Figure Q-2. The Genealogy Forum window is your gateway to a number of research
resources, including beginner assistance, surname boards, and chat rooms.

Beginners' Center

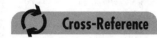

Cross-Reference

Chapters 2 and 3 examine the Beginners' Center, chat rooms, and message boards in greater detail.

Click the Beginners button to go to the Beginners' Center, which introduces you to researching your family history. It includes a Beginner's Tool Kit (which has articles and organizational tips), lessons for getting started, and a Quick Start list of questions and resources (see Figure Q-3). You can also find links to areas within AOL — such as chat rooms, message boards, and articles/tips — that are geared specifically toward members who are new to genealogy.

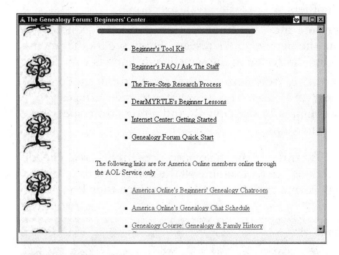

Figure Q-3. You can find information to help you start researching your genealogy at the Beginners' Center.

Message Board Center

Definition

A *message board* is an online bulletin board of sorts. You visit the message board page that suits your genealogical interest, where you can post messages and respond to others' messages. Don't forget to check back with the message board to see if anyone has responded to your postings and to see if anyone else's posts interest you.

Click the Messages button to go to the Message Board Center, which categorizes its message boards by topic within a category (see Figure Q-4). Here are the five message board categories:

▶ **Ethnic and Special Groups:** If you're looking for a place to post messages about Arab Ancestry, Creole families, the Holocaust, Orphan Trains, the Pennsylvania Dutch, or other ethnicity-related topics, this is the section to visit.

▶ **Computer and General:** This section has two message boards — one contains discussions about computers, and the other is about general genealogy.

▶ **Surnames:** Head for this section if you want to post messages about the surnames you're researching, and look for other researchers with interests in the same family lines as you.

▶ **The United States:** Here you can post questions and information about locations in the United States in which your ancestors lived.

▶ **Countries of the World:** This section has message boards where you can ask questions and provide information about countries other than the United States in which your ancestors resided.

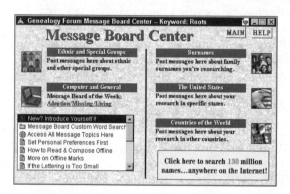

Figure Q-4. Clicking one of the buttons in the Message Board Center takes you to the actual board where you can read and post messages.

Chat Center

Click the Chats button to go to AOL's Chat Center. The Chat Center has five main chat rooms pertaining to genealogy (see Figure Q-5):

▶ Ancestral Digs

▶ Root Cellar

▶ Beginners

▶ Golden Gates

▶ Family Tree House

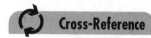 **Cross-Reference**

Chapter 3 looks closely at the Message Board Center and the Chat Center.

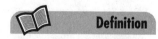 **Definition**

A *chat room* is an online area where you meet other people to discuss a common interest in *real time* (or live). You type a line of conversation, post it to the chat room, and see immediate responses from other participants in the chat.

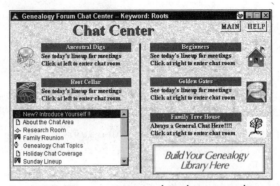

Figure Q-5. You can participate in chats about many subjects in the main genealogical chat rooms.

Drop-in-Hours are open discussion times in AOL chat rooms. They are not hosted or monitored by forum volunteers; rather, they are an opportunity for you to visit informally with other AOL members about a variety of research subjects.

With the exception of the Beginners chat room, overall you are not restricted to discussing specific topics in individual chat rooms. In fact, several topics are discussed in more than one chat room at various times during the week or month. Check the schedule of chats if you're interested in finding out when a topic is going to be discussed. Some of the topics include African Ancestry, British Isles Chat, Mid-Atlantic US Chat, Royalty Drop-in-Hour, and War Between the States Drop-in-Hour.

File Libraries Center

GEDCOM, which is short for GEnealogical Data COMmunication, is a text file format that allows genealogists who use two different genealogical software packages to share their family information easily.

Click the Files button to go to the Files Libraries Center, shown in Figure Q-6. This area holds numerous electronic files that you can download and use in your research — which help you prepare for research as well as dig around for names, facts, and documentation. The files are divided into these categories:

▶ **Logs, Newsletters, and More:** This category includes meeting minutes, various newsletters, transcriptions of lectures and chats, pictures, and other graphics.

▶ **Software and Tools:** This electronic filing cabinet contains all sorts of documents with tips about genealogical programs, reviews, programs you can use, and graphics.

▶ **Ancestors:** Here's where you find GEDCOMs that AOL members have shared, lineage files, photos, and surname archives.

▶ **History and Culture:** This category includes documents about historical and cultural events, such as the U.S. Civil War, Medieval History, and Maps, as well as recipes that have been handed down through families and shared by AOL members.

▶ **Records:** This section has documents containing tips and resources for researching, transcribed indexes and records of vital events (birth, marriage, death), transcriptions of books (including some family Bibles), and transcriptions of census schedules.

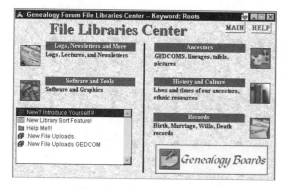

Figure Q-6. The File Libraries Center has a number of documents you can download and use in your genealogical research.

Resource Center

Click the Resources button to find a variety of resources in the Resource Center, shown in Figure Q-7. The materials are categorized as follows:

▶ **Addresses:** If you're looking for an address where you can write to request a copy of something or additional information, check out this section of the Resource Center. It contains files with addresses for various genealogical and historical societies, libraries, and other organizations.

▶ **Other Resources:** This area is a Web page that contains links to several other places that the Genealogy Forum's volunteers find useful, where you can find forms, newsletters, and other miscellaneous resources.

Cross-Reference

Ancestry.com's World Tree is a collection of GEDCOM files. You can read more about the World Tree later in this chapter.

Caution

While many of the files that are available on AOL have been scanned for viruses, it's always a good idea to run an additional virus scan to any file that you download. AOL offers an anti-virus program (Dr. Solomon's Anti-Virus) and information about viruses at Keyword: **Virus**.

▶ **Regions of the World:** In this section, select an area of the world in which you're looking for information. AOL then takes you to a list of its resources for that area or country.

▶ **Ethnic Resources:** This part of the Resource Center categorizes its listings into these areas: African-American, Hispanic, Huguenot, Jewish, or Native American. Each subsite (for example, the Hispanic Resource Center) provides links to types of resources (such as Web sites, message boards, genealogical societies, and geographic-related information).

▶ **Vital Records/Other Records:** Look here for information about various types of records and find out how to contact agencies to get more information or copies of records.

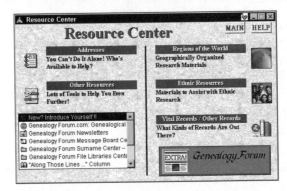

Figure Q-7. The Resource Center has a variety of resources on geographic locations, records, and other miscellaneous topics.

Internet Index

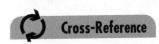

Cross-Reference

You can find more information about these and similar resources throughout this book as we walk through research examples.

Click the Internet button to go to the Internet Center. Here you find the Genealogy Forum index of links to Web sites that contain information for genealogists, as shown in Figure Q-8. The index includes sites that forum volunteers have found and sites that people like you submit for inclusion. Each site contains information that is helpful to genealogists, such as facts and stories about a person or family, or tips for researching a particular type of record. The categories in the index include Search Engines, Sites by Topic, Sites by Region/Ethnic, Mailing Lists and Newsgroups, AOL Only Links and Resources, and New Genealogy Sites.

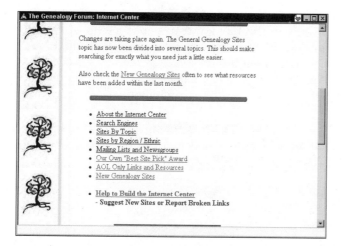

Figure Q-8. The Internet Index contains links to other Web sites that may be useful in your research.

Surname Center

Click the Surnames button to go to the Surname Center, shown in Figure Q-9, which offers links to five surname-related resources:

▶ **Message Board Center:** This is a series of online bulletin boards where you can post messages and queries about the people/surnames you're researching, and respond to messages posted by other AOL members.

▶ **Input Surname Web Sites:** This is an online form for you to complete if you have a Web site about your family history that contains information about someone with one of the 1,000 most popular surnames (as determined by the 1990 U.S. Federal Census). Your site is then added to a list of resources about that surname.

▶ **Surname Areas:** These areas contain resources about and links to the 1,000 most popular surnames so that you can see files about surnames and people who hold/held them.

▶ **Top 100 U.S. Surnames:** Here you can find information about the 100 most popular surnames in the United States (as determined by the 1990 Federal Census).

Definition

Surname is another word for your family name (last name).

▶ **Mayflower Surnames:** This interesting area provides a brief history of the Mayflower passengers who survived their journey and first winter in America. Beyond the history, the area links to resources pertaining to these survivors' surnames (25 surnames are included) and the people who are currently researching them.

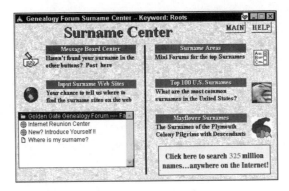

Figure Q-9. Post messages, contribute information about your personal Web site, and research files in the Surname Center.

Family Reunion Center

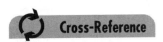

Cross-Reference

Chapter 4 explores the Genealogy Forum's Surname Center, as well as other sites that aid in your surname research.

Click the Reunions button if you're looking for information about planning a family reunion. AOL then takes you to the Family Reunion Center, shown in Figure Q-10, which shares ideas about reunions and posts schedules of virtual and real reunions. Forum volunteers and AOL members provide the contents of the Family Reunion Center; anyone can write in and share a reunion experience.

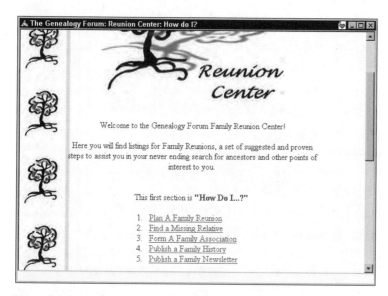

Figure Q-10. Visit the How Do I? section of the Family Reunion Center to find ideas for your next reunion and learn from other AOL members' experiences.

GenealogyForum.com

Clicking the GenealogyForum.com link takes you to the GenealogyForum.com Web site, shown in Figure Q-11. From here, you can access any of the Genealogy Forum resources described earlier in this section, but the links to these resources look a little different on the GenealogyForum.com Web site.

Definition

A *reunion* is a gathering of people who share a common bond. That bond may be familial (all are descendants of a particular person or share the same surname) or based on an experience (such as a reunion of people who attended and graduated from the same high school in a certain year). In many cases, reunions bring together people who may not have seen each other in a long period of time or may have never met.

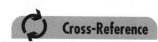

Cross-Reference

Chapter 14 provides in-depth coverage of reunions.

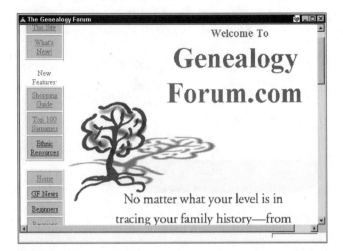

Figure Q-11. The GenealogyForum.com Web site provides access to the same resources as the Genealogy Forum in AOL.

Telephone Search Facilities

Click the Phone Numbers link to head for the Telephone Search Facilities Center (shown in Figure Q-12), through which AOL offers quick access to nine online search services. These online facilities take their information from publicly accessible directories and lists of names, phone numbers, and other contact information that they get from phone and other utility companies. They do not include information about persons who have unlisted phone numbers.

Figure Q-12. The Telephone Search Facilities gives you one-stop access to some of the most popular online directories.

Most of the resources in the Telephone Search Facilities allow you to search and display a person's phone number, address, and/or e-mail address.

Although the current directories that are available here won't enable you to contact your ancestors directly, they may lead you to relatives and other researchers who are looking for information about the same ancestors as you. That's not to say that we recommend you look up and e-mail every single person in a directory who shares your surname. Please, please don't do that! Rather, use these directories in the following situations:

▶ You've lost the e-mail address of someone who is researching the same family line or geographical area as you.

▶ You need the street address or telephone number for someone you've been corresponding with via e-mail (to send them printed copies of your research, invitations to family reunions, holiday greetings, and so on).

Search the Forum

You know from earlier in this chapter that you can conduct a general search of AOL to find areas that reference a word or term that you're interested in. However, a general search is just that — it returns hits from anywhere and everywhere within AOL. For example, if you enter the name *Sanders* as your search word, AOL generates a list of hits including all the areas in which the word Sanders is used — not just genealogical areas. When we entered the name Sanders, we got a list of 107 matching categories that included Sports (football player Barry Sanders), Science (a logician named Charles Sanders Peirce), Arts (writer Lawrence Sanders), and Home (power sanders — you know, the plural of a tool called a sander). We also got a list of 1,956 Web sites that contain the word Sanders.

Unless you've hit a brick wall and can't find anything on your surname, searching in this manner is not an effective use of your time. Most people have a limited amount of time to surf AOL for genealogical information — after all, there are only so many hours in a day. You probably don't want to spend your precious time sorting through all the hits that a general search of AOL would turn up. Wouldn't you prefer to search just the genealogical areas in your quest for family history?

That's just what Search the Forum enables you to do. Well, actually it allows you to search only the Genealogy Forum; you need to conduct a separate search to look through the Ancestry.com parts of AOL, which we cover that in more detail in a few minutes. In the meantime, here are the steps to follow for searching the Genealogy Forum:

1. Click the Search the Forum button.

   This brings up the Genealogy Forum Search window, shown in Figure Q-13. Near the top of the window is a search field where your cursor is automatically inserted.

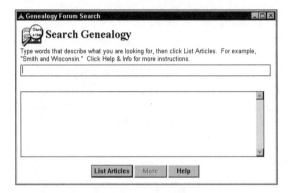

Figure Q-13. The Genealogy Forum Search window.

2. Type the name or word you want to search for in the search field.

3. Click the List Articles button.

   A list of articles and other resources containing your search term appears in the results box at the bottom of the window. Additionally, a statement appears between the search field and results box that says something like Items 1–20 of 250 out of 283 matches (see Figure Q-14). This message means that the box is displaying the first 20 hits for you to review. AOL found 283 matches total, but can display only 250.

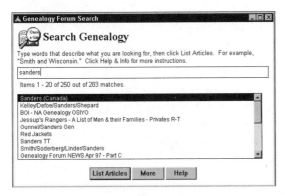

Figure Q-14. Results from a search on Sanders.

4. Scroll through the hits and click any that interest you. Remember to click the Back button when you're ready to return to this list to continue checking it out.

5. If you want to see additional hits, click the More button.

As you may guess, sorting through 253 hits is faster and easier than sorting through 1,956 hits! This is especially true if you have only a couple of hours to research on a given day. And many of the 253 resources will lead you to similar sites that you can surf to (if you have time) or plan to visit during your next trip online.

DearMYRTLE

The menu on the right side of the Genealogy Forum window offers DearMYRTLE's daily column, which takes you to writings by DearMYRTLE (an alias for Pat Richley, a computer instructor and avid genealogist). This area includes a daily column, articles about genealogical research, questions and answers, and book reviews. DearMYRTLE draws upon her own experiences and readings to help other genealogists in all aspects of family history research.

Scroll-Down List of Resources

The scroll-down list of resources in the Genealogy Forum window is a menu system that takes you to the same resources as the buttons/links in the window.

Definition

The *Back button* is the first button on the left of the navigation toolbar. It has a little arrow pointing to the left. Clicking this button with your mouse takes you back to the previous page you visited.

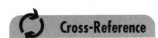

Cross-Reference

You can find out more about DearMYRTLE and her resources in Chapter 2.

Keyword: Genealogy — Discovering Ancestry.com

Note

In addition to the Keyword: **Genealogy**, you can use any of these Keywords to get to the Genealogy/Family History forum: **Ancestor, Ancestors, Ancestry, Family History, Family History Library, Family Research, FamilySearch, Family Trees, Genealogy, Geneaology,** or **Geneology**.

Using the Keyword: **Genealogy** takes you to the Genealogy/Family History window, shown in Figure Q-15, which is part of the AOL Families area. Ancestry.com, a leader in the online genealogical community, partners with AOL to bring you all of the content and resources in the Genealogy/Family History area. Ancestry.com enables you to search its resources for your ancestors' names and provides helpful sections for getting started in genealogy.

The Genealogy/Family History window doesn't look like much when you first bring it up — a search engine is centered on the left, an old-fashioned picture on the right, and a few textual links to various areas of interest to genealogists. But if you click the Ancestry.com logo, located just above the search engine, the larger and more detailed Ancestry.com@AOL Families window opens, as shown in Figure Q-16.

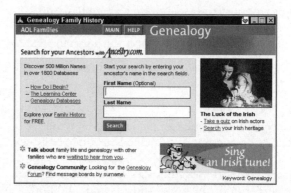

Figure Q-15. The AOL Families: Genealogy/Family History window opens up some of the resources available from Ancestry.com.

Figure Q-16. You can see more of what Ancestry.com offers by using the Ancestry.com @AOL Families view.

Ancestry.com@AOL Families also provides access to the Ancestry.com search engine, which is located near the top center of the page. The left side of the page links to various resources at Ancestry.com, including Welcome, the Learning Center, Genealogy Databases, and Shop 'n Save. The right side of the page lists all the databases that Ancestry.com makes available (some are free for a limited time to anyone who visits the Ancestry.com site), links to articles and tips, and genealogy research product information. In the center, under the search engine, you find a field where you can sign a guest registry to receive free newsletters from Ancestry.com, and a section that explains how to join Ancestry.com to gain access to even more data.

Most of the resources identified on the Ancestry.com@AOL Families page are self-explanatory, but here is a little information about each of them:

▶ **The Learning Center:** This resource offers information about how to research your genealogy. This information comes in the form of daily and weekly columns and newsletters, online tips, and Internet-based lessons.

Cross-Reference

GEDCOM is defined and discussed briefly earlier in this chapter, and in more detail in Chapter 11.

▶ **Genealogy Databases:** This resource allows you to select which databases you want to search with the name you're researching. The databases themselves contain textual information gathered from books, records, and other data sets worldwide. Some of them include census indexes, periodical indexes, phone directories, and the World Tree, which is a collection of GEDCOM files contributed by Ancestry.com users.

▶ **Shop 'n Save:** This is a future online shopping area; currently it's simply a link to an interim page.

Searching Ancestry.com

Cross-Reference

We discuss online databases like those you find at Ancestry.com in Chapter 4.

You probably want to have the option of searching only the Ancestry.com resources for the same reasons that you want to be able to search only the Genealogy Forum on AOL: Sorting through several-hundred hits is much easier than checking out thousands. For this reason, Ancestry.com makes its search engine readily available on all its pages in the Genealogy/Family History area.

The search engine is the first thing you notice when you open the Genealogy/Family History area, so the following steps walk you through using it:

1. In the Last Name field, type a surname you're interested in researching.

   You can enter a first name as well, but we recommend against doing so when you're first starting out. You'll most likely get a larger number of hits to explore if you use only a surname. Plus, including a first name restricts the search to finding information only about people with that specific name — it doesn't allow for hits that could lead you to information about other relatives with the same surname.

2. Click the Search button.

The Global Search Results page opens, listing the Ancestry.com areas in which the search word or term was found (see Figure Q-17).

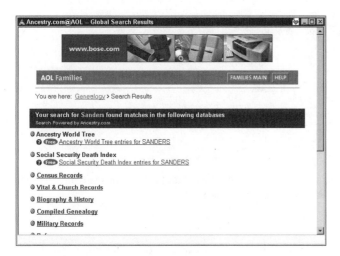

Figure Q-17. The Global Search Results page.

3. Scroll through the list and click the link for the area you want to check out.

You're transported to another search results page — this one lists all the hits within the particular area you've chosen, as shown in Figure Q-18. Along with each entry is a question mark button (which allows you to refine your search), a Free or Paid icon (which indicates whether the database is free for public use or restricted to Ancestry.com subscribers), the name of the database, and the number of times your search word or term occurred in the database.

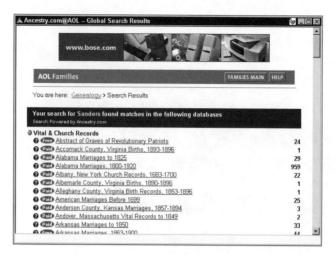

Figure Q-18. You can tell at a glance whether the resulting database is free for all to use or restricted to only Ancestry.com subscribers.

Note

Now, we don't want to hear lots of grumbling out there. Before you complain about possibly paying for genealogical information you obtain online, stop and think about how that information got on the Internet in the first place. The companies or individuals who transcribe, digitize, or index records, documents and other information to post online have to front the money to cover the costs involved in doing so — that means purchasing equipment and resources, as well as possibly paying employees. In order to stay in business and keep that information posted for your access, they've got to recoup their costs.

4. Click any links that interest you.

   You can view the results only in those databases that are free to all unless you have a subscription to Ancestry.com. If you don't have a subscription and you click the link for a pay database, a page appears that gives you information about how to subscribe.

We feel that we should forewarn you that just because you're conducting your genealogical search online doesn't mean that you won't have to pay to use some of the resources you find. For example, many of the hits that you get when searching Ancestry.com will be for information contained in databases that are restricted to Ancestry.com subscribers. However, using the Ancestry.com search engine is a fun way to see just how many database entries are available for the name you're researching and it gives you practice researching online. And you may even find that you receive so many hits in the pay databases that subscribing for at least a one month is worth it to see exactly what is available. (Or, better yet, watch for the free trial memberships that Ancestry.com offers at various times so you can explore its resources at no cost.)

Getting Started

Now you know how to

- ▶ Navigate AOL by using links, keywords, and the general search engine
- ▶ Find the genealogy areas by using the two most important keywords
- ▶ Conduct searches in the Genealogy Forum and Ancestry.com

We think you're going to find these skills exceptionally useful throughout this book. So now that you've got your feet wet, are you ready to dive in head first? We thought so. In the next chapter, you get started with the nitty gritty of planning and carrying out your genealogical research, storing your findings, and sharing your successes and lessons with the world!

PART

I

BEGINNING YOUR
JOURNEY INTO THE PAST

CHAPTER

1

SETTING GOALS

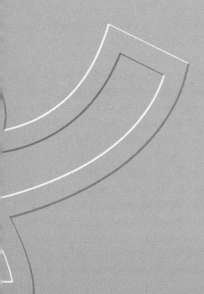

Quick Look

Chapter 1

Setting Goals

IN THIS CHAPTER

Identifying the information for which you seek

Determining where to look for information

Developing a strategy

Discovering resources through AOL

I magine you wake up one morning and decide you're going to visit a place you've never been before. You have a general idea that this place is to the west of where you live, but you're not sure how far away it is, in which state it's located, or which roads will get you there. So are you going to jump in your car and head west hoping you luck out and land in that place? Probably not. Most likely, you'll pull out a map and do a little research before heading out. If your destination is far away, you'll estimate how many hours or days it may take you to get to your destination, and you'll choose places to stop, gas up, and rest along the way.

1

Setting Goals

We like to think of genealogy as a long journey — one that requires many intermediate stops along the way. To make it to your final destination, we recommend that you set goals for the distance that you want to cover each day, consult a map that shows you the best route to travel, and determine which tools will help you get where you're going quickly.

In this chapter, we look at how to use a research plan to set goals for your online research trips. We also provide a brief introduction to AOL and Internet tools that you can use to help find success along your genealogical journey.

Tip

Setting goals helps you stay focused and use your online research time in the most efficient manner.

The Research Cycle

Although a research cycle may not sound like the most exciting topic, we think it's worthwhile because it acts as a road map for researching your family history. In fact, we use this research-cycle concept throughout this book to help you put all the different tools in perspective. Keep in mind that this research model is only a guide; you can research many different ways. Just pick a method that you feel comfortable with.

The research model that we like to use is lovingly called the Helm Online Family Tree Research Cycle. The cycle is based on common sense. And the best part about it is that it works just as well for offline, traditional researching as it does for online researching.

Here are the five phases in the Helm Online Family Tree Research Cycle:

▶ Planning
▶ Collecting
▶ Researching
▶ Consolidating
▶ Distilling

Figure 1-1 illustrates the cycle, and we discuss the five phases in the following sections.

Definition

The *Helm Online Family Tree Research Cycle* is a five-phase research model that outlines the ongoing process of genealogical research.

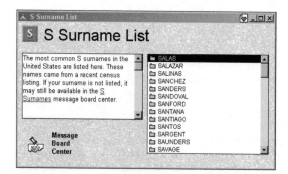

Figure 1-1. The Helm Online Family Tree Research Cycle.

Planning Your Research Strategy

We think that the planning phase is the most important one. Here is where you decide what information you're going to look for and select which resources you're going to use to find the information. Here are some examples:

▶ You may decide to find the father of your ancestor Harris Sanders. To look for this information, you may search the databases at Ancestry.com (Keyword: **Genealogy**). Or you may decide to check out the Surname Message Boards in the Genealogy Forum (Keyword: **Roots**) and look for messages posted by other researchers who are looking for information about Harris and might be willing to share their findings.

▶ Say you have many ancestors with the surname Sanders and you want to gather as much information about that name as possible. You may plan to join a mailing list devoted to Sanders discussions or visit a Web site like SurnameWeb (www.surnameweb.com) to see if you can find any Web sites devoted to that surname.

▶ Your goal may be to find out about Tippah County, Mississippi, where your ancestor lived most of his life. Information about the history of that county can add a lot of color to your genealogy. To find such information, visit the USGenWeb Project (www.usgenweb.org) and, in particular, its page for Tippah County, Mississippi.

Collecting the Information You Already Have

After you decide to research a specific individual (or group of individuals, such as a husband and wife, or an immediate family of parents and children) or a geographic location, you then collect (or gather) all the information that you currently have about that research topic. If you want to find information on Harris Sanders's father, you should first locate the facts that you currently have about Harris (such as his birth date and birthplace) that may provide hints on where you need to look for further information.

For example, if all you know about Harris Sanders is that he was born in North Carolina in 1824, this information helps you formulate your next step, searching databases of information about North Carolina around the year 1824.

Researching for More Information

During the researching phase, you visit Web sites and search the forums on AOL for information. Some other forms of researching include sending and receiving e-mail messages from other researchers, using chat rooms, posting to message boards, and reading newsgroups for leads about your family.

Consolidating New and Existing Information

Whenever you find valuable information that you want to hang on to, you should consolidate it in your files. The consolidating phase is when you take information that you've found and add it to your existing research collection, whether you keep your collection in a genealogical database on your computer or in a filing cabinet.

Distilling

After you add any newly discovered information to your genealogical database, you can then use that database to *distill* (or sort through) facts so that you can use them to plan future online research excursions. In particular, you can identify new leads, weed out inaccurate data, and see patterns. Say you discovered that the father of Harris Sanders was Nimrod Sanders, and that Nimrod was also born in North Carolina. Based on this finding, you may plan to look for additional information about

 Note

One of the keys to successful planning is to remain focused. You can easily go to a site looking for one piece of information and end up spending a lot of time browsing through pages that are unrelated to what you were originally looking for. Staying focused saves you a lot of time in the long run.

 Cross-Reference

Chapter 2 explores collecting basic information about yourself and your family that you can then use when researching online.

 Cross-Reference

Chapters 4 and 5 cover the researching process in detail as it pertains to looking for information about a particular name and looking for various types of records.

Tip

Set aside some time after each online research trip to add new information to your genealogical database. This way the data is fresh in your mind, and you won't lose the information later on.

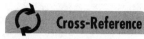

Cross-Reference

Chapters 8 and 9 discuss using a genealogical database to consolidate and store your findings.

Nimrod in North Carolina during your next online research trip. And all through this process, you should keep the information in your database as current and accurate as possible.

What Information Do You Want to Find?

What you're looking for during any given research experience — online or offline — really depends on how far along you are in your research and what information you're lacking. You have to start by assessing what you already have. Ask and answer the following questions:

> ► **What do you currently know about your family history?** You know that Harris Sanders and Emaline Crump had a son named John Duff Sanders in 1872 in Tippah County, Mississippi.

> ► **What documents do you possess that prove what you know?** You have a copy of John Sanders's birth certificate from the state of Mississippi.

> ► **What leads do you have for what you believe to be true about your family?** Your aunt once told you that Harris held an elected office in Tippah County, Mississippi, but she had nothing to back up her story.

As you answer these questions for the ancestor you plan to research, you may begin to see gaps — areas in which you need more information.

In any genealogical research (online or offline), you're generally looking for five types of information:

> ► Information about people with a particular surname
> ► Facts and stories about a specific person
> ► Information about a specific place
> ► Historical facts about a particular event
> ► Contact information for other researchers

Cross-Reference

Searching for information with an ancestor's name is covered extensively in Chapter 4.

When first starting out, many people think of researching their family histories simply as collecting information about their direct ancestors. Going back through the generations, they look only for stories and facts about those who share their bloodlines. This is one way to search for information, but it's not the only way. Often, you'll find relevant and interesting information about your direct ancestors when you research other ways. The following sections examine some of the areas you should consider researching so that your lineage is as complete as possible.

Cross-Reference

Chapter 3 examines various ways to contact other researchers.

Bloodline Research

As we've already stated, some genealogists are interested only in researching their direct line or bloodline ancestors. They're not interested in finding information about the brothers or sisters of their ancestors; nor are they interested in family stories relating to anyone other than their own ancestors. People usually research this way to support membership in a lineage society, such as the Sons of the American Revolution or the Daughters of the American Revolution. Researching your bloodline entails looking for information about particular people (your direct ancestors), often by using their names.

Family Research

Although family research uses similar methods to bloodline research (looking for particular people with certain names), it has a broader scope. Genealogists who research entire families want to know the details of not only the lives of their direct ancestors but also the collateral (or indirect) branches of the family tree. You'll find that the many stories you find in family research add a lot of color to your history, giving you more than just dates and places of events. Family researchers are usually the kind of researchers that you run into on AOL and the Internet.

Surname Research

Some genealogists are interested in researching all the individuals of a certain surname, regardless of their relationship to the researcher or where they were located geographically. This kind of research is referred to as one-name study research. As you get further into your research, you may see an occasion to find out general information about a surname, regardless of whether it directly relates to your particular family line. For example, if you're just starting to research a new family line, you may want to find out where the surname frequently occurs so that you can narrow down where the family may have originated. Also, you do general surname searches to look for clues when you hit a brick wall in your research.

Location Research

To spice up your family history and uncover leads about individuals, you may want to find out details about the geographical location in which your family members lived. This is true even if the information does not pertain specifically to your ancestors. For example, having information about a certain place at a certain time may give you insight into why your ancestor moved there, as well as help you determine where most of the people in that locality came from. It can also shed light on what the living conditions in a particular area were like for your ancestors.

Historical Research

One of the neat things about researching your genealogy is finding out how historical events affected your ancestors. For example, you may discover that one of your ancestors was present at a particular battle during the American Revolution. If you know the military unit in which your ancestor fought, you may be able to piece together what your ancestor experienced by finding a history of the battle. Although the history may not specifically mention your ancestor, it may contain details that can help you appreciate your ancestor's part in the battle.

Looking for Help

When conducting genealogical research, keep in mind that you're not alone. Hundreds of thousands of other researchers all over the world are going through the same trials and tribulations that you are. And many of them are now taking advantage of the Internet as a research tool. In fact, a good number of them are probably fellow AOL members. The chances are good that some Internet users are interested in the same family lines as you are — imagine how rewarding it is to find someone with whom you can share information and coordinate future research!

Why not try to contact some of your fellow researchers to see if they can lend you a helping hand? Likewise, why not offer to lend another researcher a helping hand? You can relate your research successes and give others hints on how they can be successful, too. By exchanging information with other researchers on the Internet, you can become a valuable member of the online genealogical community. Most of the neighborhoods in the online genealogical community are warm and inviting places, where people like to share information and get to know each other. AOL is a perfect example — it offers e-mail capabilities, user home pages, message boards, and chat rooms where you can meet others and become active in the neighborhood.

Putting Together Your Research Plan

After you decide what kind of information you're going to look for during your online trip, your next step is to create a research plan. Whether your research plan is formal or informal, written or unwritten, is strictly up to you. As long as it's realistic and helps you see the big picture of your genealogy, the research plan should serve its purpose. By realistic, we mean that the goals you set are attainable in the allocated amount of time that you'll be researching that day. For example, it's realistic to say you'll conduct a search at Ancestry.com for the name Harris Sanders and follow up on as many hits as possible. But it's not realistic to say that you'll find everything available online about Harris Sanders and his children.

Here are some things to consider including in your research plan:

▶ **A list of goals that you want to accomplish.** Some of your goals may include finding the location of your grandmother's birth certificate (so you can order a copy), checking Query Central (an online message board where you can post questions for others to review and answer) and posting responses to messages about your ancestors, and reading online about the history of Montgomery County, North Carolina.

Query Central (query
.genealogytoolbox
.com) is an online message
board where you can post
questions and comments for
other researchers to read
and respond to.

Definition

A collateral family line is one
that is related to you but not
in your direct bloodline. For
example, your great-uncle's
family would be considered
a collateral family line.

Note

Some genealogical database
programs have built-in plan-
ners or to-do lists to aid you
in your research. They're
typically easy to create, understand, and use.

▶ **The sites and resources that you want to use during that online trip.** Start with AOL and its genealogy
areas (the Genealogy Forum and Genealogy/Family
History by Ancestry.com), as well as sites that we identify in this book. As you start researching online, you'll
discover sites that you return to over and over, so you'll
add those to your list of resources.

▶ **How much time you want to spend trying to meet
each goal.** This depends on a number of factors — primarily your other time commitments. If you log on to
AOL after your kids have gone to bed, you may have a
few hours to research before your bedtime. So review
your list of goals and allocate a percentage of your research time to each one.

▶ **Information you already have that can help you
determine if and when you've met your goals.** List
facts from documents that you have in your possession
about a particular ancestor (like birth, marriage, or death
certificates, or a letter from your aunt). These documents
serve as quick references to identify whether the information you find on a Web site or other Internet resource
relates to your ancestor of the same name. For example,
the dates you glean from a birth certificate can help you
recognize whether the Harris Sanders you found in the
1850 Federal Census for Cherokee County, Alabama is
your ancestor.

▶ **A follow-up section.** This area is where you can record
the names and URLs (or other addresses) of new leads
and resources you intended to visit but didn't have
enough time to do so. You can also include other to-do
items, such as ordering copies of official records from a
certain location or reviewing your notes about a collateral line (a family line that is related to you but not in
your direct bloodline) before responding to a message
you saw online.

Table 1-1 shows a sample research plan that we like to use.

Table 1-1. Family Research Plan

My Goal:	Discover the identity of the father of Harris Sanders.
What I Know:	Harris Sanders was born in Montgomery County, North Carolina, circa 1824 (federal census records).
Resources:	Ancestry.com Database Search (30 minutes)
	AOL Surname Center (30 minutes)
	Montgomery County, North Carolina, USGenWeb page (15 minutes)
	GenealogyPortal.com Search (15 minutes)
Follow-up Leads:	

In addition to recording source information, it's a good idea to print off a copy of the Web page or e-mail message in which you found something relevant to your research. That way, you have a copy for your files that you can refer to should the page or message ever disappear (which is not unusual when you're dealing with Internet resources).

Make sure that you leave room on your research plan so that you can note the searches that you conducted and the results. And be sure when you're noting where you found something pertinent that you include a complete bibliographic citation — at the very minimum, include the name of the source, person, or organization that created it, the copyright date, and the URL where you found it. We can't stress enough that documenting your sources is very important for sound research.

Another good section to add is the follow-up leads section. Use this section to note things that you found online that did not directly relate to your goals for that particular trip. These notes enable you to return to that information at another time rather than spend the current research trip chasing down information that may be useful but doesn't accomplish your current goal.

AOL Can Help You Create a Research Plan

AOL offers some help when you're planning your research in the form of the Five-Step Research Process (see Figure 1-2). It's sort of a cross between the Helm Online Family Tree Research Cycle and the research plan we discuss in this chapter. It contains specific questions for you to consider when digging for information:

▶ **What do I already know?** Identify what you currently know about your ancestor. (This is part of the planning phase in the Helm Online Family Tree Research Cycle.)

▶ **What specific question needs to be answered?** Identify your needs or to-do items. (This is part of the planning phase in the Helm Online Family Tree Research Cycle.)

▶ **What information sources might answer my question?** Plan which resources to visit in your quest for answers. (This is part of the planning phase in the Helm Online Family Tree Research Cycle.)

▶ **What do the information sources tell me?** Record your findings from reading or using each particular resource. (This is part of the researching phase in the Helm Online Family Tree Research Cycle.)

▶ **What conclusions can I reach now?** This is where you put it all together — add new information to what you already know and draw some conclusions about your ancestor. (This is part of the consolidating phase in the Helm Online Family Tree Research Cycle.)

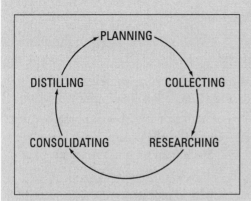

The Five-Step Research Process provides useful questions to help you with your research plan.

To get to the Beginners' Center and its resources, follow these steps:

1. Type the Keyword: **Roots** in the text box on the navigation bar, which brings up the Genealogy Forum.

2. Click the Beginners button. AOL takes you to the Genealogy Forum's Beginners' Center.

3. Scroll down and click the Five-Step Research Process link.

After you arrive at the Five-Step Research Process, you can click the links at the top of the page to jump to specific parts of the page, or you can read through the entire thing from top to bottom.

Summary

In this chapter, we looked at these topics:

- ▶ The components of the online research cycle — planning, collecting, researching, consolidating, and distilling
- ▶ The different types of searches that you can conduct while researching your genealogy
- ▶ How to develop a research plan to assist you with your online search

The next chapter takes an in-depth look at the genealogical resources provided by AOL and its partners.

CHAPTER

2

BEGINNING YOUR
GENEALOGICAL SEARCH

Quick Look

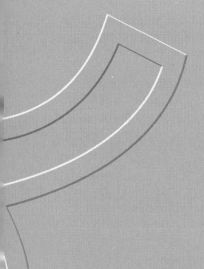

Chapter 2

Beginning Your Genealogical Search

Before you start looking for information online, you need to gather the information that you already have about yourself and your family. Having all this information at your fingertips helps you plan and stay focused when you're researching on the Internet. You will then be able to recognize leads, determine whether certain information pertains to your ancestor, and narrow down possibilities when you're dealing with a really popular name (such as Smith, Johnson, or Jones).

To begin collecting basic information, you need to sit down and record everything you already know. Start by recording information about yourself — because that's who you know the most about. List everything you can about yourself and then work your way backward through the generations — write down what you know about mom, dad, grandma, grandpa, and so forth. Working backward through the generations allows you to build on what you already know. Working backward in time also increases your odds for success when you start researching online because you're more likely to encounter more recent information (information about people in the 1800s and 1900s) than information from earlier times.

Tip

When collecting basic information, start with yourself and work your way backward through the generations.

2

Beginning Your Genealogical Search

Gathering Basic Information

As you recall facts about your life and your relatives' lives, try to find documents around the house that validate your recollections — such as birth certificates to prove dates of birth, an old letter from grandma explaining why she moved from her farm home of 40 years to an apartment in town, tax papers and business receipts from your dad's paint store, and so forth. Here is a list of the kinds of information to have at your disposal before you go online:

▶ **Names:** Full names, maiden names, and nicknames.

▶ **Dates:** Especially dates of birth, marriage, death, and other significant life events.

▶ **Places of birth, marriage, death, and more:** Don't forget other important places that figure into your family history, such as that 15 years your grandfather spent in Texas before he started a family in Oregon.

▶ **Relationships:** Be clear on how each ancestor is related to another.

▶ **Employment, military, and educational facts:** Names of schools and regiments, dates of graduation, degrees and honors, and so on.

▶ **Religious and organizational affiliations:** If your ancestor was a member of a particular church or social group, this information can be quite handy for gaining insight into his or her life and activities.

▶ **Stories and recollections:** You've probably heard lots of stories about various family members. Focus on the stories that identify particular events in which your ancestors were involved (elected offices they held, wars in which they fought, and so forth) so that you know approximate dates and names of events to look for specifically online.

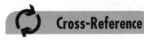

Chapter 9 covers how to enter the information you gather into a genealogical database.

Knowing exactly where another researcher discovered a fact and having a copy of the source enable you to review the information yourself should you ever question its accuracy.

You can interview and exchange information with your relatives by using AOL's e-mail service. Not only is it a fun way to correspond with your relatives, but it also creates a paper trail of sorts should you need to review something that your great-aunt told you.

After you've recorded everything you know, begin interviewing your relatives about their lives and find out what they know about your common ancestors. You may be surprised to hear some new stories. And your relatives may be able to corroborate facts or shed light on information about which you have only half the story. Ask relatives if they have records and documents that you can copy, and be sure to offer to pay for any copying and postal costs. Validating what you've learned or think you know helps ensure you're conducting sound research. You should never just take another researcher's word that something is true. The best way to validate is to have in your posession copies of all records and documents that prove facts about your ancestors.

After laying some groundwork by collecting basic information through your own recollections and interviews with family members, you're ready to move on to gathering outside information — facts, stories, documents, and leads from sources other than your immediate family. You can use a variety of resources, both online and offline. Soon you'll find yourself a patron of libraries and archives, courthouses, societies, Web sites, mailing lists, newsgroups, and chat rooms, just to name a few.

Using AOL as Your Guide

AOL has many resources to help you begin your genealogical journey — tips on what information to look for (not to mention how to look for it) and how to organize your research and findings. AOL can, in essence, serve as your mentor if you're new to genealogy. America Online provides helpful information, and its volunteers and other members provide feedback when you have questions or want to discuss research problems.

AOL has resources for beginners in both of its genealogy areas — the Genealogy Forum and the Genealogy/Family History area, which was created by Ancestry.com. The following sections examine each area.

The Genealogy Forum's Beginners' Center

The Genealogy Forum (Keyword: **Roots**) has a special section designed just for beginners, which is called, appropriately enough, the Beginners' Center (see Figure 2-1). In this center, you can find a variety of resources, most of which give you background information on how to research. You can find some of these resources on AOL, some at GenealogyForum.com, and others elsewhere on the Internet.

The resources are divided into these categories:

- ▶ Beginner's Tool Kit
- ▶ Beginner's FAQ/Ask the Staff
- ▶ The Five-Step Research Process
- ▶ DearMYRTLE's Beginner Lessons
- ▶ Internet Center: Getting Started
- ▶ Genealogy Forum Quick Start

Caution

The front page of the Beginners' Center in the Genealogy Forum reiterates a warning we always give at lectures and in publications: The Internet is only one of many tools that you will use in researching your genealogy. In other words, don't expect to find your entire family history online.

2

Beginning Your Genealogical Search

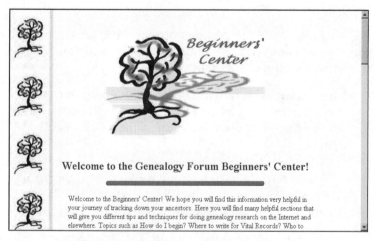

Welcome to the Genealogy Forum Beginners' Center!

Welcome to the Beginners' Center! We hope you will find this information very helpful in your journey of tracking down your ancestors. Here you will find many helpful sections that will give you different tips and techniques for doing genealogy research on the Internet and elsewhere. Topics such as How do I begin? Where to write for Vital Records? Who to

Figure 2-1. The Genealogy Forum's Beginners' Center.

Additionally, you can find these links to areas where you can post questions and participate in discussions:

- ▶ America Online's Beginners' Genealogy Chatroom
- ▶ America Online's Genealogy Chat Schedule
- ▶ Genealogy Course: Genealogy and Family History Centers
- ▶ New? Introduce Yourself! Message Board
- ▶ New to AOL? AOL Tips to Get You Started

To get to the Beginners' Center and its resources, follow these steps:

1. Type the Keyword: **Roots** in the text box on the navigation bar, which brings up the Genealogy Forum.
2. Click the Beginners button. The Genealogy Forum's Beginners' Center opens.
3. Scroll down and click the link for the resource you're interested in. The following sections give you an overview of the resources you can choose from.

Beginner's Tool Kit

The Tool Kit area of the Beginners' Center is divided into eight parts — each one with a separate, but similar, function. Here's an overview of the different areas:

- ▶ **Information on Getting Started:** This section contains articles that give you basic background information and research tips. Here are a few of the articles you'll find:
  - • **Welcome to the Genealogy Forum:** This article explains how the forum works. It covers who the volunteers are and what their roles are, as well as tells you about the forum's monthly newsletter.
  - • **How to Get Past the "Stone Wall Syndrome":** This article offers information about the different types of documents you can use to substantiate a particular event (such as a date of birth, death, or immigration) or characteristic (such as ethnicity or religion). It also lists items you can use to find out more about significant locations.

- **Naming Trends:** This article provides a brief overview of some past naming trends, as well as lists some kinship or relationship terms that you may encounter while researching.

▶ **Making Sense of It All:** This section links to research aids that help you learn the relationship or kinship terms (phrases or words like *second-cousin* and *third-cousin, once removed*) that you'll encounter in your genealogical research as well as find sites that are written in foreign languages. You can also find information about the Soundex indexing system and about deciphering discrepancies in calendars and dates. The calendar we use today was converted in 1752 (from Julian to Gregorian), so the further back you go in your family's history, the more likely you'll encounter problems with dates. See the "What's the big deal about calendars?" sidebar for more information.

Definition

The Soundex is an indexing system that groups together names that sound alike but are spelled differently and then gives them a unique code. The code includes the letter that the name begins with, followed by three numbers that are determined by a formula.

What's the Big Deal about Calendars?

When you first start out on your genealogical journey, calendars don't seem like a big deal. Initially, you're focusing on ancestors who lived during times that, for the most part, conformed to the calendar you're accustomed to using (which is called the Gregorian calendar).

But when you go back far enough — possibly just a generation or two — you'll encounter dating problems of the calendar variety. These challenges are courtesy of a conversion to the Gregorian calendar from the Julian calendar. And the conversion was necessary because of the earth's relationship with the sun and shifting seasons (winter, spring, summer, and autumn).

Here's the deal — in plain English. The earth takes 365.2422 days to revolve around the sun. How do we account for the partial day? If we had a calendar that was a straight 365 days a year, we'd fall short almost a quarter of a day per year. The result would be a shift in our seasons of more than 24 days every century.

Continued

Find It Online

You can find more information about calendars as well as a program that converts dates for you at the Calendar Conversions Web page (www.genealogy.org/~scottlee/calconvert.cgi). The converter adjusts dates for other calendars besides just the Julian and Gregorian calendars. And if you still want to read more about the Julian to Gregorian conversion, check out the Leap Years and Our Calendar page at www.ips.oz.au/papers/richard/leap.html.

What's the Big Deal about Calendars? *(continued)*

To address this shifting-season problem, Julius Caesar created the Julian calendar around 46 BC; this calendar had 12 months in a year, and every fourth year included a *leap day* to account for the .2422 of a day left over at the end of the year. This all meant that every fourth year was 366 days long instead of 365. Unfortunately, the little mathematical difference between 365.2422 and 365.25 created another problem. Every 128 years, the seasons would shift by one full day.

To remedy this second shifting-season problem, Pope Gregory XIII introduced a reformed calendar in 1582. He took away ten days in October to make up for past differences in time and put the seasons back on track. Then he mandated that the calendar would have a leap day during those years that can be divided by 4, but not by 100 *unless* they can be divided by 400. This means that the year 2000 has a leap day (because it can be divided by 4 and 400), but 1800 and 1900 did not. The end result is the calendar we use, which makes a year 365.2425 days long — close enough to the actual 365.2422 that not many people worry about a third shifting-season problem. (Thank goodness!)

The ten missing days in October are what throws a lot of genealogists off. And to add to the confusion, not every country accepted the Gregorian calendar in 1582 when it was introduced. Many didn't begin using it until 1752 or later. This means you need to know which calendar was commonly used in the time frames and locations in which your ancestors lived in order to accurately determine dates for their life events.

▶ **Obtaining Information:** This area provides research aids and tips that you can use when corresponding with others about your family. You can find a list of the types of records to look for when researching births, marriages, deaths, and relationships, as well as a sample letter to use when writing to agencies requesting copies of documents. The Family Folklore page contains information taken from the Smithsonian Institution's Folklore

Program to help you interview family members and learn about your family's folklore. You can also find out information about the usefulness of genealogical and historical societies, and how to use probate records, Social Security information, and the Soundex.

▶ **Organizational Ideas:** This section contains an Everton Publishers article about organizing your research with pedigree charts, family group sheets, and individual data sheets.

▶ **Organizing Information:** If you're looking for background articles and advice about getting organized, then you may want to check out this section. You can find out information about keeping a journal (not a research journal, though) and selecting genealogical software, as well as links to DearMYRTLE articles about organization.

▶ **Other Genealogy Forum Centers:** This area contains links to other parts of the forum, most of which are covered in various sections of this book. They include the Internet Center, Resource Center, DearMYRTLE, File Libraries Center, Message Boards, Search the Forum, and Phone Search Facilities.

▶ **Other Related Forums:** When you're ready to wander out of the Genealogy Forum, the Other Related Forums area contains links to various other resources that the forum volunteers recommend. The links take you to various AOL forums, such as the Adoption and Fostering Forum, the Civil War Forum, the International Channel, and the Revolutionary War Forum. In addition, you can follow links to the Hispanic Online Web site, the Jewish Community Web site, and the Language Dictionaries and Resources Web site.

▶ **DearMYRTLE:** In addition to linking to DearMYRTLE from the organization areas of the Beginner's Tool Kit, you can access her site directly from the front page of the Tool Kit as well as directly from the main page of the Beginners' Center. On the main page of the Beginners' Center, click the DearMYRTLE's Beginner Lessons link and then click the Beginning Genealogy Lessons link on the next page. DearMYRTLE's beginner topics include Previously Compiled Genealogies, which warns you not to take the word of others as gospel but to use information you glean from compiled genealogies as clues for finding the truth. Interviewing Relatives provides a list

Note

DearMYRTLE is a genealogical column and Web site produced by computer instructor and avid genealogist, Pat Richley. Drawing on Richley's personal experiences, DearMYRTLE provides simple lessons in genealogical research and answers readers' questions. You can get to DearMYRTLE from the main Genealogy Forum page (on the scroll down menu) and the Beginners' Center.

of ideas for interview topics or themes for a particular session. Wills and Probate Records explains the usefulness of wills and probate records in tracking your ancestors and gives you some common will and probate terminology.

Beginner's FAQ/Ask the Staff

The Frequently Asked Questions (FAQ) section of the Beginners' Center is more interactive than the resources available in the Beginner's Tool Kit. In addition to providing information about interpreting abbreviations used on AOL, getting Social Security records, and finding sites on the Internet, the Beginners' Circle FAQ also addresses the following topics:

▶ Research issues and resources, including information about hiring someone online to help you do your research

▶ Accessing private resources, including information about the Mormon Library — and, yes, you can use it even if you're not Mormon

▶ Technology questions, including information about Zip files and downloading documents from the Internet

▶ Examples of a Tiny Tafel (a software-generated summary of your genealogical research)

▶ Using the AOL message boards, alphabetizing messages, and finding posted messages

If your specific question isn't covered in the FAQ, you can pose it to the staff of the Beginners' Center. You can post your own questions via e-mail and receive responses from the Genealogy Forum's volunteers. Follow these steps to use the Ask the Staff resource:

1. Click the Ask the Staff link on the Frequently Asked Questions page, which brings up a Write Mail window. The Send To field automatically contains the e-mail addresses of the Ask the Staff volunteers, as shown in Figure 2-2.

Definition

A FAQ, or Frequently Asked Question, is just what it sounds like — a place where you can review standard answers to the most frequently asked questions on a Web site. FAQs are standard not just on AOL, but on just about every Web site you visit on the Internet.

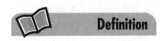

Definition

A Tiny Tafel is a numbering system that is generated by genealogical software, which summarizes the facts (names, dates, and places of people you're researching) in your database.

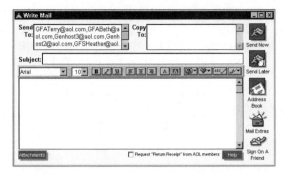

Figure 2-2. The Ask the Staff Write Mail window.

2. In the Copy To field, enter e-mail addresses for anyone you want to carbon copy on this message. You can click the Address Book button, which is centered on the right side of the window, to use your e-mail address book.

3. Type a brief description of your question in the Subject field. For example, if your question pertains to finding church records from when your grandfather was a minister in Indianapolis, you might type **church records for Indianapolis, IN** in the subject line.

4. In the large box at the bottom of the window, type your message.

5. Click in the Request Return Receipt from AOL Members check box if you want to receive confirmation that the Ask the Staff volunteers received your message.

6. After you've completed your message, click the Send Now or Send Later button, depending on when you want the message sent.

After reviewing your message, one of the Genealogy Forum volunteers will respond directly to you via e-mail.

The Five-Step Research Process

The Genealogy Forum outlines a five-step research process for you to use when collecting genealogical data. Because we cover all the steps in this section of the Beginners' Center in Chapter 1, we won't make you sit through it again. Simply take a gander back at Chapter 1 for a review.

Cross-Reference

Chapter 3 delves into e-mail and other forms of Internet communication in greater detail. It includes how to use AOL Mail Features (enhancements designed specifically for e-mail).

Tip

If you need any help preparing your e-mail to Ask the Staff, click the Help button in the Write Mail window.

DearMYRTLE's Beginner Lessons

DearMYRTLE is a genealogical column in the Genealogy Forum News and is also a Web site that contains online lessons and questions/answers. In addition to accessing all the DearMYRTLE resources through the Online Lessons from DearMyrtle link on the Beginners' Center main page, you can get to various parts through related areas, such as the Beginner's Tool Kit and the main Genealogy Forum window in AOL.

DearMYRTLE's online genealogy lessons are divided into these categories:

- ▶ Beginning Genealogy Lessons
- ▶ Finally Get Organized
- ▶ Kid's Genealogy
- ▶ Step By Step
- ▶ Using LDS Family History Centers
- ▶ Writing Your Personal History

When putting together her various resources, DearMYRTLE incorporates practical advice, her own experiences, and information she's read in recent and tried-and-true genealogical publications. Many of her articles provide interesting background information about particular types of records or sources you may be using for the first time.

Internet Center: Getting Started

Similar to the Other Related Forums section of the Tool Kit, the Internet Center: Getting Started section provides links to other resources you can use. The links offered here are Web site recommendations from Genealogy Forum volunteers. Some of the Web sites are the same resources that we recommend in the "Getting the Most from Other Online Beginner Resources Online" section, later in this chapter.

Genealogy Forum Quick Start

The Genealogy Forum Quick Start is a guide to getting your search underway in the shortest amount of time. It briefly explains how and why to search by topic, as well as how to use the Surname Message Boards, navigate the File Library Center, and explore other parts of the Genealogy Forum.

Meeting Other Researchers Online

You can meet other researchers on AOL in several ways, but if you're a beginner, check out the Beginners' Genealogy Chatroom and the New? Introduce Yourself! Message Board, which are described in the following two sections.

AOL's Beginners' Genealogy Chatroom

A *chat room* is a real-time forum where you can carry on electronic discussions with others. The Beginners' Genealogy Chatroom is devoted to topics of interest to AOL members who are new to genealogy. To enter the Beginners' Genealogy Chatroom, click the America Online's Beginners' Genealogy Chatroom link on the main page of the Beginners' Center (see Figure 2-3). You can also access this chat room from the Chat Center — which you can access on the main Genealogy Forum page (Keyword: **Roots**).

On the left side of the window, you see messages that have been posted, and as new messages are posted, older ones scroll up. At the bottom of the window, you can select the font you want to use. The blank field in the bottom-left corner is where you type your message — just click the Send button when you're ready to add your message to the discussion. The box on the right side of the window lists everyone who is logged on to the chat room at that moment.

Figure 2-3. The Beginners' Genealogy Chat room.

Tip

To find out the schedule of topics for the Beginners' Genealogy Chatroom, click the America Online's Genealogy Chat Schedule link. This link is near the bottom of the main page of the Beginners' Center.

Cross-Reference

Chapter 3 discusses chat rooms, message boards, and other communication tools in depth.

New? Introduce Yourself! Message Board

A *message board,* like a chat room, is a good place to meet others and discuss topics of common interest. However, the discussions on message boards don't take place in real time. Instead, a researcher posts a question to a Web site, which is organized like a bulletin board, and others can respond whenever they read the initial message — whether that's five minutes or five days after the initial message is posted.

The New? Introduce Yourself! Message Board is designed specifically for beginners in genealogy and newcomers to AOL. To use this message board, click the New? Introduce Yourself! Message Board link on the main page of the Beginners' Center. A window opens up that allows you to read other users' postings as well as post your own messages.

To read a message, click the message you're interested in and then click the Read Post button in the bottom-left corner of the window. To post your own message, click the Create Subject button at the bottom of the window. In the new window that pops up enter a brief description of your message's topic in the Subject text box and enter your message in the large text box. Click the Send button when you're done composing the message.

Taking a Look at What Ancestry.com Offers

The Genealogy/Family History Forum produced by Ancestry.com devotes two areas to beginners: Getting Started and the Learning Center. You can access these two areas through the forum's main window by using the Keyword: **Genealogy**.

Getting Started

Click the How Do I Begin? link to go to the Getting Started page, which briefly explains how the site works, which resources you can use for free, and how to subscribe to Ancestry.com for more services. The site tour is an excellent way to get an overview of the numerous databases, articles, and other research aids that Ancestry.com offers.

The Learning Center

To get to the Learning Center, click the link by the same name in the Genealogy/Family History window. The Learning Center is divided into these six categories (see Figure 2-4):

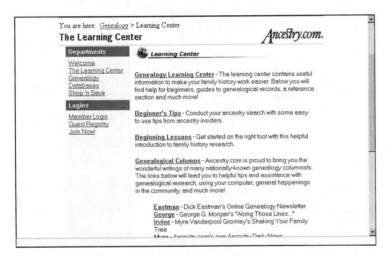

Figure 2-4. The Learning Center has six categories.

- ▶ **Genealogy Learning Center:** This series of articles walks you through the research process. You start off with the How Do I Begin? article and then move on to The First Steps, The Genealogical Network, The Geographic Dimension, The Historical Dimension, Organizing Data and Putting It into Perspective, Computer and Genealogy, Etiquette, Ethics, and Legal Considerations. All the articles provide excellent information and are worth checking out.

- ▶ **Beginner's Tips:** This section (also called Genealogy Help) contains articles such as First Steps, Finding Evidence of Your Ancestor, and Using Your Computer. You also find a Genealogy Lessons link, which takes you to the articles in the Genealogy Learning Center.

- ▶ **Beginning Lessons:** Clicking this link takes you to a list of online lessons by DearMYRTLE. These are the same lessons you can access through the Genealogy Forum, as described earlier in this chapter.

- ▶ **Genealogical Columns:** Here you'll find links to all the online columns and newsletters associated with Ancestry.com: the Ancestry Daily News, articles by Sherry Irvine, DearMYRTLE's genealogy column, Eastman's Online Genealogy Newsletter, George G. Morgan's "Along Those Lines . . .," and Myra Vanderpool Gormley's "Shaking Your Family Tree."
- ▶ **Ancestry Magazine:** This section contains online information about the print publication.
- ▶ **Library Signup:** The Library Subscription Page provides information for libraries that are interested in subscribing to Ancestry.com to use its subscription-based databases and other resources.

Getting the Most from Other Online Beginner Resources

In addition to the beginner resources on AOL, other Web sites provide helpful information for new genealogists. The following few sections give you brief introductions to these sites.

Ancestors

The Ancestors site (www.kbyu.org/ancestors) is the companion site for the PBS series of the same name. This site offers research suggestions in the Tips and Tricks, Resource Guide, and Blank Charts and Forms areas, as well as provides information about the original series and the new series, which is scheduled to air in June 2000.

Beginner's Guide to Family History Research

The Beginner's Guide to Family History Research (biz.ipa.net/arkresearch/guide.html) is an electronic version of the book by the same name. The entire book is geared toward beginners, but two chapters that are especially helpful when you're just starting out are the Home and Family Sources chapter and the Organizing Your Family Records chapter.

Genealogy.com

The Genealogy.com site (`www.genealogy.com`), which is produced by the creators of Family Tree Maker and other popular genealogical software, offers all sorts of resources. Of particular interest to beginners are the How-To Articles page and the If You Are Just Beginning page. The How-To Articles page covers just about everything — researching census records, conferences and associations, documenting sources, immigration research, photographs, reunions, technology, and more. The If You Are Just Beginning page has information about beginning your research and creating a family tree, finding family members online, and discovering new books and products that can aid you in your genealogy. It also provides links to the Genealogy SiteFinder (a comprehensive list of genealogical sites on the Internet).

Genealogy Toolbox

Combining nine sites under one roof, the Genealogy Toolbox (`www.genealogytoolbox.com`) offers practical resources for researching on the Internet. The Journal of Online Genealogy has articles about all aspects of researching, as well as book and product reviews. GenealogySoftware.com contains information about genealogical software programs and the companies that produce them. Query Central is the oldest genealogical message board that allows surname posts, and GenealogyPortal.com is a search engine that indexes only those Web sites containing genealogical information.

RootsWeb.com

RootsWeb.com (`www.rootsweb.com`) hosts a variety of Web sites that you'll undoubtedly use throughout your genealogical pursuits. Beginners will be particularly interested in RootsWeb's Guide to Tracing Family Trees and the GEN-NEWBIE mailing list. The Guide to Tracing Family Trees is a collection of interactive lessons covering various aspects of research. And the GEN-NEWBIE is a mailing list devoted to discussions of interest to those who are new to computers and genealogy.

Find It Online

You can access the How-To Articles through various, clearly marked links on the Web site or go directly to the back issues at `www.-genealogy.com/backissu.html`.

Find It Online

Click the New to Genealogy link in the middle column of the main Genealogy.com Web page to get to the If You Are Just Beginning resources. Or go directly to the page at `www.genealogy.com/newstart.html`.

Find It Online

You can find the Guide to Tracing Family Trees at `www.rootsweb.com/~rwguide`.

Find It Online

The GEN-NEWBIE Web page explains more about the mailing list and how to subscribe to it. You can access this Web page at `www.rootsweb.com/~newbie/`.

To find other beginner resources online, we recommend that you use a comprehensive index of genealogical sites, such as the Genealogy SiteFinder. Follow these steps to use the Genealogy SiteFinder:

1. In the text box on the navigation toolbar, type **www.genealogysitefinder.com** and press the Enter key. The AOL Web browser opens up and takes you the Genealogy SiteFinder.

2. Scroll through the list of categories and click the How-To and Help link. The How-To and Help page pops up, as shown in Figure 2-5.

3. Click the Beginner Guides link. Clicking this link brings up a list of sites that contain information of interest to genealogy beginners.

4. Review the list of sites and select one to visit.

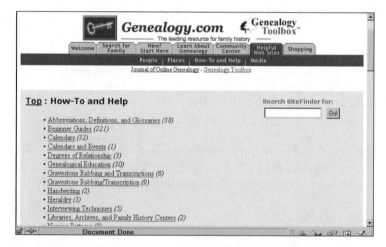

Figure 2-5. You can find sites that are categorized as Beginner Guides through the How-To and Help area.

Netiquette Lessons

What is netiquette? It's net etiquette — manners or consideration of others on the Internet. Although the term netiquette applies to all aspects of the Internet, you'll most likely encounter references to it in discussions about e-mail (including mailing lists and newsgroups) and postings to message boards.

In the very simplest terms, the overarching rule of netiquette is the golden one — treat others as you would like to be treated. Here are a few other guidelines to keep in mind:

▶ Only send messages that you don't mind the world seeing. Assume that the general public can potentially see any e-mail you send — after all, you never know when a recipient might forward your note to a mailing list or other large group. Would you want a hateful e-mail message to or about you circulated to the world?

▶ If someone does send you (or a group) an e-mail that attacks you on a personal level (also called a *flame*), try your best to ignore it. Most flames eventually fizzle out, and trading insults back and forth doesn't do anyone any good.

▶ Always use mixed-case letters when writing your message. In other words, don't write IN ALL CAPS. Using all uppercase letters indicates that you're shouting.

▶ Be careful about using information from books, other e-mails, and Web sites in your e-mail messages. You may be violating copyrights by doing so.

▶ Be judicious when clicking the Reply button. If you intend for your message to go to only one or two people, don't use the reply feature to address a message that arrived from a mailing list. If you do, you're likely to send your message to a lot of people who aren't interested in your response.

▶ To overcome the inability to use body language or vocal inflection to express emotion over the Internet, use *emoticons* (emotional icons) to convey your feelings in e-mail messages. Emoticons are the little faces that are made out of characters on your computer's keyboard — such as the sideways smiley face :-) .

Note

Although you don't want to use all uppercase letters when writing a general e-mail message, using all caps for a surname is appropriate in some instances. Using all caps makes the surname you're researching stand apart from the rest of your message so readers can easily determine whether your question/message may interest them.

Find It Online

To use emoticons in your e-mail on AOL, just click the Mail Extras button in your Write Mail window and then click the Smileys button. Scroll through the list of emoticons and select the one you want to use.

Summary

Your research is underway. You've learned how to begin with yourself as a resource and then move on to interviewing relatives to acquire all the knowledge you can. And you've discovered resources — on AOL and the rest of the Internet — that can help you learn the fundamentals of genealogical research. Additionally, you found out more than you probably ever wanted to know about the big calendar conversion from Julian to Gregorian, and you've picked up some helpful tips about netiquette.

So where do you go now? You're ready to get down to the nitty gritty of actually using the information about your ancestors that you've learned and collected in this chapter. Get ready to use this information to research a particular individual by name.

CHAPTER

3

COMMUNICATING
WITH OTHERS

Quick Look

▶ **Using E-Mail to Enhance Research**   **page 67**

One of the most effective ways to share information and discover new resources for your genealogical search is to communicate directly with others. E-mail is a fast, efficient way to get information about genealogical research or about your family history.

▶ **Messaging Your Way to Success**   **page 76**

Posting queries on genealogy-specific message boards allows the whole world (or at least that portion of the world conducting genealogical research online) to see your research interests. You may quite possibly find another researcher who is interested in the same family lines as you and who you can then use as a research resource.

▶ **Chatting Around**   **page 80**

If you think that the millisecond lag between the moment you send an e-mail and the time it's received on the other side of the world is slowing down your research, try using a chat room. Chat rooms allow you to communicate with other researchers in real time. In fact, chat rooms allow you to talk to several people at a time, which can really increase your research productivity. (Talk about fast!)

▶ **Using Newsgroups and Mailing Lists**   **page 83**

When you want to communicate with a larger audience, newsgroups and mailing lists may be the solution. Each resource allows you to post a single message that is in turn read by several people.

Chapter 3

Communicating with Others

IN THIS CHAPTER

Using e-mail effectively

Posting your research questions to message boards

Learning to use chat rooms

Reading information from mailing lists and newsgroups

Although most of the stories you hear about researching genealogy online focus on the many databases and family histories that are available, one of the most important aspects of Internet technology is the ability to contact another person (or a group) directly. All over the world, individuals who live thousands of miles away from each other and who have never met face-to-face correspond on a regular basis by using Internet technology to communicate and coordinate research toward a common goal.

This chapter looks at the many different ways that you can use AOL and Internet resources to communicate with other researchers, to exchange family lore with relatives living far away, and to otherwise contact the many researchers who are waiting to hear from you. Not only can you communicate with researchers and family members in your own geographic area, but you can also send messages to people all around the world. In fact, informal research groups commonly are created as a result of e-mail correspondence and message-board activity.

Discovering E-Mail

The basic building block of online communication is electronic mail, better known as *e-mail*. E-mail allows you to send a message to a single individual or multiple people at the same time. You can use e-mail to correspond with:

- ▶ **Other researchers:** Some of these researchers may be related to you while others will be unrelated people who are interested in the same family lines or geographic areas as you.
- ▶ **Relatives:** Your relatives may or may not be interested in genealogy, but surely they'll enjoy hearing from you and getting to know you better.
- ▶ **Organizations:** These include genealogical and historical societies, family associations, libraries, archives, and other such entities that you may contact to get membership information or information about records that are available from the organization.

You've Got Mail

Whether you use AOL or another Internet service provider (ISP), one of the first things that you probably do each time you log on to the Internet is check to see if you have e-mail messages. If you're using AOL, you don't even have to look to see if you have new mail because you hear a familiar voice telling you, "You've got mail," when you log on. Here are some other ways to tell that you have new e-mail after you're logged on:

▶ The mailboxes that appear on the Welcome screen and the AOL toolbar have mail coming out of them, and the red flag is raised, as shown in Figure 3-1.

▶ If you have mail, the friendly Welcome screen says so. If you don't have new mail, the mailbox directs you to the Mail Center instead.

Figure 3-1. This is the first screen you see when you log on to AOL. The mailboxes notify you that you have e-mail.

▶ For Mac users, a mailbox flashes in the upper-right corner of your screen.

Checking your e-mail is just as easy as figuring out that you have new mail. Just do one of the following:

▶ Click the mailbox icon on the Welcome screen.

▶ Click the Mail Center button on the AOL toolbar and then choose Read Mail from the menu that appears.

▶ Click the mailbox button on the AOL toolbar.

▶ Press Ctrl+R (press the Ctrl key and R key at the same time). Mac users press ⌘+R.

After you open your mailbox, you see a screen with three tabs, as shown in Figure 3-2. The New Mail tab contains a list of your new e-mail messages. To read a message, simply click a message to highlight it and then click the Read button at the bottom of the Mailbox window. Or you can just double-click the message you want to read.

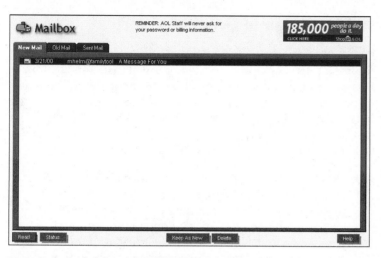

Figure 3-2. You find three tabs in the AOL Mailbox window.

To respond to e-mail, click the Reply button on the right side of your message window, as shown in Figure 3-3. A reply window opens so that you can type your response in the box provided. After you finish typing your reply, click the Send Now button in the upper-right corner of the window.

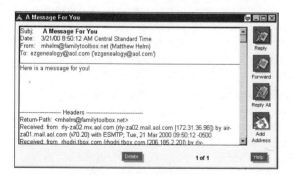

Figure 3-3. The Reply button is located at the top right of the open e-mail window.

Tip

The AOL e-mail program does not automatically include the text of the original or previous message in your reply. To include the text, right click on the previous message and click Select All. After the text is selected (highlighted), choose copy from the Edit menu. Return to the screen for the new message and choose Paste from the Edit menu to include the text from the previous message into your reply.

3

Communicating with Others

Writing Original E-Mail

For more details on what kinds of information to put into a query, see Chapter 4.

Offering a polite salutation, such as "Hello," and signing your name can go a long way to adding a friendly, professional tone to your person-to-person e-mail correspondence. Writing the entire message in ALL CAPS can come across as shouting and really put people off.

Everyone seems to be using e-mail these days. All the more reason for a refresher course in writing e-mail that conveys your message well and doesn't unnecessarily annoy others. You may want to think of e-mail the way you think of a letter you receive in the mail. Obviously, you're more inclined to read it if it's clear, friendly, and contains information you consider relevant. Consider the following when you send e-mail:

▶ **Clarity:** Writing e-mail is a lot less of a chore if you start by making your communication as clear as possible; the more clear your writing is, the more likely you are to receive a good response. Start by stating the purpose of your e-mail in the subject line. The body of your e-mail should only be as long as necessary to convey the important details. Check your message for spelling and grammar. If want a response from the addressee, then ask for it.

▶ **Tone:** Remember, people can't hear the laughing tone of your voice or see your smiling face over the Internet (well, not yet, anyway), so you should avoid making off-color or sarcastic jokes that don't translate well into writing. Someone may misunderstand your intentions and send you an unnecessarily nasty response. Likewise, if you receive an e-mail message that makes you angry, hold off before you respond. E-mail is so immediate and can't be taken back, so do everything in your power to avoid regretting your actions or overreactions.

▶ **Relevance:** E-mail as a form of communication is here to stay, which means that you're going to receive more and more messages as time goes on. This is why using good judgment about when to send an e-mail message to begin with is imperative. Before you send an e-mail message, ask yourself if you can find the answer to your question elsewhere yourself. Also, determine if the addressee is likely to have the answer. If you can think of any reason why the addressee of your e-mail might not understand your message, think about using another form of communication. If the content of your message is personal, then use another form of communication. (Who says the e-mail will reach its intended destination or that the recipient won't forward it to several other people?) Finally, never pass chain letters on. They are annoying and generally contain inaccurate information.

Now that you've had a short course in e-mail basics you can get down to the fun part — composing messages of your own. Creating e-mail in AOL is simple; just follow these steps:

1. Click the Write button on the AOL toolbar.

   The Write Mail window appears.

2. By default, the cursor blinks in the Send To box. Type the e-mail address of the person to whom you want to send the message. If you are sending the e-mail to more than one person, separate their e-mail addresses with a comma.

   If you're sending e-mail to another AOL user, you only need to type the user's screen name — in other words, everything that appears before the @ symbol. (For example, if you're sending e-mail to someone@aol.com, all you have to type in the Send To box is someone. AOL then automatically delivers it to your special someone.) However, when you send e-mail to people who use another e-mail program, you need to include their entire e-mail address (for example, someone@somewhere.com).

3. If you want to send a copy of your message to someone else, press the Tab key or use your mouse to click in the Copy To box. Then type the screen name or e-mail address of the individual(s) you want to copy.

4. Using your mouse, click in the Subject box (or press the Tab key again) and then enter the subject of your message.

5. Click in the large box (or press the Tab key again) and begin typing the text of your message.

6. After you finish composing your message, click the Send Now button.

Forwarding E-Mail

If you receive a message from one person and think that it may interest another person, you can forward it. To forward e-mail, open the message in the Mailbox window and then click the Forward button (the second button from the top on the right side of the screen) and type the e-mail address of the person to whom you're forwarding the e-mail. You may choose to add an introduction to the forwarded e-mail message, as well. When you're finished, click the Send Now button.

Tip

You don't have to be in the Mail Center to compose new e-mail. Just click the Write button on the AOL toolbar; then select Write Mail. And no matter what part of AOL (or the Internet) you happen to be visiting, a blank e-mail window appears on your screen.

Tip

Make the subject of your e-mail as informative as possible. Simply calling the subject of an e-mail Genealogy may not mean much to someone who receives several e-mails a day about genealogy. A better subject line would be the name of the ancestor to whom your message pertains, dates for that individual, and a location where the ancestor lived. For example, your subject line might read: HELM, George (1723-1749) Frederick County, Virginia.

3

Communicating with Others

Tip

You can adjust the font used in your message (change the font size and add bold, italic, underline, and so forth), the alignment of the text, and the text and background color, as well as insert pictures, a favorite URL (from your list of favorite places), or a signature file by using the buttons located just above the text box.

It's always a good idea to get permission from the author of an e-mail message before forwarding it to other researchers. This way, you don't step on anyone's toes by sharing words that the author may be sensitive about other people seeing.

Sending E-Mail Attachments

As you progress in your research and meet fellow researchers online, you'll probably want to send a copy of a genealogical database, word processing file, spreadsheet, or other type of electronic file along with e-mail. To do this, you have to attach the file to your e-mail. If you're a Windows user, follow these steps to attach a file to your e-mail message:

1. In the Write Mail window, click the Attachments button in the bottom-left corner.

   The Attachments window appears.

2. Click the Attachments button, located just below the large box, to add an attachment.

   This step launches the Attachments dialog box, shown in Figure 3-4, which allows you to select the file to attach.

3. Select a file by double-clicking its name.

   You then return to the Attachments window, which displays the location of the file that you selected.

4. Click the OK button.

   At the bottom of the screen to the right of the Attachments button, the title of the attached file appears next to a small diskette.

If you're a Mac user, follow these steps to attach a file:

1. In the Write Mail window, click the Attachments tab at the top of the screen.

2. Click the Attach File button.

3. Select the file you want to attach and then click the Attach button.

   You should see a small disk icon at the top of the Write Mail window. The name of the attached file appears in the attachment box.

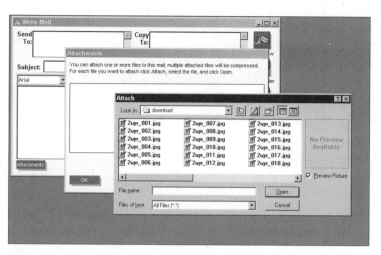

Figure 3-4. The Write Mail window with a file attached.

Deleting E-Mail

If you no longer need a message, you can delete it. You can delete any message in the Mailbox window by selecting the message and clicking the Delete button at the bottom of the window. If the message is open, you can simply click the Delete button at the bottom of the window.

Using the Personal Filing Cabinet

Eventually, you may receive a large number of e-mails about the different family lines in your genealogical research. Wouldn't it be great if you could set up e-mail file folders for each family line? Well you're in luck! That's where AOL's Personal Filing Cabinet comes in handy.

When you open the Personal Filing Cabinet, you see three main file folders and a few subfolders underneath them. The main folders are Mail, Newsgroups, and Download Manager. For the purpose of organizing e-mail, we're interested in the Mail folder.

Note

If you want to send multiple files as e-mail attachments, AOL automatically compresses the files into a ZIP file. (Compressing a file is when one or more files are reduced in size and packed into a new file.) The recipient of your e-mail must have a program that can decompress the ZIP file, such as the shareware program PKUNZIP (which is available at www.pkware.com).

Tip

If you accidentally delete an e-mail that you want to keep, you can retrieve it as long as you deleted it within the past 24 hours. To retrieve your inadvertently trashed e-mail, click the Mail Center button on the AOL toolbar and choose Recently Deleted Mail from the drop-down menu.

Caution

The Personal Filing Cabinet stores e-mail on your computer's hard drive. So make sure that you have enough hard drive space to accommodate all the e-mail that you intend to store.

Tip

When you want to read mail that is stored in the Personal Filing Cabinet, simply click the Mail Center button on the toolbar and choose the Read Offline Mail and Incoming/Saved Mail options from the drop-down menu.

Tip

In addition to setting up folders for surnames, you can set up folders for geographic locations. Then you can store messages pertaining to a location or about more than one ancestor from that location in the appropriate file.

Storing E-Mail Files in the Personal Filing Cabinet

Given the large amount of e-mail that AOL members receive each day, AOL can only store messages for so long. Any e-mail that you have read and not deleted remains available online for a few days. New e-mail that you haven't read is available for about four weeks.

Follow these steps to save your e-mail to your Personal Filing Cabinet (for Windows and Mac users):

1. Click the Mail Center button on the toolbar.
2. Choose Mail Preferences from the drop-down menu.

    The Mail Preferences window appears, as shown in Figure 3-5.
3. Select the check boxes labeled Retain All Mail I Send in My Personal Filing Cabinet and Retain All Mail I Read in My Personal Filing Cabinet. Then click the OK button.

    If you're a Mac user, select the check boxes labeled Save the Mail I Send and Save the Mail I Read.

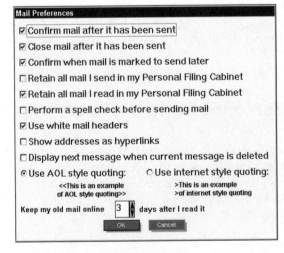

Figure 3-5. The Mail Preferences window.

Adding New Folders to the Personal Filing Cabinet

After you begin receiving e-mail by the boatload, you're going to want to create additional files to organize your genealogy-related research and to keep it separate from your personal correspondence. You'll probably want to add a mail folder for each major family group you're researching. To begin with, why not set up a folder for the surnames of each of your grandparents? To create new files in the Personal Filing Cabinet:

1. Click the My Files button on the toolbar and choose Personal Filing Cabinet from the drop-down menu.

   The Personal Filing Cabinet appears, and the Mail folder is highlighted, as shown in Figure 3-6.

2. To add a folder, click the Add Folder button (the second button in the bottom-left corner of the window).

3. Type the name of the folder (such as one of the surnames you're researching) and then press Enter or click the OK button.

   The new file subfolder appears under the Mail folder.

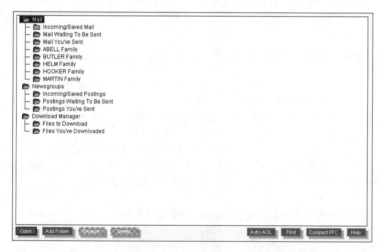

Figure 3-6. Keep track of your e-mail with the Personal Filing Cabinet.

Mac users can add a folder by following these steps:

1. Click the My Files button on the toolbar and choose Personal Filing Cabinet from the drop-down menu.

2. Double-click Offline Mail and click the New Folder button.

3. Type the name of the folder (for example, one of the surnames you're researching) and then press Enter.

   The new file subfolder appears in the Personal Filing Cabinet in alphabetical order.

3

Communicating with Others

To save a message to a folder in the Personal Filing Cabinet, open the message that you want to save and then choose File from the menu bar. Choose Save to Personal Filing Cabinet and select the file folder in which you want to save the message.

Using Message Boards

Message boards are another crucial resource for genealogists. You can reach thousands of other genealogists who may have answers to your questions just by posting a message on a single message board. Another benefit of message boards is that other researchers may read your message days and even months after you post it. That way, even if you don't get a response immediately, you shouldn't lose hope — you may receive one a couple of months down the road.

Genealogy Forum Message Board Center

A good place to gain some experience with message boards is the AOL Genealogy Forum Message Board Center, shown in Figure 3-7. The Message Board Center contains a variety of areas that enable you to contact other genealogical researchers. To get to the center, type the Keyword: **Roots** and then click the Go button. Click the Messages button in the Genealogy Forum window (the second button in the far-left column).

Tip

Check a message board for responses to your posting weekly for about the first six weeks after you've posted it. After that, check for responses about once a month for six months to a year. Then consider reposting your message, adding any new information you have to share or other questions that you have.

Note

The length of time that your postings remain available to the public depends on the message boards to which you've posted them. Be sure to look over the message board instructions and/or FAQs to see the specific details about that forum.

Figure 3-7. The Genealogy Forum Message Board Center window.

In the Message Board Center, you see icons for five main message board areas, as well as a scrollable window, listing message board resources. The main five message board areas are

- ▶ Ethnic and Special Groups
- ▶ Computer and General
- ▶ Surnames
- ▶ The United States
- ▶ Countries of the World

Each of these board areas contains a set of message boards that further break down the topic, and even these second level boards can contain their own boards. For example, the Surname message board (discussed in Chapter 4) contains several boards — one of which is dedicated to discussion of surnames beginning with the letter *A*. Under the A Surnames board, you find message boards that are dedicated to specific surnames, such as the Abbott Message Board. Look around the message boards and read the posts from other researchers. Doing so helps you familiarize yourself with the structure and tone of the messages.

When you're ready to post a message, you may want to begin by posting to the New? Introduce Yourself! board. Here's how:

1. Type the Keyword: **Roots** in the text box on the navigation toolbar and then click Go.

   The Genealogy Forum window appears.

2. Click the Messages button.

   The Genealogy Forum Message Board Center appears.

3. Double-click the New? Introduce Yourself! message board in the scrollable list, which is located just below the Computer and General message board icon.

   This step launches the New? Introduce Yourself! window.

4. Click the Create Subject button (the fourth button from the bottom left of the window).

5. Type your subject in the Subject box. Make sure that the subject is detailed enough to interest fellow researchers.

6. Press the Tab key to go to the message text box. Type your message and be sure to use full names and include

dates and places of events (such as birth and death) that can help other researchers determine if they can help you.

7. Click the Send button to post your message to the message board.

Of course, you want to do more than just post messages. You also want to read the postings of other researchers to see if they share your interests. After you enter a message board, you can find messages that interest you in a couple of ways:

▶ You can open up a message board and scroll through the list of the subjects until you find something of interest.

▶ You can use the Find By drop-down list (located in the bottom-right corner of the window) to search through posts for specific words.

In the following section, we describe another site that serves the same purpose as the Message Board Center in the Genealogy Forum.

GenForum

The largest genealogical message board site is GenForum (www.genforum.com), which is hosted by Genealogy.com. It currently has a collection of over 3.7 million messages from genealogists around the world. Message boards, called forums, address individual surnames, geographic locations, and general topics (such as computer software, historical periods, and so forth). Follow these steps to locate a forum:

1. Type **genforum.genealogy.com** in the text box on the navigation toolbar.

   AOL opens a new window and takes you to the GenForum home page.

2. Click a link under the Surnames, Regional, or General Topics heading.

   For example, if you're interested in looking at messages about the Helm surname, click the H link under Surnames. A new page with a list of surnames on it then appears.

3. Click the link for the topic.

   In our example, we would click the Helm link.

After you find a forum that interests you, scroll through the list of messages until you find a subject of interest. Then click the message link to see the full text of the message. If you want to reply to a message, click the Click Here to Post a Followup Message button. Fill out the form that appears and then click the Post Message button.

In addition to the Genealogy Forum's Message Board Center and GenForum, check out these other message board sites. They work similarly.

Tip

Another way to find a forum is to use the Forum Finder. On the GenForum home page, enter the topic you're researching in the Forum Finder box and then click the Find button.

Query Central

The oldest of the general query boards is Query Central (query.genealogytoolbox.com), which is located at Helm's Genealogy Toolbox. It contains an archive of messages dating back to 1995 and allows you to post new messages through its Open Queries pages.

FamilyHistory.com

One of the newest general-purpose message boards is located at FamilyHistory.com (www.familyhistory.com) and is part of the Ancestry.com family of Web sites. Here you can post messages on surname, state and county, and general research topic message boards.

GenConnect

GenConnect (cgi.rootsweb.com/~genbbs/) is a system of message boards used by several different types of genealogical sites. You can find surname, geographic, and special project boards at GenConnect.

GenExchange

GenExchange (www.genexchange.com) has message boards on geographic locations and surnames, and keeps growing more and more each day.

3

Communicating with Others

Participating in Chat Rooms

Sometimes just posting a message and hoping for a reply isn't enough. You may want to have a real-time conversation with another researcher. That's where chat rooms come in. Chat rooms are areas where groups of people can meet online to discuss a certain topic. Chats can be scheduled events or informal meetings that occur on the spur of the moment.

Genealogy Forum Chat Center

You can get your feet wet with the Genealogy Forum's regularly scheduled chats. These chats, which are monitored by a host, include topics such as ethnic groups, geographic regions, computers and the Internet, and historical periods. You can access all of these chats in the Genealogy Forum Chat Center.

To enter one of the Genealogy Forum's chat rooms, do the following:

1. Type the Keyword: **Roots** in the text box on the navigation toolbar and click Go.

   The Genealogy Forum window launches.

2. Click the Chats button (the third button in the first column).

   The Chat Center window appears, as shown in Figure 3-8.

If you're interested in getting to know other members of the AOL community, type the Keyword: **Chat** to visit the People Connection. The People Connection links you to chats of all kinds. From here, you can learn the ropes and see the variety of topics being discussed all the time.

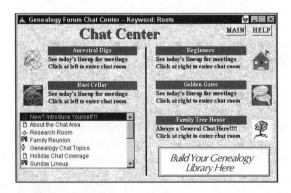

Figure 3-8. The Chat Center in the Genealogy Forum.

3. Select one of the five chat areas by clicking the appropriate icon.

   The chat room window appears. The chat room window contains a brief overview of the chat room and some guidelines on what you can expect from the chats. On the right side of the window, you find an icon that leads you to the chat room schedule and another icon that allows you to enter the chat room.

4. Click the icon for the chat room (which is usually labeled the name of the chat area; for example, the icon for the Ancestral Digs Conference is labeled Ancestral Digs).

   This step launches the chat window.

On the left side of the window is a box that displays the current conversations going on in the chat room, as shown in Figure 3-9. If you want to say something in the chat, type your message in the small text box at the bottom of the window (located just to the left of the Send button). After you type your message, click the Send button, and your message appears in the chat window. On the right side of the screen is a small scroll box. This box tells you the screen names of the other members who are currently in the chat room. Beneath that box are some buttons that allow you to customize your chat experience.

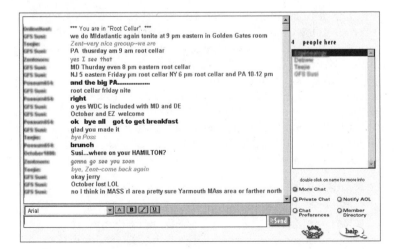

Figure 3-9. A chat window in the Roots Cellar chat area.

3

Communicating with Others

At some point, you're likely to find another member in the chat room who has a research interest similar to yours. Rather than using the general chat area to discuss a topic that is of concern only to you and the other researcher, you may want to have a private chat instead.

You can begin a private chat two different ways:

▶ If you're already in a chat room, click the Private Chat button located beneath the scroll box to launch the private chat window. In the space provided, type the name that you want to call your chat (or, if another member sends you a notification of a chat, type in that exact name) and click the Go Chat button.

▶ Click the People button on the AOL toolbar and then choose Start Your Own Chat from the drop-down menu. Then click the Private Chat button.

To see a copy of the chat schedule for the Genealogy Forum, click the Genealogy Chat Topics option in the scroll box at the bottom of the Chat Center window. This schedule provides details on the times and locations for all the genealogically related chats that are regularly scheduled. You can also see the daily lineup of chats by selecting one of the lineups in the scroll box.

Internet Relay Chat

Another popular method of chatting is Internet Relay Chat. Internet Relay Chat (IRC) is similar in concept to the chat rooms in the AOL Genealogy Forum. However, the individuals using IRC are from the Internet community at large rather than just the AOL community. In order to use IRC, you must have a software program that allows you to connect to a chat server. mIRC is a popular IRC client that you can download from Winsock Central (Keyword: **Winsock**). After you install the software, you need to find a chat server to log on to. Here are some servers you may want to try:

▶ AfterNET (`irc.afternet.org:6667`) - #GenealogyForum, #Genealogy-n-UK, #Genealogy-Native

▶ DALnet (`irc03.irc.aol.com`) - #Canadian Gen, #genealogy-events, #genealogy-help, #Genealogy_IRC

▶ EFNet (`irc02.irc.aol.com`) - #genealogy

▶ NewNet (`irc.newnet.net:6667`) - #family_history, #genealogy101

Don't Forget Mailing Lists and Newsgroups

Two other resources that we need to tell you about are mailing lists and newsgroups. Mailing lists and newsgroups are at opposite extremes in terms of how you receive information.

Mailing Lists

You may have sent an e-mail to two or three people, but can you imagine sending a single e-mail message to thousands of people? That's exactly what happens with a mailing list.

Mailing lists address a number of topics including surnames, geographic areas, ethnic groups, and methods of researching genealogy. To join some of the larger mailing lists, you need to subscribe. Subscribing consists of sending a message to an e-mail address with specific text in it that allows you to join the mailing list. After the host server receives your message, it sends you a confirmation notice with details on how to post messages, as well as how to unsubscribe from the mailing list. You can then send a message to a central address that is then sent to everyone on the list.

Keep the guidelines we offer about e-mail earlier in this chapter in mind when you're sending messages to a mailing list because your message may be read by a large audience. Here are some additional tips:

▶ Make sure that your posts to the mailing lists are appropriate for that list. For example, if you subscribe to a mailing list that discusses genealogical research in Frederick County, Virginia, don't post messages about the migration patterns of Canadian geese.

▶ Keep in mind that carrying on a one-on-one e-mail conversation is sometimes preferable to addressing the list as a whole. One-on-one conversations usually take place when researchers exchange several e-mails on a topic that is of interest only to them.

Definition

A mailing list is formed when a group of people who have common interests decide to exchange ideas through e-mail. To avoid placing hundreds of people in the To line of the e-mail, they put together a list of all the group members' e-mail addresses, and this list can then be accessed with a single e-mail address.

3

Communicating with Others

Newsgroups

Newsgroups are similar to mailing lists in that a group of people form a newsgroup to discuss topics that interest them. However, with newsgroups, the messages are not sent to your mailbox. Instead, messages are posted to a news server. In order to read newsgroups, you need to have software that allows you to connect to a news server.

Tip

AOL has a newsreader built in, so you don't have to worry about installing any other software if you want to participate in newsgroup discussions.

You can find several newsgroups that are dedicated to genealogy. You can access 26 newsgroups in the soc.genealogy hierarchy that tackle topics such as ethnic groups, geographical areas, surnames, and computers (see Figure 3-10). You can also find some specialized newsgroups in other hierarchies, including some foreign language newsgroups.

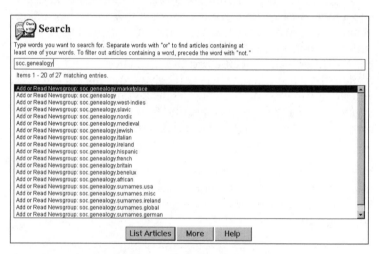

Figure 3-10. The soc.genealogy hierarchy of newsgroups.

To access a newsgroup, you need to add the newsgroup to your newsgroups list by following these steps:

1. Type the Keyword: **Newsgroups** in the text box on the navigation toolbar and click the Go button.

   This step launches the Internet Newsgroups window.

2. Click the Search All Newsgroups button.

   The Search All Newsgroups window appears.

3. Type the subject that you're interested in — such as *genealogy* — and click the List Articles button.

In the lower box, you see any matches to your search criteria. In our case, the search turned up 41 newsgroups related to genealogy.

4. Double-click a newsgroup that interests you.

(We picked the `soc.genealogy.italian` newsgroup.) This step brings up the Add or Read Newsgroup window.

5. If you just want to read messages from this newsgroup, click the List Articles link. A list of articles then appears, as shown in Figure 3-11. If you want to add the newsgroup to your My Newsgroups list (so that you can always refer to it quickly through a shortcut), then click the Subscribe to Newsgroup link. (Selecting this option takes you to a new window where you can define your newsgroup preferences).

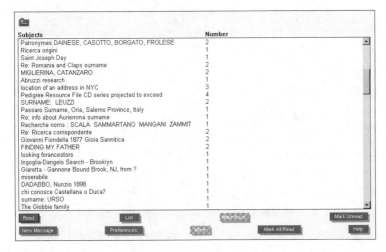

Figure 3-11. Messages from the `soc.genealogy.italian` newsgroup.

After you subscribe to a newsgroup, you can view it by going to the Internet Newsgroups window (Keyword: **Newsgroups**) and clicking the Read My Newsgroups button.

Meeting Research Buddies Online

We all have buddies, right? People with whom we speak or correspond frequently — chums, pals, compadres. Well, AOL provides a wonderful little feature (appropriately called Buddies) that you can use to communicate quickly with your research buddies.

The Buddies feature notifies you when another AOL buddy is signed on. You can then contact that person to discuss your genealogical research or life in general, if you desire. Here is how you create a Buddy List:

1. Click the People button on the toolbar and choose View Buddy List from the drop-down menu (or type the Keyword: **Buddy**).

   This launches the Buddy List window. The default window has three categories of buddies: Buddies, Family, and Co-Workers.

2. Click the Setup button just beneath the Buddies List window.

   The Buddy List Setup box appears.

3. To create a new Buddy List category (for example, you may want to create a category for researchers of a particular family line), click the Create button.

   This step launches the Create a Buddy List Group window.

4. Type in a Buddy List Group Name and then the screen name of an AOL member you want to add to your Buddy List. Then click the Add Buddy button.

5. Click the Save button after you finish entering screen names.

If a person designated as a buddy logs on to AOL, his/her screen name appears in your Buddy List. When the name appears in your Buddy List, you can initiate an instant messaging session or a buddy chat session to communicate with the fellow researcher.

Some people have privacy concerns about people knowing when they log on to AOL and what parts they are visiting. If you share this concern, then you can adjust your privacy preferences. To do this, click the Setup button in the Buddy List box. Then click the Privacy Preferences button. You are presented with five different levels of privacy that you can implement when you're online.

Summary

This chapter told you the basics of Internet communication tools. We've covered using e-mail, posting information to message boards, participating in chat sessions, and using mailing lists and newsgroups. Additionally, we showed you how to set up storage files for your e-mail messages and how to use AOL's Buddy feature, which is fun and handy. Now it's time to put your new knowledge to use — the next chapter shows you how to use some of these communication tools in your actual research when you're searching using your ancestor's name.

3

Communicating with Others

P A R T

II

GATHERING
AND SHARING ONLINE

Quick Look

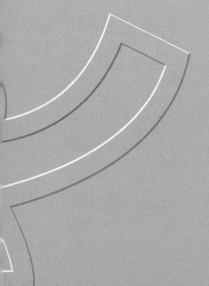

Chapter 4
Searching for Family by Name

The majority of genealogical research online involves using a family member's name to find information. That's because it's relatively easy to learn some of the surnames in your family either from your own recollections or from other relatives. Also, you can be reasonably sure of the accuracy of at least a couple of surnames with which you'll want to start — your father's surname and your mother's maiden surname. With this in mind, you need to have a good understanding of how to research by name so you can conduct searches effectively.

Researching an Individual by Name: Why and How

Searching for information about people by using their names is logical — that's how they're known and how information about them is recorded. For the most part, the process of re-searching a name is relatively easy: You find out your ancestor's name and then use that name to look for records and other documents that contain information about the person. Some complications, however, may make searching by name more challenging. Here are a few ways to avoid potential problems:

▶ **Start with what you think you know.** You have to start somewhere. Use a surname that you're sure of or have heard used in your family when you begin re-searching. Only in the process of finding records about relatives whose names you know can you discover the names of other ancestors.

▶ **Take into account variations in spelling.** Many names have more than one spelling — take Helm and Helme, for instance. Some names that don't necessarily sound the same were used interchangeably over time — like Sanders and Saunders. Keep in mind that you may have to try a variety of spellings to find the records that pertain to your relative.

▶ **Consider name changes.** People change names under a variety of circumstances. Name changes commonly oc-cur when a woman exchanges her maiden name for her married name, her husband's surname. Name changes also occur when adopted children take their adoptive parents' surname. Another common reason that names change is because of immigration — immigrants often shorten names or take on new names to make it easier for others to understand or pronounce their names, or to reflect the culture of their new country. And even some name changes aren't necessarily at the choice of the name-holder — it's not unusual to find a person's name changed when a clerk or other record keeper mis-understood or wasn't very diligent about recording cor-rect spellings.

 Definition

A surname is a person's last name. Generally, it is the family name passed down from one's father or taken from one's spouse.

Tip

Researchers looking for information about immigrant ancestors commonly discover that their surnames have been Americanized or short-ened after arriving in the United States or Canada. Many immigrants did so in an attempt to assimilate into their new culture and to make it easier for record keepers to spell their names.

4

Searching for Family by Name

Tip

If you're not sure about the variations of the surname you're researching, surf over to CPROOTS.COM Genealogy Resource Center: What's in a Name? site at `www.cproots.com/ nameindx.htm` to see if your surname is included in their database — they include information about the origins of some 6,900 surnames and variations for many of them.

Tip

John Fuller and Christine Gaunt provide spelling variations for many of the surnames for which there are mailing lists. To see if your surname is included, check out Genealogy Resources on the Internet's index of Mailing Lists at `www.rootsweb.com/ ~jfuller/gen_mail .html#SURNAMES`.

Tip

Starting with a name that's not too popular or too unique gives you a better chance of finding relevant and useful information about that name online. Think about using your own surname or the full name of one of your grandparents.

Picking a Name to Start With

When you begin your online research, pick a name that increases your odds of success. Select a name that is not so popular that you're overwhelmed with matches but, at the same time, not so unique you can't find anything about it. Also, it's a good idea to make a list of possible spelling variations or extensions of that name that were used by your ancestors that you can also use in your search. For example, if you're looking for information about someone with the surname Sanders, be sure your list of spelling variations includes Sander, Saunders, Sounder, Souder. If possible, wait until you have a little experience with the name-based resources online before searching with common surnames.

Think first about using your own name. Is your surname really common? Smith, Jones, Johnson, Miller, and Cook are examples of very common names that may result in an incredible number of hits or matches online. While identifying really popular names is pretty easy, figuring out which names qualify as unique is more difficult. That's why we recommend that you use a site like Hamrick Software's Surname Distribution to determine how popular your name is. See the sidebar, "How Popular Is Too Popular?" for more on this site.

If your name qualifies as too popular or too unique, consider using one of your maternal grandparents' names (that means the name of your mom's mother or father) to begin your online research.

Having Extra Information at the Ready

The fact is, until you conduct your search, you won't know for sure whether the surname you've chosen is too common or not common enough to give you the information you need. To avoid ending up in a situation that we call *resource overload* —

an overabundance of sites to check out — we encourage you to try these strategies to increase your odds of success:

▶ Recognize when to use a person's full name instead of just his or her surname.

▶ Know something about your ancestor, such as his or her date or place of birth.

Popular Is Too Popular?

How do you determine whether the name you want to research is too popular? Or not very popular at all? Check out Hamrick Software's U.S. Surname Distribution site at `www.hamrick.com/names` (see Figure 4-1). Here you can enter a surname and search by year to see how many people in various areas of the United States had that name during a particular time period. You can look for the surname in 1850, 1880, 1920, and 1990, or in all years. Data for the earlier years comes from federal census records, and the 1990 information comes from phone directories. Here's how you use the site:

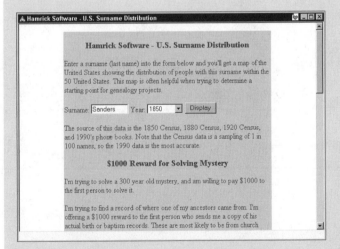

Figure 4-1. Hamrick Software's U.S. Surname Distribution site.

Continued

Popular Is Too Popular? *(continued)*

1. Enter a surname in the Surname field.

2. Choose a year from the pull-down menu. If you choose the All Years option, the site rotates through maps for each of the years available so that you can see how distribution of the surname changed over time.

3. Click the Display button. The resulting page illustrates the percentage of the population that had the surname. For example, in most states in 1850, only 1 in 10,000 people used the surname Sanders, but in Alabama, 1 out of 100 people used it, as shown in Figure 4-2.

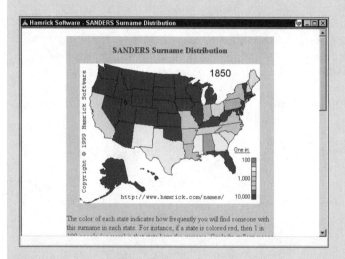

Figure 4-2. One out of every 100 people had the surname Sanders in Alabama in 1850.

When to Search for a Full Name

Imagine researching an ancestor with a common name like William Jones. You're likely to find many, many leads. But what if you search just for the surname Jones? You're likely to come up with an overabundance of sites containing information about anyone and everyone with that name — probably too many leads to sort through in a reasonable amount of time.

But think about what you may encounter if you're researching an unusual name, such as Absolum Looney. You may get just one or two leads by using his full name. But if you use just the surname Looney, you're likely to find several more resources pertaining to Looneys — some of those Looneys may be related to Absolum or their references may even contain information about Absolum that hasn't been indexed under this spelling of his first name. (That's right — first names can have various spellings too, which can make your search even more challenging!)

What to Know about Your Ancestor

Knowing at least one or two things about the person you're researching online can improve your results because you can quickly recognize leads that pertain to your ancestors. For example, if you know that your great-grandfather William Jones lived his whole life in Estill County, Kentucky, this information can help you narrow down which online resources to use. Why not start with resources that have information about William Joneses who lived in Kentucky? You may need to rely on what you've heard or can recall about a particular relative, and play some guessing games about which resources to use, especially if these recollections help you approximate when William Jones was born or when he died.

Tip

Knowing important information, such as dates and places of residence, can help you quickly determine whether a particular site contains information that is pertinent to your research. You can use this information to help narrow a search, or you can use it to verify that you've found the right person.

Tip

Searching online with only a surname increases the number of hits you get, thus increasing your choices of sites to visit and potentially find information. Using a full name, on the other hand, reduces the number of hits you get, which can be helpful when you're dealing with a popular surname, such as Smith, Jones, or Miller. We recommend that you use only surnames when searching with an uncommon name, and use full names when you're looking for information about someone with a really common name.

4

Searching for Family by Name

Knowing Which Online Resources Are Right for You

You've got a name picked out and you're ready to get started, but where do you begin? To make your search worthwhile, you need to know which sites are right for you. Actually, all the sites that we discuss in the following sections are right for you, but you should start with the Web sites that contain the most information, such as online databases. After that, you can identify potential sites to visit by using comprehensive genealogical indexes and search engines. Here's a list of resources you can use:

▶ Online databases

▶ Genealogical indexes

▶ Search engines

▶ Message boards

▶ One-name studies

▶ Mailing lists

For more information about the types of resources available and how to find them, take a look the following sections.

Searching Online Databases First

When you conduct your first genealogical search for a surname, you want to start from the largest pool of information possible. Databases are great because they hold large amounts of information that can lead you to the next step. Here's a list of great online databases you can use:

▶ **Ancestry.com** (www.ancestry.com) is one of the best online database sites, and it's available right at your fingertips! This AOL partner brings you the Genealogy/ Family History part of the AOL Families area. Ancestry .com has a collection of free and subscription-based databases with more than 500 million names. Wondering how to find and use it from the AOL Welcome page? Skip ahead to the next section to find out how.

▶ **Genealogy.com** (www.genealogy.com) has over 470 million names. Like Ancestry.com, some of the Genealogy.com databases are free to the general public, but many are restricted to subscribers of the Genealogy-Library.com service. The search interface for GenealogyLibrary.com uses the same technology as and is similar in look to Genealogy.com's Internet FamilyFinder search engine, which we examine in greater detail in "Finding Name-Related Sites," later in this chapter.

▶ **FamilySearch Internet Genealogy Service** (known simply as FamilySearch, www.familysearch.com) from the Church of Jesus Christ of Latter-day Saints (also known as the Mormons) also has several databases. Simply because of its popularity, this site warrants further examination. See the section on searching its databases to find out how.

Searching Ancestry.com Databases from the AOL Welcome Page

To get started with the database at Ancestry.com, follow these steps:

1. Type the Keyword: **Genealogy** in the text box on the navigation toolbar and click the Go button. The Genealogy/Family History window appears, which has a search interface in the center.

2. Enter the name(s) of the person you're researching in the appropriate fields.

3. Click the Search button. This step takes you to a Global Search Results page that lists the Ancestry.com areas in which the search word or term was found.

4. Scroll through the list and click an area that you want to check out. Another search results page pops up, listing all the hits within the particular area you've chosen. Each entry includes a question mark (which allows you to refine your search), a Free or Pay icon (which indicates whether the database is free for public use or restricted to Ancestry.com subscribers), the name of the database, and the number of times your search word or term occurred in the database.

5. Click any links that interest you.

Tip

Are you wondering which of these three databases you should use? Use all three. No database in the world can hold all the information you need, and these three only scratch the surface.

Tip

Always verify information that you find online against original records. Until you can prove the information is true (either by getting a copy of the record through traditional means or by downloading a digitized version), treat the information you find on the Internet only as a lead (not as gospel).

Note

The First Name field is optional, and whether or not you use it depends on whether you need to expand or narrow your search.

Searching FamilySearch.com Databases from the AOL Welcome Page

To find information by using the databases at FamilySearch.com, follow these steps:

Note

Unless you have a subscription to Ancestry.com, you can only view the results that are free to all Internet surfers. If you don't have a subscription and you click the link for a pay database, a page appears, giving you information about how to subscribe.

Note

The more fields that you complete, the more restricted your search becomes, and the more likely you'll have fewer hits than if you search simply by surname or first and last name. If you enter quite a bit of information and have fewer than five hits, try again, this time limiting the amount of information you enter.

1. Enter the FamilySearch URL — `www.familysearch.com` — in the text box on the navigation toolbar and click the Go button. This step brings you to the main Web page of the FamilySearch site, as shown in Figure 4-3.

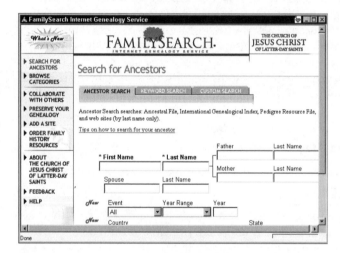

Figure 4-3. The main page of the FamilySearch site.

2. Enter the complete last name of your subject in the Last Name field. If you're searching for a common name, such as *Jones*, you should also enter additional details that may aid you in finding information specifically about your ancestor.

   You can add your subject's first name, his father's first and last names, his mother's first and last names, and his spouse's first and last names. You can also choose dates of events (and choose from various events), as well as the countries in which the events took place.

3. Click the Search button to submit the search or click the Clear button to cancel it and begin again. A results page displays matches in all four of the databases compiled and maintained by the church. You also see links to Web pages that fit your search term from the FamilySearch index of genealogical sites.

4. Scroll through the results and click any links that interest you. Clicking a link takes you to a new Web page that provides information about the person (sometimes just a name and date) and the source of the information (as well as the database from which the information was taken). If the information is available on CD-ROM, you may want to order a copy of the CD-ROM if you find the information valuable.

Note

As with genealogical information that you find on any Web site, you should always be sure to double-check what you find at FamilySearch against original records. Individual researchers, some of whom don't always cite their sources, contribute much of the information in the FamilySearch databases. There's no way to tell from a simple online search whether the information you're viewing is well documented with reliable records or merely hearsay. We discuss the different kinds of records you can use to verify your research in Chapter 5.

Finding Name-Related Sites

You can find thousands upon thousands of Internet resources that contain information about people by their names. And there are two types of sites that can help you find these resources: comprehensive genealogical indexes and genealogical search engines. We take a look at these types of sites and show you how best to use them in the sections that follow.

Comprehensive Genealogical Indexes

Don't let the long name of this type of site intimidate you in any way — *comprehensive genealogical indexes* are simply lists of links to other Internet-based resources that have value to family historians. The lists are set up like directories (similar to AOL's directory system for conducting searches) and have various categories and subcategories into which all the links are sorted. Figure 4-4 shows you the People page of the Genealogy SiteFinder, the index that currently has the most links to genealogical resources on the Internet.

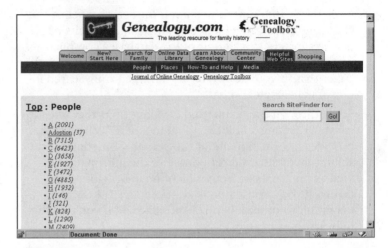

Figure 4-4. Use the People category to look for individuals by name in the Genealogy SiteFinder.

Definition

A comprehensive genealogical index is a list of Internet resources of interest and value to genealogists and family historians.

To find online resources related to the specific surname you're researching, follow these simple steps:

1. Type **sitefinder.genealogytoolbox.com** in the text box on the navigation toolbar and then click the Go button. This takes you to an entry point for the Genealogy SiteFinder.

2. Scroll down the page a little and click the link for the People category. The People page of the Genealogy SiteFinder appears. On it, you find links for each letter of the alphabet, as well as some general links to other Web pages at the bottom.

3. Click the link for the first letter of the surname you're researching. A page appears, listing links to other Internet resources that contain information about surnames beginning with that letter. The list is sorted alphabetically by surname, and each entry states the surname and the name of the Internet resource.

   Next to each resource listed is a brief description of the information available if you use the resource. This information gives you an idea whether a particular site is likely to have any information about your ancestor.

4. Scroll through the list and see if you can find any links for your surname.

5. Click any links that interest you to go to those Internet resources.

Here are some other comprehensive genealogical indexes to check out:

▶ Cyndi's List of Genealogy Sites on the Internet (`www
.cyndislist.com`)

▶ Genealogy HomePage (`www.genhomepage.com`)

▶ Genealogy Resources on the Internet (`www-personal
.umich.edu/~cgaunt/gen_int1.html`)

Search Engines

Search engines are programs that index the contents of Web sites. When you visit a search engine Web site and enter a keyword or term in the search field, the search engine searches its index for results that match your request. Genealogical search engines take this process one step further by limiting the indexing to only those sites that contain information of interest to genealogists and family historians.

For the same reason that we recommend you use more than one comprehensive genealogical index, we recommend that you always use more than one genealogical search engine. Here are a few to check out:

▶ GenealogyPortal (`www.genealogyportal.com`)

▶ GenPageFinder (`www.ancestry.families.aol.com/
databases/genpagefinder.htm`)

▶ Internet FamilyFinder (`www.genealogy.com/
ifftop.html`)

The following steps show you how to use the Internet FamilyFinder search engine, but you can follow these general steps to search any genealogical search engine:

1. Type `www.genealogy.com/ifftop.html` in the text box on the navigation toolbar and then click the Go button. The Internet FamilyFinder search engine Web page appears, as shown in Figure 4-5.

Note

If you'd rather not click a series of links, you can use the Genealogy SiteFinder's search engine, which allows you to enter a surname or a full name and quickly get a list of resources to visit. However, if you're dealing with a name that has more than one possible spelling, you will see results that closely match (but aren't exactly the same as) what you enter in the search box. You can find the Search SiteFinder field in the upper right of the Genealogy SiteFinder's People page or from any of the pages at the Genealogy SiteFinder.

Tip

Because of the large number of genealogical and geographical Web sites available, you can't possibly find all the information you need from one comprehensive index. For this reason, we recommend that you use several sites when researching.

Definition

A genealogical search engine is a program that indexes the text of genealogical Web sites and then allows you to search the index for particular keywords.

4

Searching for Family by Name

Note

Two of these genealogical search engines allow you to search by more than just names. This capability is handy when you're looking for genealogical information by location or type of resource (such as library, primary records, or software).

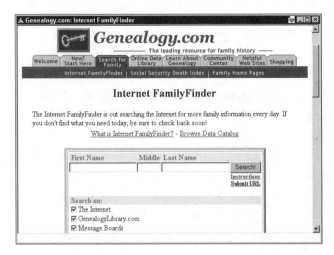

Figure 4-5. The Internet FamilyFinder allows you to search the Internet for Web pages for information about a particular name.

Tip

General search engines are programs that index sites all over the Web and return search results that link to those sites. Some examples of general search engines are Google, AltaVista, Lycos, and HotBot.

2. Enter the name(s) of the individual you're researching in the name fields. Exactly which fields you complete depends on whether you're searching with your ancestor's full name or just his or her surname.

3. In the Search On section of the page, use your mouse to select which resources you want the search engine to search. If you put a check mark in a check box, the search engine searches this resource. If you don't put a check mark in a check box, the search engine skips that resource. Keep in mind that the more resources you search, the more hits the search returns.

4. After you finish completing the search form, click the Search button. A page pops up, displaying a list of links that match your search criteria (see Figure 4-6).

5. Scroll through the page and click any links that look promising or interesting.

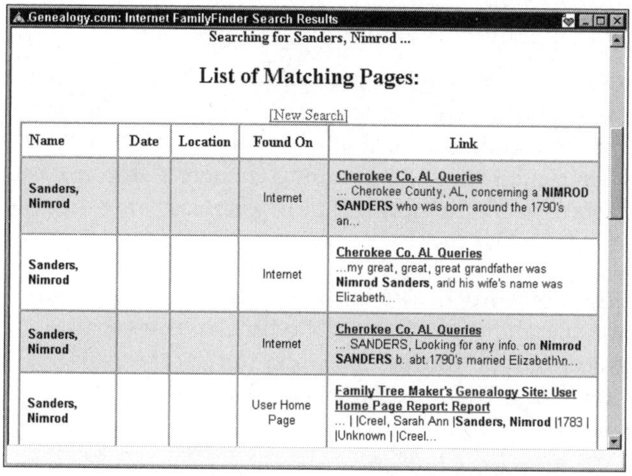
Genealogy.com: Internet FamilyFinder Search Results

Searching for Sanders, Nimrod ...

List of Matching Pages:

[New Search]

Name	Date	Location	Found On	Link
Sanders, Nimrod			Internet	Cherokee Co. AL Queries ... Cherokee County, AL, concerning a **NIMROD SANDERS** who was born around the 1790's an...
Sanders, Nimrod			Internet	Cherokee Co. AL Queries ...my great, great, great grandfather was **Nimrod Sanders**, and his wife's name was Elizabeth...
Sanders, Nimrod			Internet	Cherokee Co. AL Queries ... SANDERS, Looking for any info. on **Nimrod SANDERS** b. abt 1790's married Elizabeth\n...
Sanders, Nimrod			User Home Page	Family Tree Maker's Genealogy Site: User Home Page Report: Report ... | |Creel, Sarah Ann |**Sanders, Nimrod** |1783 | |Unknown | |Creel...

Figure 4-6. The results page for a search on the name Nimrod Sanders.

Using Surname Message Boards

You can use surname message boards to gather information about people, as well as find others who may be researching the same family lines as you. Most surname boards allow you to post a message stating who you are researching and the geographic locations in which they lived. You can also respond to other peoples' postings.

Although you can find other surname message boards by using comprehensive genealogical indexes and genealogical search engines (which we discuss in the two preceding sections), we suggest that you begin with the surname message boards at the Genealogy Forum on AOL because they're easy to use. AOL's message boards are located in two areas of the forum. One area has boards only for the most popular names, and the other has boards for all names for which people have submitted messages. We discuss each type of message board in the following sections.

Popular Name Message Boards

AOL's popular name message boards allow you to keep up with the Joneses, the Smiths, the Johnsons, and countless other family historians with common surnames. If you don't know how popular the surname you're researching is, there's only one way to find out. Here's how to view the most popular name message boards:

1. Type the Keyword: **Roots** in the text box on the navigation toolbar and then click the Go button. You can also press Ctrl+K, type **Roots**, and press the Enter key on your keyboard. Then the Genealogy Forum window pops up.

2. Click the Surnames button to open the Surname Center window.

3. Click the Surname Areas icon. A second Surname Center window appears; this one has a scrollable list that offers alphabetical links to files of popular surnames, as shown in Figure 4-7.

Figure 4-7. Alphabetical links to the files of popular surnames in the Surname Center.

4. Double-click the file for the first letter of the surname you're researching. A window with the most popular surnames beginning with that letter pops up.

5. Scroll through the list and see if the surname you're researching is represented. If it is, double-click it. A window for that name appears, from which you can choose to use the message board, upload a GEDCOM file or check out other files that have been contributed, or link to relevant Web sites.

6. Open the message board by double-clicking the link. You can read messages posted by other people (and respond to them) or create a new message yourself.

General Surname Boards

If you're interested in finding out what people have to say about surnames, or you want to see if your less-popular name is listed, then general surname boards are for you. To get to these message boards, follow these steps:

1. Type the Keyword: **Roots** in the text box on the navigation toolbar and click the Go button. You can also press Ctrl+K, type **Roots,** and press the Enter key on your keyboard. The Genealogy Forum window then pops up.

2. Click the Messages button to open the Message Board Center window. You can also get to this level by clicking the Surnames button in the main Genealogy Forum window and then clicking the Message Board Center icon.

3. Click the Surnames icon to bring up the main Surname Message Board window, which has a scrollable list of alphabetical links.

4. Scroll through the list and click the first letter of the surname you're researching. A window pops up that alphabetically breaks down the surname boards even further, as shown in Figure 4-8.

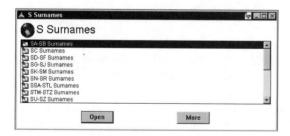

Figure 4-8. A second-level categorization of surname message boards.

5. Scroll through the list and click any message boards that pertain to your research. You can read messages posted by other people (as well as respond to them) or create a new message yourself.

Posting Your Message

Posting a message on a message board can be an art form — and rightfully so. After all, you want to creatively and concisely state exactly what you're researching so that others can understand and hopefully help you.

Here's how you should craft your message:

1. Follow the numbered steps in either of the preceding two sections ("General Surname Boards" or "Popular Name Message Boards") to find the message board to which you want to post your message.

2. Click the Create Subject button. This brings up the Post New Message window, shown in Figure 4-9.

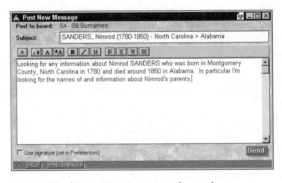

Figure 4-9. The Post New Message window is where you construct your message and post it to the message board.

3. In the Subject field, enter the subject of your message in this format: First type the surname in all uppercase letters, followed by the first name, which can be lower-cased. Additional information, such as dates of birth and death, if you know them, can follow in parentheses. You may also choose to include the location for which you're seeking information after the dates in parentheses. Your subject line should look similar to this: "SANDERS, Nimrod (1780-1850) - North Carolina > Alabama" (refer to Figure 4-9).

Note

If you know the exact dates of birth and/or death for the person you're researching, be sure to use them instead of years only. For example, if you know your ancestor was born on May 5, 1780 and died sometime in 1850, use "(5 May 1780–1850)" instead of "(1780–1850)."

Caution

Be sure to use four digits when you record years in genealogical research. Don't leave others guessing whether you mean 1780, 1880, or 1980 by using '80.

Tip

Always enter your ancestor's surname in all uppercase letters so that other researchers can easily identify the surname you're researching.

4. Tab down to the large box at the bottom of the window and type your message. You should make your message as clear as possible — cut to the chase and state your question or message simply. Don't forget to include as much information as you can to help other researchers recognize if they can help you. Here's an example (refer to Figure 4-9):

"Looking for any information about Nimrod SANDERS who was born in Montgomery County, North Carolina, in 1780 and died around 1850 in Alabama. In particular I'm looking for the names of and information about Nimrod's parents."

You can change the font and format of the message by using the toolbar above the message window.

5. After you've completed your message, click the Send button.

After you've posted some messages on AOL about the names you're researching, be sure to post similar messages on some other boards. Doing so helps you reach researchers who may not have access to the AOL boards or who use only one or two of these other boards. Here are some other message boards that you may want to check out:

▶ FamilyHistory.com (www.familyhistory.com)

▶ GenConnect (cgi.rootsweb.com/~genbbs)

▶ GenForum (genforum.genealogy.com)

▶ Query Central (query.genealogytoolbox.com)

Making the Most of Mailing Lists

The role of mailing lists in researching ancestors by name is much like that of message boards — mailing lists allow you to post messages that can put you in contact with other researchers who may be interested in the same family lines as you. The real difference is in how you access the messages. When you post questions to a message board, other researchers visit the board, see your message, and respond. When you post questions to a mailing list, your question is automatically sent via e-mail to all of the list's subscribers. But first you have to find a list and subscribe to it.

Caution

Include as many basic details as you can about your ancestor to help other researchers determine whether they have any information that pertains to your research (such as names, dates, and places). But make sure you don't go overboard by providing lots of nonessential information, such as grandpa's personal habits. Save those for one-on-one correspondence with other researchers who inquire about grandpa based on this posting.

Tip

In addition to using our guidance here, you can get a feel for how to craft your messages by reviewing what others have posted. See how they phrased the notes they posted and summed up the subjects of their messages.

Note

Be sure to check back at the message boards to see if anyone has responded to your posting(s). Initially, check at least once a week. After about six weeks, you can start checking monthly. And consider reposting your message after six months to a year so you can update information with any of your own findings, as well as reach out to new visitors to the message board.

Finding a Mailing List and Subscribing

We think the best resource for finding mailing lists for the surname you're researching is to take a look at the mailing list section of Genealogy Resources on the Internet (`www.rootsweb .com/~jfuller/gen_mail.html`). This comprehensive genealogical index has an extensive list of the mailing lists that are available. Just follow these steps to select a mailing list:

Tip

Mailing lists give you an instant audience for your research question because every posting is automatically sent to all of the list's subscribers.

1. Type `www.rootsweb.com/~jfuller/gen_mail.html` in the text box on the navigation toolbar. This brings up the Mailing Lists page of the Genealogy Resources on the Internet site.

2. Scroll to the bottom of the Web page until you see the alphabetical links for surname-related mailing lists, as shown in Figure 4-10.

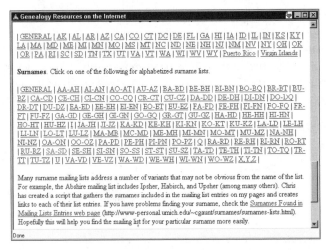

Figure 4-10. Links to surname-related lists appear at the bottom of the Mailing Lists page of Genealogy Resources on the Internet.

3. Click the appropriate link for the surname you're researching. A new Web page pops up that contains links for the names that fit in that alphabetical category.

4. Scroll through the list of names and click the one that you're researching. This takes you to a page that provides information about the mailing list and its focus, as well as explains how to subscribe to it.

5. Follow the online instructions to subscribe to the mailing list.

Learning the Ropes Before You Post to a Mailing List

After you subscribe to a mailing list, you may be tempted to jump right in and post your own messages — after all, the sooner you can make contact with other researchers, the better, right? Wrong. If you don't follow the protocol for posting to some mailing lists, you could be setting yourself up for negative responses from other subscribers (which doesn't help anyone in their genealogical research). Why do other subscribers get so easily annoyed? How would you feel if you got several e-mails a day asking questions that you have no earthly idea how to answer or that you shouldn't have to answer? Here's a list of things you should do to avoid subscriber backlash:

▶ Monitor the mailing list (this activity is often called *lurking*) for a little while — just until you get a feel for the way things are done on a particular mailing list. The best way to learn the ropes is to watch the pros. The amount of time you should lurk depends on the mailing list. If you subscribe to a list where you receive daily postings, you may need to lurk only for a day or two. But if you subscribe to a list from which you get postings only once a week, you may need to wait a week or two.

▶ Read the mailing list's FAQs (or Frequently Asked Questions) if it has some available. Typically, the FAQs are included in the confirmation message(s) you receive when you subscribe, or the confirmation message tells you where you can find them. Never post a question about how things work before checking this essential document.

▶ Read over any tips that the mailing list offers regarding how to format a message.

AOL's Help resources give you some mailing list etiquette. Go to the Help menu and choose Member Services Online Help. From the list that appears, choose Internet. Then choose Mailing lists to see an index of information available on using mailing lists.

After you're familiar with the protocol for that mailing list, jump on in and begin posting your messages.

Tip

Hold on to the confirmation message that you receive when you join a surname mailing list so that you know where to address your posts, and where you can unsubscribe should you ever desire to do so.

Caution

Monitor (or lurk on) the mailing list for a little while to learn the culture and format for posting.

Posting to a Mailing List

Posting your messages to a mailing list is generally easy. You simply send an e-mail to the e-mail address supplied in the e-mail you received upon subscribing to the mailing list.

The subject line of your e-mail and the text of your message should resemble the message board posting that we discuss earlier in this chapter.

Subject: SANDERS, Nimrod (1780-1850) – North Carolina > Alabama

Message: Looking for any information about Nimrod SANDERS who was born in Montgomery County, North Carolina in 1780 and died around 1850 in Alabama. In particular I'm looking for the names of and information about Nimrod's parents.

Replying to messages posted to the mailing list is just as simple. All you generally have to do is click the Reply button, type the e-mail message, and click the Send button.

Checking Out One-Name Studies and Family Associations

Two additional sources of information that you should consider (especially if you're researching a more popular surname) are one-name studies and family associations. These types of Web sites devote themselves to collecting information about a particular name. Here's some information on how these sites work:

▶ **One-name study Web site:** This type of site devotes itself to a collection of any and all information about a given surname, regardless of where the people with that surname lived. The information contained on such a site often includes details such as the history and origination of the particular surname, a list of places where the name has been traced, and stories and facts about various people who used the name (including famous people).

▶ **Family association Web site:** This site typically has information about a single surname. However, the information is usually limited to a particular branch of the family tree (such as the Joneses who trace themselves through

Caution

Be careful when replying to mailing list posts. If the information you're providing will be of interest only to the author of the message, make sure that you reply only to that person and not to the entire list.

Note

When you reply to someone else's posting, be sure the existing text in the Subject field of the e-mail pertains to the subject to which you want to reply. For instance, if you have information about someone's posting about *SANDERS, Nimrod (1780–1850) – North Carolina > Alabama*, make sure the subject of your heading reads: **Re: SANDERS, Nimrod (1780–1850) – North Carolina > Alabama.**

Caution

If you subscribe to the digest mode of a mailing list, be sure to look over the topics covered in the digest-mailing before deleting it. For more information about digest modes, look back over our discussion of mailing lists in general in Chapter 3.

George Jones of Georgia, 1761) or to a geographical area (such as Joneses of the Pacific Northwest). You can generally find facts, stories, and histories about the specific family on the Web site, along with information about how to join the family association.

Finding one-name studies and family associations is relatively easy — just follow the steps in "Finding Name-Related Sites," earlier in this chapter. These steps walk you through the process of using comprehensive genealogical indexes and genealogical search engines. Typically, the results from searching these types of sites yield at least a few Web sites that qualify as one-name studies or family associations.

Looking through Non-Surname Sites

You may also find information about particular surnames on sites that focus on topics other than surnames. For instance, you may find a site that has the history of a county in Texas and amid the text, you find a reference to your great-great-grandfather who was elected to office there in 1850.

Your best bet for finding sites like these is to use a genealogical search engine. Because a search engine indexes all the text at a given site, it picks up your ancestor's surname even on sites that are not surname-oriented. So keep your eyes open for sites like these as you're sifting through the results of your search.

Summary

You've learned a lot about names in this chapter, including how to select which name to begin your online research with. You've also mastered conducting searches online and using comprehensive genealogical indexes to find sites about surnames, as well as learned how to use various types of online resources in your research.

In the next chapter, we help you build on what you've learned here and begin searching for various types of records by name *and* location.

You can visit one-name study and family association sites to gather leads and find other researchers who are interested in the same surname as you so you can contact them and collaborate.

The reliability of content on one-name studies and family association sites varies immensely, so we can't really tell you exactly what information you can expect to find and how you should use it effectively.

4

Searching for Family by Name

CHAPTER

5

FOLLOWING THE
PAPER TRAIL

Quick Look

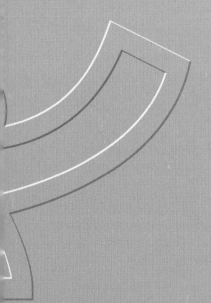

Chapter 5

Following the Paper Trail

It seems that every time you want to make contact with the government, you have to fill out a form. Sometimes filling out this paperwork is frustrating and something you would rather not do. However, this bureaucratic process has benefited genealogists for many years; in other words, it can be a good thing.

Whenever you complete a piece of paperwork for the government — or any other institution for that matter — you're leaving a paper trail. Future generations can use this trail to find out information about you for their genealogies.

This chapter focuses on how to use AOL to locate records that can provide a trail of your ancestors' lives. We also look at the many different types of records and methods that you can use online to find them.

Why Locating Original Records Is Important

You may find your job as a genealogist similar to that of a detective, because good detectives seek clues leading to solid evidence that they can use to solve crimes. Your challenge is to examine records for evidence that proves facts about your ancestors.

Of course, detectives occasionally use circumstantial evidence to solve crimes, and circumstantial evidence always leaves open the possibility that someone may be falsely accused of a crime when he or she is actually innocent. Similarly, some genealogists may intentionally or unintentionally take shortcuts — failing to prove their research. Their work often contains inaccuracies and details that cannot be proven. Unfortunately, you may run across unconfirmed, incomplete research when you conduct your genealogical research online.

Types of Sources

When gathering evidence, genealogists consult a number of resources, such as interviews with relatives and copies of government records. As you research your genealogy, you're likely to run into three types of sources:

- ▶ **Primary source:** A source that records an event at or shortly after the time it occurred
- ▶ **Secondary source:** A source that records an event some time after it occurred or is recorded by someone not present at the event
- ▶ **Tertiary source:** A source that guides you to primary or secondary sources (such as an index or compilation of records)

Primary Sources

Primary sources are sources of information that are created or compiled at or near the time an event occurred. They include certain documents, photographs, tape recordings, film, and oral accounts (such as an interview with an eyewitness the day an event occurred).

 Cross-Reference

After you find some good sources of information on your ancestors, don't forget to place the information (along with the source of the information) into your database. See Chapter 9 for details on entering facts into your genealogical database.

 **Tip**

The only way to ensure that your research is accurate and sound, is to validate all the data that you come across. You do this by finding and maintaining as many original records as possible. These records serve as evidence of the accuracy of your research.

 **Note**

Never assume that a source is a primary source without also considering the context of the information. In some instances, records that are usually considered primary have been recreated. Re-creations of original documents can be considered secondary sources, because they may not have been provided by a witness to the event or may have been recollected a long time after the event actually occurred.

Definition

A primary source is a record or an account of an event created at or near the time of the event. A witness or someone with first-hand knowledge provides the information about the event. Sometimes the source is created by a person whose job it is to record the event based upon the testimony of witnesses.

Find It Online

See the Historian's Sources page at the Library of Congress Web site (`lcweb2.loc.gov/ ammem/ndlpedu/ lessons/psources/ pshome.html`) for more on primary sources.

Definition

A secondary source is a record or account of an event created some time after an event took place or for which the information is provided by someone who was not a witness.

A birth certificate is a good example of a primary source for your genealogical research. When a person is born, a birth certificate application is completed, usually by the doctor who delivered the child. The application itself is also a primary source because it's usually completed immediately after the child's birth and then submitted to a county clerk who issues a birth certificate. Even though the birth certificate may be issued a few days after the birth, it is considered a primary record because it was created near the time of birth.

Secondary Sources

Secondary sources are records, documents, and other accounts that were created some time after the original event occured or were created by someone who was not actually present at the event.

On some occasions, a document that you would ordinarily consider a primary source (such as a birth or marriage certificate) really isn't. Say the courthouse that stored your great-grandfather's birth certificate was destroyed in a fire, and you can find no other evidence of his birth. Your great-grandfather may have completed some new paperwork to recreate evidence of his birth, but unfortunately, this record is a secondary source if no witness who was also present at the birth has verified its accuracy.

Unless the individual died as a young child, you can use a death certificate as both a primary source and as a secondary source of information about an ancestor. Here's how:

▶ Under normal circumstances, the date of an individual's death is usually certified by a physician shortly after it occurs, making it a primary source of information.

▶ If the death certificate also contains information about the individual's date and place of birth, this birth-related information is a secondary source. You can't trust the information as a primary source because this information is often supplied by a relative of the deceased who probably was not a witness to the birth. (Sometimes this information is even supplied by the children of the deceased.) Under the circumstances, the person supplying the information may not have taken time to verify its accuracy.

Tertiary Sources

Tertiary sources are documents that point you to primary and secondary sources. Often they come in the form of indexes and bibliographies. You see a lot of tertiary genealogical sources online. For example, several Web sites provide indexes to census records for certain geographical areas or periods of time.

Note

Although the information provided on the death record points you toward the approximate date of an individual's birth, you should always confirm birth information with a birth record, instead of relying on the information from a death record.

Types of Records Useful to Your Research

Many different types of records are useful to genealogists. We discuss some of the more popular ones that you're likely to encounter in the following sections.

Definition

A tertiary source merely points you in the direction of a primary or secondary source.

Vital Records

Vital records (also called civil registrations) are records created during the landmarks of a person's life. These records include the following:

- ▶ Birth records
- ▶ Marriage records
- ▶ Divorce records
- ▶ Death records

Usually, these records are created at the local level — that is, the county or parish level — although some higher-level governments (such as state governments) are starting to centralize the storage and preservation of these records.

For the most part, you won't find large collections of vital records online. Instead, you are more likely to find indexes of record sets and guides that tell you how to order copies of vital records.

Vital records are often difficult to obtain because of privacy issues. Because these records are created and maintained at the local level, local laws may vary. For example, in the United States, some states have rather strict laws for obtaining copies

Find It Online

If you're looking for repositories of vital records in the United States, try the Vital Records Information for the United States page at `www.vitalrec.com/index.html`.

Find It Online

A great site for discovering land records for the eastern part of the United States is the Bureau of Land Management's Government Land Records Office site at `www.glorecords.blm.gov`.

of vital records — even records pertaining to deceased individuals. In some cases, you may have to prove that you are related to an individual before the records will be released to you.

Land Records

Some of the most plentiful records are land records. If your ancestor owned quite a bit of land, it's quite possible that you may find four or five land transactions for each year he owned the property. Land records include the following:

- ▶ Records of the original purchase of government land
- ▶ Applications for land patents
- ▶ Land surveys
- ▶ Claims
- ▶ Sales of land
- ▶ Grants of bounty lands for service in the military

Although land records may not contain many personal details about your ancestors, they do provide geographic details that you can use to find other records that contain more information (see Figure 5-1) — such as the exact location of the land and the land office where the deed was recorded. They are especially handy for tracking the migration of your family, because families often moved to secure land in other areas. You can find indexes to land records and digitized copies of federal government land records online.

Figure 5-1. The land record of Jacob Helm from the Bureau of Land Management Land Patents site.

Census Records

Census records are a staple in genealogical research in the United States. A federal census has been carried out every ten years in the United States since 1790. The National Archives and Records Administration maintains microfilm copies of census records from 1790 to 1920 for public use.

The United States census does have some holes in its data. Here are a couple of examples:

▶ Almost all of the 1890 U.S. census was destroyed, and portions of the census from other years are missing.

▶ U.S. census records prior to 1850 include only the names of the head of households. After 1850, every person in the household was enumerated.

Census records contain a variety of information, depending on the year you're looking at (see Figure 5-2). Early census records tend to have the least amount of information. Later records include details such as age, occupation, place of birth, amount of personal property owned, race, naturalization date, and language spoken. You can find a variety of online resources pertaining to census records.

Definition

Enumeration is the act of recording individuals in the census record (called schedules). People who go house to house gathering information for the census are called enumerators.

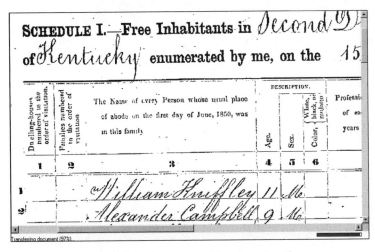

Figure 5-2. An 1850 U.S. federal census record from GenealogyLibrary.com.

Find It Online

You can find an index to on-line census resources at Census Online (www.census-online.com).

Find It Online

One interesting project is the Civil War Soldiers and Sailors System maintained by the National Park Service. Currently, you can search for soldiers who served in the United States Colored Troops regiments (shown in Figure 5-3). Eventually, the database will contain basic data on 5.4 million soldiers and sailors who served during the war. You can find this resource at www.itd.nps.gov/cwss.

Military Records

If your ancestor served in the military, records reflecting that service are likely to exist. Military records come in many forms, including

- ▶ Muster records
- ▶ Service records
- ▶ Pension records
- ▶ Military census records
- ▶ Unit rosters
- ▶ Cemetery records
- ▶ Regimental histories
- ▶ Casualty lists

Each type of military record contains different information that is of use to genealogists. Typically, the most useful records are the pension records, which often provide details on spouses and family members. In some cases, pension records include narratives from the service members as proof of service.

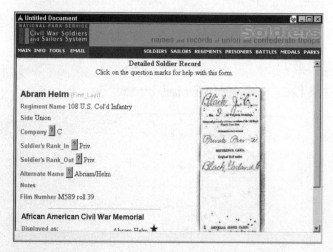

Figure 5-3. A database entry from the Civil War Soldiers and Sailors System.

Employment and Business Records

Employment and business records are some of the most over-looked records by genealogists — probably because they are rather difficult to locate. In the past, a lot of businesses didn't establish archives or see the need to preserve their records in the same way that governments did, so many of their records have simply vanished. Typically, the employment records that do exist were maintained by individual employees or business owners.

Note

Online, you generally can find only an occasional list of members of a certain profession taken from census records, city directories, or records of unions and trade organizations.

Educational Records

Don't overlook educational records when conducting your genealogical research. Educational records range from class rosters, yearbooks, and graduation lists to payment records and class photographs.

Also, many educational institutions maintain archives of their holdings and important historical information about their towns and local regions. You can often gain access to educational institutions' holdings, especially at the university level.

Immigration and Naturalization Records

Unless all your ancestors were born in the same country that you currently reside in, you have ancestors who immigrated. If your ancestor immigrated recently, then there probably are records of your ancestor's entry into the country, intent to become a citizen, and confirmation of citizenship.

If your ancestors immigrated before formal immigration laws were created, you can look for passenger lists of the ships that they arrived on. Because much of immigration processing occurred at the local level, not many compilations of immigration records are available online. However, several transcribed passenger lists and a few indexes to naturalization records are available online (see Figure 5-4).

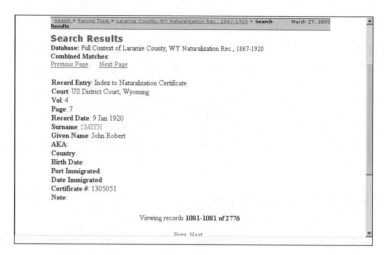

Figure 5-4. A record from a naturalization index at the Ancestry.com site.

The National Archives and Records Administration has Web pages that describe the immigration and naturalization records that it houses. You can find these pages at `www.nara.gov/genealogy/immigration/immigrat.html` and `www.nara.gov/genealogy/natural.html`.

Court and Civil Records

Your ancestors didn't have to have rap sheets to be mentioned in court records. Your law-abiding ancestors may have been called upon to testify or required to file documents in court. They may have been called to testify as character witnesses in a criminal trial or testify about land boundaries in a land dispute. If your ancestors held positions within the local government, they may be listed in civil records (such as when they were sworn in or had monetary claims). You can find some transcribed criminal and civil records online, as well as indexes to archives, libraries, and courthouses that house them.

Tax Records

Tax records are useful sources for genealogists because they can often fill in the gaps when other records are not available. Some online sites contain transcribed tax lists or indexes to tax records.

Other Records

Several other types of records are useful to genealogists, including religious group records, adoption records, and fraternal organization records.

You can often find explanations of these types of records, pointers to archives that house them, and some transcribed records and indexes online. Here is a list of some of these records:

- ▶ Family bibles
- ▶ Legal documents, such as mortgages, titles, deeds
- ▶ Insurance policies
- ▶ Wills
- ▶ Family letters
- ▶ Obituaries and newspaper articles
- ▶ Diaries
- ▶ Baptismal certificates and other church records
- ▶ Membership cards
- ▶ Passports
- ▶ Adoption records
- ▶ Fraternal organization records

Knowing the Difference: Digitized versus Transcribed Records

As you investigate resources on the Internet, you're bound to come across both transcribed and digitized documents. *Transcribed records* are created when a researcher copies the contents of an original record into a new document. For example, someone who types the contents of a microfilm census record into his or her word processor is transcribing the record. *Digitized records* are electronically scanned from the original record or a representation of the original record. If you use a scanner to electronically copy your grandmother's birth certificate and make it available online, then you have created a digitized record.

Definition

A transcribed record is one in which a researcher has copied information from an original record into a word processor and shared it on the Internet or printed it out.

Definition

A digitized record is a digital representation of an original record.

Currently, several projects — many of which are volunteer efforts that take an immense amount of time — are underway to transcribe records. Not surprisingly, you won't find a lot of completely transcribed records. And you'll find even fewer digitized records online — at least at the moment. We think that you'll see many more digitized records within the next year or so as more companies commit to spending the money necessary to digitize records.

Because we are seeing more and more of each type of record online, a debate is emerging regarding which type of record is preferable to genealogists. Here are the two sides of the argument and how they affect your research:

▶ **Transcribed records pros:** You will soon see more transcribed records online to help your research efforts. You can search transcribed records by using a Web site's search functions, which can speed up the research process.

▶ **Transcribed records cons:** Transcribers must make judgment calls when they transcribe records because not every line of a record is easily readable. Thus, at their very best these records are secondary sources and are often tertiary sources.

▶ **Digitized records pros:** The main benefit of digitized images of original documents is that they can be considered primary sources. Each individual researcher can immediately interpret the record.

▶ **Digitized records cons:** Digitizing records is expensive. Special scanners are needed to digitize microfilm records, and large-scale storage facilities are required to store large collections of digitized files. Unless they are indexed, digitized records aren't searchable.

The bottom line is that we recommend that you confirm every transcribed record against a primary record — regardless of who transcribed it.

Finding Records Online

You can locate records online several different ways. Each way
has its advantages and disadvantages, so we recommend that you
try each one. Here are some of the ways to find records online:

▶ File libraries

▶ Index sites

▶ General and genealogy-specific search engines

▶ Geographic sites

Genealogy Forum File Libraries Center

Often groups of researchers form a file library in which they
pool their resources and contribute information for the good of
the group. These libraries aren't of the traditional variety —
rather, they are libraries of files online.

The AOL Genealogy Forum File Libraries Center is a good example of this type of file library system. The File Libraries
Center is broken down into five main categories that can give
you information and background information to support your
research. The most useful category when you're looking for
records is (aptly) called Records. The Records category contains these six sections:

▶ Bible, Birth, and Marriage Records

▶ Death Records, Obits, and Wills

▶ Genealogical Records

▶ National Archives Library

▶ Genealogy Tips and Resources

▶ State Archives File Library

Each of these sections contains files of transcribed records and
other resources that you can download to your computer.
Follow these steps to locate and download a resource:

1. Type the Keyword: **Roots** in the text box on the navigation toolbar. The Genealogy Forum window appears.

2. Click the Files button. The Genealogy Forum File
   Libraries Center appears, as shown in Figure 5-5.

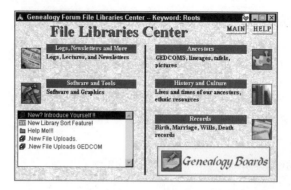

Figure 5-5. The Genealogy Forum File Libraries Center window.

3. Click the Records icon. This launches the Records window, where you see the six sections that we just mentioned.

4. Double-click a topic that looks interesting. In our case, we double-clicked the Bible, Birth, and Marriage Records folder. This launches another window with a list of files available for downloading.

5. Double-click a filename to see a description of the contents of the file.

6. When you're ready to download a file, click the Download Now button.

In the File Libraries Center, you can find a variety of transcribed records from a wide range of geographic locations. It's worthwhile to check the file libraries frequently for new or updated files, as well as contribute your own files when you have the time. That way other researchers can benefit from your efforts.

Index Sites

A comprehensive genealogical index site contains tens of thousands of links that are specifically categorized for genealogists. Some of these sites are categorized by topic, whereas others are structured by type of Internet resource. Two of the largest comprehensive genealogical indexes are the Genealogy SiteFinder (sitefinder.genealogytoolbox.com) and Cyndi's List (www.cyndislist.com). The Genealogy SiteFinder currently has over 75,000 fully-categorized links, and Cyndi's List has over 60,000 categorized links.

Tip

To see additional file listings in the Records window, click the List More Files button. If the List More Files button is not active, all the available files are already listed in the window.

Cross-Reference

We discuss creating a genealogical database to store your findings in Chapter 9. You can then share copies of your files from this database in a File Library. We cover how to generate these files and other reports in Chapter 11.

You may be familiar with sites, such as Yahoo! (www.yahoo
.com), that have several-thousand links that are organized into
browsable categories. You can use any of several general-purpose sites that have links to genealogical sites. However, these
sites generally don't provide as many quality links as the comprehensive genealogical index sites.

When looking for records on these types of index sites, you can
search under a specific record type (such as census records or
vital records) or by geographic location (such as Virginia or
Scotland). The following example shows you how to search for
records on the Genealogy SiteFinder site:

1. Type **sitefinder.genealogytoolbox.com** in the text
    box on the navigation toolbar. A list of links to the
    Genealogy SiteFinder appears.

2. Click the Places/Geographic link. This takes you to the
    Places subcategory page in the Genealogy SiteFinder, as
    shown in Figure 5-6.

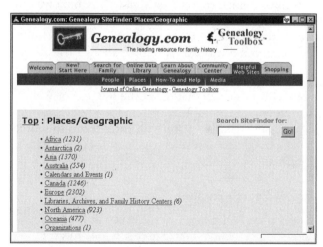

Figure 5-6. The Places/Geographic page on the Genealogy SiteFinder site.

3. Select a geographic location where one of your ances-
    tors lived. Clicking this link takes you to the specific geo-
    graphic location page. For example, if you select the
    geographic location United States, you are taken to the
    United States page.

Tip

Browsing index sites can be very time consuming because some of the information may be five or six pages deep into the site. If an index site includes a search mechanism, we suggest that you start with it first. That way, you don't need to learn the whole indexing scheme of the site just to find the link you're looking for.

Tip

It's especially a good idea to save or print out digitized or transcribed records that you find online. The image or printout of digitized records can serve as documentation for your research and the copies of transcribed records can be used to verify the information against the original record.

4. Select a geographic subcategory if necessary. For example, if you selected the United States in Step 3, you may need to select a state to narrow your search.

5. Browse the links on the page and select one that looks promising.

One drawback to using index sites is that you have to think like the person or persons that created the index. In most cases, you can figure out the indexing scheme fairly quickly, even if the links aren't categorized the way that you would categorize them. Some index sites have accompanying search mechanisms that help you find specific pages quickly.

Search Engines

Index sites tell you only so much information about a site — even if a site description is listed. For example, if you're looking for a census record for John Smith and you see a link to Frederick County, Virginia, 1820 Census Index, the only way to know if John Smith is listed on that site is to actually visit the site. However, if you decide to visit every site in the hope of finding something, you'll waste a lot of time and get frustrated.

Search engines can help you avoid these problems. Search engines are sites with programs that index the full text of Web sites. The search engine's computer system then compiles the text into a searchable database. After you enter terms to search for in the database, you see a results page that lists links that match your terms.

Whole-Internet Search Engines

If you have ever used AOL Search or sites such as Lycos, AltaVista, and Google, then you have used a whole-Internet search engine. These search engines look for certain categories of information in sites all across the Web. You can conduct a search on AOL Search by following these steps:

1. Type the search term (the information you're looking for) in the text box on the navigation toolbar and then click the Search button (located to the right of the text box). This launches the AOL Search window.

2. In the list of results found by AOL Search (as shown in Figure 5-7), click a link that looks promising. To determine what a site has to offer, read the short description following the link.

Definition

Whole-Internet search engines index all types of sites, regardless of what subjects they contain.

Note

You may hear people refer to whole-Internet search engines as general search engines.

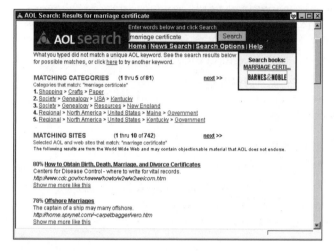

Figure 5-7. The results page from AOL Search.

Genealogy-specific Search Engines

For genealogical research purposes, whole-Internet search engines may require you to sift through lots of results that have nothing to do with genealogy. To avoid this unnecessary work, try a genealogy-specific search engine.

Genealogy-specific search engines operate just like regular search engines, with one exception — instead of indexing every Web site, they index only those sites of interest to genealogists. As a result, the number of extraneous search results is greatly reduced.

You can find several genealogical sites that have search capabilities, but only three sites are bonafide genealogy-specific search engines:

▶ GenealogyPortal.com (`www.genealogyportal.com`)
▶ GenPageFinder
  (`www.ancestry.families.aol.com/databases/`
  `genpagefinder.htm`)
▶ Internet FamilyFinder
  (`www.genealogy.com/ifftop.html`)

Searching with genealogy-specific search engines is easy —
even though they typically are not as flexible as whole-Internet
search engines. The following example shows you how to use
the GenPageFinder search engine:

1. Type `www.ancestry.families.aol.com/databases/`
   `genpagefinder.htm` in the text box on the navigation
   toolbar. The GenPageFinder site appears.
2. Type your search term in the Keyword text box.
3. Click the Search button.
4. On the search results page (shown in Figure 5-8), click a
   link that looks interesting.

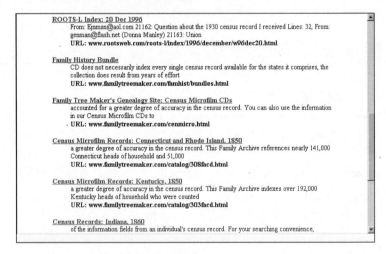

Figure 5-8. Results from the GenPageFinder.

Each genealogy-specific search engine has it's strengths and
weaknesses. So, we suggest that you use several of them until
you find what you're looking for.

Geographic Sites

Another way to look for records is through a geographic site. These sites usually contain links to databases and other resources that are relevant to a search in a specific geographical area. By visiting geographical sites, you may discover additional record sets that are useful to your research.

Although several geographic sites are useful to genealogists, you may want to check out a group of volunteer projects that attempt to provide resources for every county in the United States, for every province in Canada, and for every country in the world. These projects are called the USGenWeb (`www.usgenweb.org`), Canada GenWeb (`www.canadagenweb.org`), and WorldGenWeb (`www.worldgenweb.org`) projects.

The following is a sample search of the USGenWeb site:

1. Enter **www.usgenweb.org** in the text box on the navigation toolbar to go to the USGenWeb site. The first section on the left side of the page (labeled State Pages for the Project) takes you to links for each of the United States.

2. Click the link titled The Project's State Pages. A new page appears that identifies three ways to access the state USGenWeb pages: graphical map, table of states, or text only list.

3. Select the Text Only State List link. This link takes you to a page with a list of states and the URLs associated with each state page, as shown in Figure 5-9.

Tip

Searches that don't yield any useful results don't necessarily mean that no information is out there. Sites that contain the information you're looking for may not have been indexed yet. You may want to routinely search these search engine sites because they index new pages every day.

Caution

Because volunteers maintain the USGenWeb and WorldGenWeb sites, the quality and aesthetics of the sites may vary immensely from one state to another and, in some cases, from one county to another. And — now for our standard warning — it's a good idea to verify any information you find on these sites.

Note

The pages contained in the USGenWeb, Canada GenWeb, and WorldGenWeb projects are not the only quality geographic resources. Some independent pages provide better resources than those found in these volunteer projects. So, make sure that you look for every available geographic site — not just the ones covered in these projects.

Figure 5-9. The state listing from the USGenWeb site.

4. Click the link for a state in which one of your ancestors lived.

5. On the USGenWeb state page for the state that you chose, look for a link to the type of record you're looking for.

Dealing with Online Databases

You access many of the records that are currently available online through databases. Some databases are maintained by individuals, some by groups, and others by companies. Although the types of information that you can find in online databases is varied in subject and quality, the databases themselves generally fall into two categories: free databases and subscription databases.

Free Databases

Free databases, as opposed to subscription databases, are open for anyone to explore. Even though this information is free to users, the site maintainer had to donate the time, space, and money required to place the database online. In some cases, the maintainer receives money from a sponsor, for running banner advertisements on the site, or from donations. In others, the maintainer has some subscription databases or other products that offset the cost of the free databases. And, of course, some site maintainers place databases online out of the kindness of their hearts or as a public service.

A good example of a free database that contains a wealth of records is the General Land Office Federal Land Patents Records database, which is maintained by the Bureau of Land Management. This site enables you to search the more than 2 million federal land title records for the Eastern States Office issued between 1820 and 1908. Recently, the database expanded to include serial patent records issued after 1908, but this is an ongoing project. Follow these steps to use this database:

1. Type the URL **www.glorecords.blm.gov** in the text box on the navigation toolbar. This brings up the Official Federal Land Patents Records Site.

2. Click the Search Land Patents link in the upper-left column of the page. This loads a screen that requires you to enter a zip code.

3. Type your zip or postal code in the appropriate field and click the Continue button. The land patent search screen appears.

4. Select the state that you want to search from the State drop-down list box. Then enter the name of the person who bought the land in the Patentee Last Name and First Name fields.

5. Click the Search button. The Search Results page loads.

6. Click the Details button to see the full record, which appears on the Land Patents Detail screen.

7. To see the digitized image of the document, click the Document Image tab and click the button of the appropriate graphics file type (select a small GIF if you're just browsing the image because it downloads more quickly).

Tip

You can find thousands of free databases on the Internet. The easiest way to locate them is by using a comprehensive genealogical index site such as those mentioned in the "Finding Records Online" section, earlier in this chapter.

Tip

Some subscription database sites open up their databases for free for a limited time once a year. Usually word of these free trials appears on some of the more popular newsgroups and mailing lists. This free trial is a good opportunity to evaluate the quality of the databases.

Cross-Reference

Visit Chapter 3 to learn how to find newsgroups and mailing lists.

Subscription Databases

There are a few subscription database sites available on the Internet. Each site's contents has unique record sets, so it's a good idea to investigate what each site has before making a decision. The price structure of each site is different, but the price for a yearly subscription ranges from $40 to $100. Some sites also have monthly and quarterly subscriptions.

The two most popular of these sites are Ancestry.com and GenealogyLibrary.com. Both services have over 2,000 databases. Ancestry.com's collections include U.S. Census indexes, the Periodical Source Index, slave narratives, birth records, land records, church records, death records, obituaries, and military records. GenealogyLibrary.com's collection focuses on rare family histories, military records, obituaries, census indexes, digitized census records, and vital records.

To get an idea of how subscription databases work, follow these steps to use the Ancestry.com site:

1. Type the Keyword: **Genealogy** in the text box on the navigation toolbar and click Go. This brings up the Genealogy/Family History area of AOL maintained by Ancestry.com.
2. Click the Ancestry.com logo to go to the Ancestry .com@AOL Families page. Scroll down to the middle section called Search Over 550 Million Names.
3. Click the Advanced Link under the Search button, which takes you to a Web page where you can enter search terms for a more complex search than you can conduct from the main Genealogy/Family History window or the Ancestry.com@AOL Families main page.
4. Type your search term in the First Name and Last Name fields and select a locality from the drop-down list box. You can also designate the types of databases you want searched, the proximity of words to look for, and the date range. See Figure 5-10.

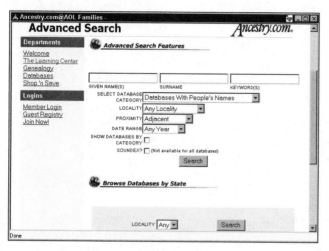

Note

Using the Advanced search interface at Ancestry.com @AOL Families, you can see the databases that are available by state. Simply use the Locality pull-down menu to select a state and click Search in the section called Browse Databases by State.

Figure 5-10. The Advanced search interface at Ancestry.com@AOL Families.

5. Click the Search button.

6. The Search Results page loads, which includes links to Ancestry.com databases that include your search term. This page also notes whether the database is free or for subscribers-only, as well as lists folders for record sets that you can explore.

7. Click a database that looks interesting. The page containing the record is displayed. If it's a subscription database, then you are required to enter your username and password.

Summary

In this chapter, we showed you the three types of sources available in genealogy research and explained the importance of finding primary sources to verify and prove your findings. In addition, you learned the difference between transcribed and digitized records. You also found out about the variety of records that genealogists encounter when researching online, as well as the types of online sites that can lead researchers to these records. Finally, we introduced you to two categories of databases and showed you how to use them. In the next chapter, we turn to another type of record — photographs.

CHAPTER

6

ENHANCING YOUR WORK
WITH PICTURES

Quick Look

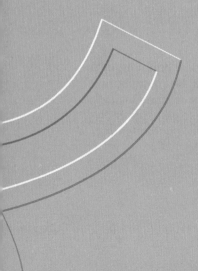

Chapter 6

Enhancing Your Work with Pictures

A family history that consists of only a list of people and dates of events can be pretty boring. One way to jazz it up a bit is to add some multimedia elements, such as pictures, audio, and video. This chapter discusses ways that you can implement multimedia elements, as well as tools that you can use to generate them.

Enhancing Research with Photos

If you've ever looked through a relative's attic and run across a picture of an ancestor, you know how inspiring old pictures can be. There's just something about being able to see what your ancestor looked like that adds a whole new dimension to your research.

Looking at the Details

If you look closely at photographs, they can provide unique details and clues about an individual's life, and their significance goes well beyond merely the representing the likeness of your ancestor.

Say you discover a picture of your great-grandfather wearing a uniform, holding a hat, and carrying a sword. On the reverse side of the picture is the stamp of the photographer who took the picture. All of these details, plus the condition, color, and texture of the photo itself, can be clues about your great-grandfather's life.

When you first examine the picture, you notice that the uniform looks like military garb. However, upon closer evaluation, some of the symbols on the uniform don't quite fit with what you know about military uniforms. By paying attention to these details, you're on to a whole new path in your genealogical research, and after researching the symbols on the uniform and its unique style, you discover that your great-grandfather was in a fraternal organization — one that you never knew he belonged to. Table 6-1 shows you some things to look for in photographs.

Photographs are great tools to take along when interviewing a relative because they can often jog that person's memory to remember important family stories that can help you in your research.

Your first clue to finding out when a picture was taken is the color and texture of the picture. Certain photographic processes can be traced to specific time periods. The stamp on the back of the photo is also a clue. You can do some research to determine the time period in which that particular photographer took pictures, and you may even be able to find some records of when that specific picture was taken.

6

Enhancing Your Work with Pictures

Find It Online

For more information on dating old photographs, take a look at the City Gallery site (see Figure 6-1) at www .city-gallery.com.

Table 6-1. *Looking for Details in Photographs*

Look For	Example	Tells You	Example
Clothing style	A woman in a Victorian-style dress	The general time period the photo was taken	The woman may be wearing short sleeves because the picture was taken in spring or summer in a temperate climate.
Props that individuals are holding	A hat	Something unique about a particular time period	More details may help you determine the social standing of the person and the occasion of the photograph.
A building or other structure	A man and woman standing in front of a wooden structure with a sign that reads General Store	The time period and/or the location of the photo	Your grandmother may recognize the building as the old store near her childhood home and remember that it burned down around 1931.
Writing on the back of the picture	Initials, and the year 1897	Who may have been in the picture	The initials belong to your grandmother's older sister, who died before you were born and who was about 16 in 1897.

Look For	Example	Tells You	Example
The quality of the writing on the back the picture	The initials are written in ballpoint ink.	The information was recollected long after 1897.	If you know who wrote down these names, you of can find out more information from this person.
A stamp or imprint from the photographer	The stamp says Stuart Smith, Hel, MT.	Some information about the photographer (when he lived and where he worked)	Your grandparents lived in Bozeman, Montana, before moving to Helena in 1861.
Objects, vehicles, or other technological instruments	You see a horse-drawn cart in front of a barn, next to an old Model T.	The time period	The picture was taken after the invention of the automobile but before horse-drawn carts had outlived their usefulness.
Characteristics of the photograph	The photo is very glossy or has a silver tint.	A fading pattern may suggest the date of the photograph. Also look for texture, color, and tint.	A daguerreotype has fine details that can help you determine the time period in which the picture was taken.
Anyone in the picture you recognize	Your grandmother's smile was unmistakable, even when she was a teenager.	The age of the picture	If your grandmother died last year at age 75, the picture is probably about 60 years old. Use this information to identify the people you don't recognize.

Dating Photographs

You can usually determine a general time frame for a photograph based on the type of picture you're viewing. Here are some of the general types of photographs that you may run into:

▶ **Daguerreotypes:** Daguerreotype photos were taken between 1839 and 1860. They required a long exposure time and were taken on silver-plated copper. You usually find these photos enclosed in a plastic or leather case, and the photographic image appears to change — going from light to dark — when tilted.

▶ **Ambrotypes:** Ambrotypes used a much shorter exposure time and were produced between 1858 and 1866. The image was made on thin glass and usually had a black backing.

▶ **Tintypes:** Tintypes were produced between 1858 and 1910. They were made on a metal sheet, and the image was often coated with a varnish. You usually find them in a paper cover.

▶ **Cartes-de-visite:** Cartes-de-visite were small paper prints mounted on cards. They were often bound together into a photo album. They were produced between 1858 and 1891.

▶ **Cabinet cards:** Cabinet cards were larger versions of cartes-de-visite. They sometimes included dates on the borders of the cards. The pictures themselves were usually mounted on cardboard. They were manufactured primarily between 1865 and 1906.

▶ **Albumen prints:** Albumen prints were produced on thin pieces of paper that were coated with albumen and silver nitrate and were usually mounted on cardboard. These prints were used between 1858 and 1910 and were the types of photographs found in cartes-de-visites and cabinet cards.

▶ **Stereographic cards:** Stereographic cards were curved photographs that rendered a three-dimensional effect when used with a stereographic viewer. They were prevalent between 1850 and 1925.

▶ **Platinum prints:** Platinum prints had a matte surface that appeared embedded in the paper, and the images were often highlighted with artistic chalk. They were produced mainly between 1880 and 1930.

▶ **Glass-plate negatives:** Glass plate negatives were used between 1848 and 1930. They were made from light-sensitive silver bromide immersed in gelatin.

The City Gallery site (`www.city-gallery.com`), shown in Figure 6-1, can help you date photos. After you determine the approximate time frame for the picture, you can then begin looking for other details that may point you to a more specific date.

Figure 6-1. An old photograph of an American Civil War soldier from the City Gallery Web site.

For more hints on preserving your pictures (and other types of valuable documents), check out the Library of Congress Preservation page at `lcweb.loc.gov/ preserv/careothr.html`.

Preserving Your Photographic Treasures

After finding some precious photographs, your next step is to make sure that they survive for future generations to see. You can help curb the photographic aging process several ways. If you have photographs that are significantly deteriorating, you may need to have them restored or copied to ensure that they survive. Here are a few suggestions for preserving your photographs:

▶ Store your photographs in an area that has a constant temperature between 65 and 70 degrees Fahrenheit. Fluctuations in temperature can cause deterioration.

▶ Try to keep the relative humidity in storage areas to between 30 and 40 percent. Anything above 60 percent accelerates the deterioration process.

▶ You're better off storing pictures in a closet rather than in an attic or basement, where temperature and humidity levels fluctuate.

▶ Don't expose photographs to unnecessary light. If you want to display a photograph of your ancestors, we recommend that you make a copy of it and display the copy.

▶ Store photographs in acid-free containers.

▶ Avoid using harsh chemicals near your photographs (especially oil-based paints, varnishes, and shellac). Fumes from these chemicals can deteriorate photographs.

▶ Make sure that you remove any rubber bands, paper clips, or other products that may adhere to a photograph over time.

▶ Keep photo negatives separate from photographs so that hopefully you don't lose both in the event of a fire, a flood, or another disaster.

▶ Avoid using magnetic or no-stick (plastic-pocket) photograph albums, which typically are not made with acid-free materials.

▶ Have an experienced restorer fix your photographs instead of trying to make the repairs yourself.

▶ Wear gloves when handling delicate photographs because the oil and acid from human skin can deteriorate photos.

Quite a few companies sell photo preservation and conservation supplies, which are a convenient way of ensuring that your photographs stand the test of time. Consult a comprehensive genealogical index site for links to these companies.

Understanding Scanners and Digital Cameras

Another way of preserving photographs is to digitize them. *Digitization* is the process in which an electronic copy of an object is produced. You can then store this electronic copy on your computer's hard drive or on other magnetic media.

The two main pieces of hardware used to produce digitized images are scanners and digital cameras. Scanners digitize objects that already have a physical form, such as paper documents or microfilm. Digital cameras create original digital images through their lens.

Scanner Types

Scanners are popular with genealogists because they make the task of preserving and storing documents a lot easier. Many scanners allow you not only to scan documents but also to fax and copy them, which is great for genealogists who don't have the space (or money) for three separate machines.

A variety of scanners are available, including snapshot, sheetfed, flatbed, and, on occasion, handheld scanners. Most newer scanners are color scanners — although you can still find some black-and-white models. The computer requirements for scanners vary greatly, so make sure that you have the required hardware before purchasing one. Additionally, each scanner requires software to make it work, so carefully read the software's system requirements and capabilities as well. Here's a quick rundown of the major types of scanners:

▶ **Snapshot scanners.** Snapshot scanners are designed to quickly scan photographs that are 5 x 7 inches or smaller. They are very compact and either fit inside your computer or attach to it through one of your computer's external ports. This type of scanner is pretty simple to operate: You feed the photograph into the scanner, and then the scanner captures an image before sending the photo back out. Some snapshot scanners have removable tops that you can use as handheld scanners in order to capture images larger than 5 x 7 inches.

Tip

The Photography Forum on AOL is a good resource for further information on photographs. You can reach it through the Keyword: **Photography**.

6

Enhancing Your Work with Pictures

▶ **Sheetfed scanners.** Sheetfed scanners are designed to scan a standard sheet of paper (8½ inches across). These scanners are compact and hook into an external port on your computer. To scan a document, you place it in the feeder on the scanner. The scanner captures an image as the document passes through it. Like some snapshot scanners, some sheetfed scanners have removable tops that you can use as handheld scanners to capture images larger than 8½ inches across. Again, exercise caution when using these scanners with fragile photographs.

▶ **Flatbed scanners.** In the past, flatbed scanners were large and bulky, but new models are more compact. To operate a flatbed scanner, lift the lid of the scanner and place your document or photograph on the bed, close the lid, and tell the scanner (through your software) to capture the image. These scanners are safer for old photographs because you place them on the scanner bed rather than feed them through the scanner.

▶ **Handheld scanners.** You may still be able to find a few handheld scanners on the market. When these scanners first came out, their relatively low cost and flexibility made them great for genealogy. You can use them not only to scan photographs and paper documents, but also to scan books. Handheld scanners are external and compact, which makes them particularly convenient for on-site research because you can carry them in the same bag as your notebook computer. To scan with a handheld, slowly move the scanner over the object while holding down a button. As the scanner passes over the image, the accompanying software puts the image together. The only downside to handheld scanners is that the quality of the scanned image depends greatly upon how steady your hand is, how good the lighting is where you're scanning, and the original size of the document.

Before purchasing a scanner, it's a good idea to figure out exactly what you will be using it for. Will you be scanning documents larger than 8½ x 11 inches? Is speed necessary? What software comes with the scanner? Will you be using the scanner with a notebook computer? After you answer these questions, check out some reviews of scanners to make sure that the model that you choose will work for you.

Caution

We suggest that you do not use snapshot or sheetfed scanners to digitize old, fragile photographs. Photographs may become damaged when they're fed through the scanner.

Using the Scanner Decision Maker

If you want to purchase a scanner but you're not sure which one is best for your needs, consult the AOL Scanner Decision Maker. This unique area takes you step-by-step through an interview that helps you select the scanner that best fits your needs. To use the decision maker, follow these steps:

1. Go to the AOL Computing Forum by entering the Keyword: **Computing**. The AOL Computing window appears.

2. Select the Scanners topic from the Try Our Easy-to-Use Decision Maker drop-down list box (located near the center of the window) and then click the Go button. This launches the AOL Scanner Decision Maker window.

3. Click the Q&A button (on the right side of the page) to begin the interview.

4. The first page of the interview, shown in Figure 6-2, asks you which platform you want to connect to, PC or Mac. Select the appropriate check box for your response and then click the Next box in the lower-right corner of the screen.

Find It Online

If you want to see what kinds of scanners are currently available, use the Keyword: **Scanner**, which takes you to the scanner collection in the AOL Shop area. For reviews of scanners, check out the Arts and Image Scanning area on AOL by using the Keyword: **Scanning**.

6

Enhancing Your Work with Pictures

Figure 6-2. The AOL Scanner Decision Maker Q&A window.

Continued

Using the Scanner Decision Maker *(continued)*

5. Complete the rest of the interview pages by selecting the appropriate check boxes for your responses and clicking the Next button on each page.

6. After answering five questions, you see a page that lists the scanner models matching your responses, as shown in Figure 6-3. To see more information about a particular scanner, click the scanner's name.

7. If you want to send this scanner list to another individual, click the Send button. Or you can save the list by clicking the Save button. Both of these two buttons are located just above the scanner list.

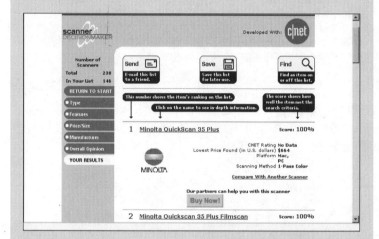

Figure 6-3. The final screen of the Decision Maker, where you can save your results.

Using the decision maker allows you to compare different models in different price ranges. If you don't see a model you want the first time you try the decision maker, try it again, this time using different responses to see other models that may be suitable. If you want to compare two scanners side-by-side, click the Compare button in the first Scanner Decision Maker window.

Digital Cameras and Camcorders

If you get really involved in researching your family history, you may end up traveling to a cemetery to look for the tombstones of your ancestors. Rather than spending time creating the traditional tombstone rubbing, you can just pull out your digital camera, snap a few pictures, and download the images onto your computer so that you can send electronic copies of the pictures to interested researchers and relatives. Digital cameras make it easy to document research travels, share the results with other researchers, and maintain the records in your genealogy database.

Digital cameras are fairly easy to operate — in fact they're very similar to traditional cameras. After you take a picture, the digital image is saved in the camera's storage area, which can vary depending on the individual camera. Most cameras store the pictures in the memory built into the camera, or on compact flash cards (small memory cards that are inserted in the camera), or on 3½-inch floppy disks.

To download the pictures from a digital camera with built-in memory, you hook up a cable between your camera and your computer (normally through the serial port), which contains software that downloads the images to your hard drive. With a compact flash card, you simply take out the card and insert it into an adapter that fits into your computer. The software then downloads the images. And, of course, with a 3½-inch disk, you just insert the disk in the floppy drive and download the images to the computer's hard drive. After the pictures have been downloaded, you can edit them with graphics software and then save them to a CD-ROM or disk for more permanent storage.

Here are some questions to consider when buying a digital camera:

▶ Does the camera support extra or removable memory?

▶ What is the resolution of the digital images? (The higher the resolution, the better the picture quality.)

▶ How long is the battery life?

▶ Does the camera have a video-out port (which you can use to display the images on an external monitor)?

▶ What is the quality of the LCD screen (the screen where you can view the images that your camera is making) for viewing pictures?

Note

Purchase a camera with the highest resolution you can afford, especially if you'll be using the camera mainly to document your genealogy research. However, remember that if you upload images to the Internet so that you can share them with others, the higher the resolution, the longer the image takes to appear on-screen. So, you may need to reduce the resolution of the image with photo software before placing it on your Web site.

Tip

Shop around and read reviews for different digital camera brands, styles, and manufacturers, as well as the software that is bundled with them. You can begin by entering Keyword: **Digital Camera** to go to an informative area called "Are Digital Cameras Ready for Prime Time?" For more specific advice, type Keyword: **Digital Photo** to take a trip to AOL's Digital Photography Forum.

6

Enhancing Your Work with Pictures

> ▶ Is the software that is bundled with the camera current and easy to use?

> ▶ Does the camera software support my computer platform (PC or Mac)?

As with any other purchase, make sure that your computer meets the requirements for the digital camera and its software.

Downloading Digital Images through AOL

A handy feature in AOL Versions 4.0 and 5.0 is the capability to download digital images from your digital camera or scanner directly through AOL. This feature saves you a lot of time if your main goal is to download a digital image to send to other researchers via AOL e-mail. The main requirement for using this feature is that you must have a TWAIN driver for your scanner or digital camera (which most of them come with) installed on your computer.

AOL 5.0 users can follow these steps to download a digital image through AOL:

1. From the Edit menu on the AOL menu bar, choose Capture Picture. This launches the Capture Picture window.

2. Click the Settings button (located at the bottom of the window), and then from the menu that appears, choose Picture Capture Device and the name of your digital camera or scanner, as shown in Figure 6-4.

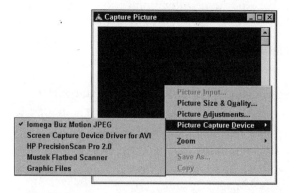

Figure 6-4. Choosing the Picture Capture Device from the Settings menu.

3. Position the item that you want to scan on your scanner or insert the memory card for your digital camera into your computer.

4. Click the Capture button at the bottom of the window. This launches your scanner or digital camera software.

5. Complete the steps necessary for your software program to create the digital image.

6. After you create a digital image, choose your software's option to return to AOL (if you're using HP PrecisionScan Pro software, you choose Scan from the menu bar and then choose Return to AOL). The digital image should appear in the space previously occupied by the large black square in the Capture Picture window.

7. From the File menu on the AOL navigation bar, choose Save As to save the digital image to your hard drive.

After saving the file to your hard drive, you can then attach the file to an e-mail message and send it to your fellow researchers.

AOL 4.0 users can follow these steps:

1. Choose Open Picture Gallery from File menu on the AOL menu bar. This launches the Picture Gallery window.

2. Click the Settings button at the bottom of the window, and from the menu that appears, choose Picture Capture Device and then the name of your digital camera.

3. Position the item that you want to scan on your scanner or insert the memory card for your digital camera into your computer.

4. Click the Capture button at the bottom of the window to launch your scanner or digital camera software.

5. Complete the steps necessary for your software program to create the digital image.

6. After you create a digital image, choose your software's option to return to AOL (if you're using HP PrecisionScan Pro software, you choose Scan from the menu bar and then choose Return to AOL). The digital image should appear in the space previously occupied by the large black square in the Capture Picture window.

7. Choose File from the AOL navigation bar and then choose Save As to save the digital image to your hard drive.

After you save the file to your hard drive, you can then attach the file to an e-mail message and send it to your fellow researchers, or add the file to your genealogical database.

Using "You've Got Pictures"

If you don't want to deal with scanning current pictures or using digital cameras, you can use AOL's "You've Got Pictures" feature (Keyword: **Pictures**) to create digital pictures. The process is really simple; just follow these steps:

1. Take your film to a participating photo developer. You can find a list of participating developers by using the Keyword: **Pictures** and selecting the link to photo developers.

2. When the film is developed, the developer creates your traditional prints as well as sends digital images of these prints to your AOL account.

Tip

A "You've Got Pictures" icon sits just below the now-famous You've Got Mail icon — it's a little roll of film. When your pictures are ready, a photo pops out of the side of the roll of film, as shown in Figure 6-5.

Note

When your pictures are ready for viewing at "You've Got Pictures," you receive an e-mail message from AOL.

Figure 6-5. A little photo extends from the "You've Got Pictures" roll-of-film icon when your pictures are ready for viewing.

You can view your pictures by clicking the "You've Got Pictures" icon on the Welcome screen or by choosing My Files⇨"You've Got Pictures" from the AOL toolbar.

If you have more than one roll of film at "You've Got Pictures," select the one you want to view first by clicking the radio button next to roll (see Figure 6-6). Then click the View button, which brings up a Roll Viewer page with thumbprint images of the photos, as shown in Figure 6-7.

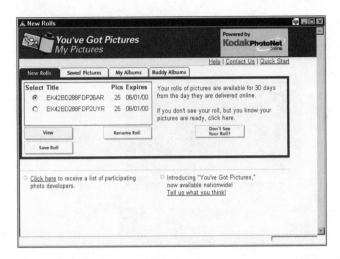

Figure 6-6. You can choose which roll of pictures to view if you have more than one in "You've Got Pictures."

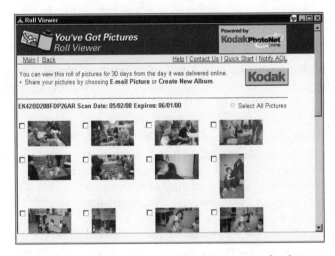

Figure 6-7. The Roll Viewer shows you thumbprint images of each picture on a roll of film.

Click any image to see the full picture (see the example in Figure 6-8). You can use the Next Picture and Previous Picture buttons to navigate through the images, or click the Back button to return to the Roll Viewer.

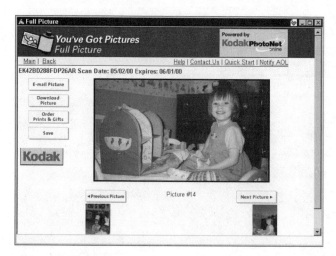

Figure 6-8. The Full Picture screen allows you to see a full-sized image, as well as gives you some options for downloading and sharing it.

On the Roll Viewer or Full Picture pages, you can do any of the following by clicking a button and following several simple steps:

> ▶ **E-mail Picture:** To e-mail a picture to another person, simply click the E-mail Picture button at the bottom of the Roll Viewer page or on the left side of the Full Picture page. On the Roll Viewer page, you must select the check box for the picture(s) you want to e-mail.

> ▶ **Save:** Clicking this button adds the picture(s) to your Saved Pictures file. You can store up to 50 photos in your Saved Pictures file, and all you have to do to see them is click the Saved Pictures tab on the main You've Got Pictures page. On the Roll Viewer page, you must select the check box for the picture(s) you want to save.

> ▶ **Download Picture:** You can download a copy of a picture for your own use. You have three resolution choices — e-mail and Web page quality (free), print quality (free), and premium offer ($1 each with a $3 minimum). On the Roll Viewer page, you must select the check box for picture(s) you want to download.

> ▶ **Order Prints & Gifts:** You can order a copy of a picture or have the image produced on a mug, jigsaw puzzle, mouse pad, or t-shirt. The cost of the service varies depending on which item you're ordering.

Instead of e-mailing digital copies of pictures to friends and family, you may want to consider setting up a digital photo album, which is another option on the Roll Viewer page. Others can view your digital photo album and order their own prints of the pictures. This option is especially handy for users who don't have color printers but may want to have a color print of that tombstone picture you sent them. Here's what you do:

1. On the Roll Viewer page of "You've Got Pictures," select the photos you want to include in your digital photo album by selecting the check boxes next to the pictures.

2. Click the Create New Album button at the bottom of the screen. This brings up a Create New Album page that shows thumbprint images of the photos you've chosen. It also shows you how many spaces you have available to fill with pictures in your digital album.

3. Click the Customize button to add or remove pictures, write a title or caption for a photo, rearrange the layout, add a particular background color, or rename your photo album.

4. After you have your digital photo album set up the way you want, click Save. This brings up an Archive and Copyright Policy that you should read before clicking OK.

5. Upon finishing, you can View the album (to see how others will see it), Share it (by inviting others to stop by and see it), or click Done.

Making the Most of Clipart

Photographs are not the only objects that can spice up your family history. Clipart can also add color and humor to your research and reports. Clipart consists of small graphics that are frequently used in publications to accentuate text. You can also use them in your own publications, such as large family histories or small newsletters. No matter where you want to use clipart, AOL has you covered through its royalty-free clipart download libraries in the AOL Computing Forum (Keyword: **Computing**).

6

Enhancing Your Work with Pictures

 Note

The digital photo album uses spaces in your Saved Pictures file so you are limited to 50 images total.

 Note

Family, friends, and fellow researchers who are not AOL members can access your photo albums at no charge. And if they want a copy of a particular picture, they can order it directly from "You've Got Pictures."

Clipart comes in a number of different graphics file formats. So, the first step is to decide which file formats your word processor (or whatever program you intend to insert the clipart into) supports. The graphics formats that are available in the AOL Computing Forum include:

- ▶ Computer Graphics Metafile (CGM)
- ▶ Graphics Interchange Format (GIF)
- ▶ Zsoft Image (PCX)
- ▶ Tagged Image Format (TIF)
- ▶ WordPerfect Graphic (WPG)

After you find a piece of clipart that you like, you need to download it and then place it into the document that you're working with. Here is an example:

1. Go to the AOL Computing Forum by using the Keyword: **Computing**.

2. Click the Download Center button to open the Download Center window.

3. In the Download Catalogue list on the right side of the screen, double-click the Desktop Publishing option, as shown in Figure 6-9. The Desktop Publishing window appears.

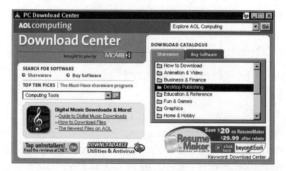

Figure 6-9. The Download Catalogue with the Desktop Publishing topic highlighted.

4. On the right side of the screen, double-click a graphics file format for the clipart that you're interested in. For example, if you want a GIF file, double-click the GIF (Monographic) topic.

5. Highlight the name of a graphic that interests you and then click the Download Now button.

6. Type in or browse to the location on your computer where you want the clipart saved and then click the Save button.

7. Open the program where you want to place the clipart and insert the clipart just as you would insert any graphics file.

Depending on the program in which you're inserting the clipart, you should be able to adjust the clipart's size to fit nicely within your text. If the program does not allow you to edit the clipart image, then you can edit it by using a graphics program such as Paint Shop Pro or Photoshop.

Capturing Aunt Betty's Essence with Multimedia

Eventually, you may want to take the next step and add more multimedia elements to your genealogical database or Web page. For example, you may want to create audio clips or video clips of portions of interviews with family members. The real limitation with multimedia is whether your computer can produce the multimedia elements that you'd like to have. If you're not sure what you need in terms of multimedia hardware, or just have questions about multimedia in general, you should stop by the Animation & Video Community (Keyword: **A&V**). In this community, you can find resources for producing multimedia presentations, as well as chat rooms and message boards dedicated to the subject.

You can find genealogy-specific clipart by typing the Keyword: **Roots.** Click the Files button to go to the File Libraries Center. In this center, click the Software and Tools icon, and then double-click the Genealogy Clipart option. Scroll through the clipart to your heart's content.

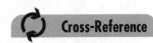

We cover creating reports and Web pages, in which you might like to include clipart, in Chapters 11 and 12.

Summary

In this chapter, you found out how to use photographs to spice up your family research, how to preserve photographs, and how to digitize photographs and documents. You also looked at the "You've Got Pictures" feature, located clipart on AOL, and discovered how to find resources on multimedia on AOL. In the next chapter, we tell you how to find helpful resources online that will keep you in the genealogical community loop.

CHAPTER

7

GAINING ACCESS TO
GENEALOGY PERIODICALS

Quick Look

► **You Needn't Ponder about Paper Periodicals**   **page 163**

If you still prefer your reading material to come in a paper form, never fear!
We tell you about some genealogical magazines in this chapter, too.

► **Have News Delivered to You**   **page 164**

Having news delivered directly to your doorstep or, in this case, to your virtual
doorstep, via e-mail, helps you remain informed of developments in
the genealogical community.

► **Do you Know the Difference Between an E-Zine and an Online
Newsletter?**   **page 164**

This chapter examines the various types of online news sources, including
e-zines, columns, and newsletters, and tells you where to find them.

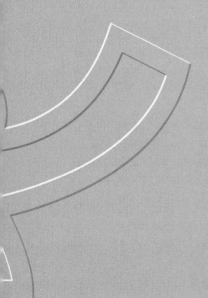

Chapter 7

Gaining Access to Genealogy Peridicals

By reading this book, you recognize some of the benefits of perusing the written word. Reading can be a very relaxing and rewarding activity — not to mention educational.

When you take up a hobby or interest, you probably find yourself wanting to know more about it. That's usually the case with budding family historians, and that's one reason why you can find several genealogical publications online and in the "real world." These publications can answer your questions about research methods, provide you with support and reassurance when you encounter a challenge, and entertain you. Publications help you stay abreast of new technology and products in the field and explain issues that you're likely to encounter in the genealogical community — online and offline.

Now that we've convinced you that reading genealogical publications is a good idea, you may be asking, "Just what qualifies as a genealogical publication, and how do I find these valuable resources?" Those are great questions — ones we're eager to answer. So sit back and keep reading.

Printed Books and Periodicals

Printed sources are what you traditionally think of in terms of genealogical publications — books, magazines, journals, newsletters, or any written sheets of paper that are bound together in some way. This book is a printed source.

Although our main focus in this chapter is finding *online* resources for genealogical research, first we want to take a brief look at a few of the better-known printed genealogical sources. Here are four that you may want to check out:

▶ *Ancestry* **magazine:** Published by Ancestry.com, *Ancestry* magazine is a bimonthly publication that is available by subscription as well as at newsstands. It typically has general research articles and some regular columnists. For more information about Ancestry and to see sample articles online, visit www.ancestry.com.

▶ *Family Chronicle: Family Chronicle* is a bimonthly publication from Moorshead Magazines Ltd. in Canada. In each issue, you'll find articles on every aspect of genealogical and family history research. You can subscribe to the magazine or purchase it at newsstands. The *Family Chronicle* Web site, which you can find at www.familychronicle.com, tells you more about it.

▶ *Family Tree Magazine:* This is a new magazine from F&W Publications. Its publication schedule is not clear — the first two issues came out in January 2000 and April 2000. It has articles on all aspects of family history, and is available by subscription and on newsstands. For more information about *Family Tree Magazine,* check out its Web site at www.familytreemagazine.com.

Definition

Printed and online resources, such as magazines, newsletters, journals, and columns, are often referred to as *periodicals* because they are published at fairly regular intervals throughout the year.

7

Gaining Access to
Genealogy Periodicals

▶ *Genealogical Computing:* Published by Ancestry.com, *Genealogical Computing* is a quarterly journal that focuses on the use of computers and technology in genealogical research. It's available by subscription only. You can find more information about it at `www.ancestry.com`.

To find family or society newsletters, follow the same instructions that we provide in dealing with online newsletters later in this chapter.

Tip

If you're looking for books about genealogy, check out the family history section of your nearest public library or bookstore.

Checking Out E-Zines and Online Columns

You can find several online sources of information about issues and changes in genealogical research and technology. Some of these sources are set up like printed magazines on the Web and thus are called electronic-magazines or e-zines. They have several articles on various topics related to family history research, sometimes organized around a particular theme (such as international research, computers and other technology, or certain types of records). Here are a few e-zines that you may want to check out:

Definition

An *e-zine* is an electronic magazine that you access on the Web.

▶ **Journal of Online Genealogy** (`www.onlinegenealogy.com`): This is our e-zine, and it has been around since mid-1996. Typically, it's published monthly; although that schedule has varied some in the past year due to our personal time constraints and competing projects. The *Journal* features articles on a variety of topics, including beginner and advanced research, international and U.S.-based research, current events and issues, and software and book reviews. The *Journal* is free and open to the public.

▶ **The Global Gazette** (`globalgazette.net`): Published by the good folks at GlobalGenealogy.com (formerly Global Genealogical Supply) in Canada, new issues of this e-zine (shown in Figure 7-1) are posted on average a couple of times a month. The *Gazette* has been around since late 1997, and you can access all back issues online. You can find articles on almost every aspect of

genealogical research — how-to research, geographic research, book and software reviews, document and photo
preservation, and news and issues. The *Gazette* is free
and open to the public.

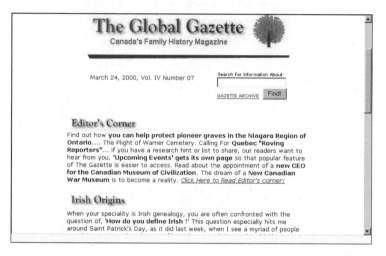

Figure 7-1. New issues of the free e-zine called the Global Gazette are posted twice a
month.

Other online sources are individual columns that appear on a
Web site — some are posted daily, and others are posted
weekly. Here are the genealogical columns available through
AOL's Genealogy Forum, as well as a few others that we recommend checking out:

▶ **Pat Richley's DearMYRTLE** (Keyword: **DearMYRTLE**):
  Pat answers research questions and shares information
  from her own experiences in this AOL genealogical column, which is updated daily. You can also find
  DearMYRTLE at **www.dearmyrtle.com**, where you can
  subscribe to receive the column via e-mail.

▶ **Uncle Hiram's Adventures in Genealogy (www**
  .stategensites.com/unclehiram): Bill Hocutt
  writes this monthly column that you can access through
  the Genealogy Forum at AOL. In it, he shares his
  thoughts and explains how to carry out various research
  activities. Hocutt writes this easy-to-understand column
  in a fun, humorous way.

▶ **Diana Smith's Pilgrims, Pioneers, & Aliens**
(**members.aol.com/dianahome/index.htm**): In her
monthly column, which you can access through the
Genealogy Forum at AOL (shown in Figure 7-2), Diana
provides guidance on how to research ancestors who
migrated from country to country, state to state, and
even county to county.

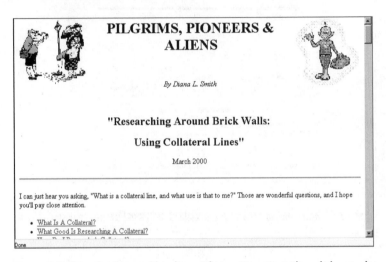

Figure 7-2. Diana Smith's monthly column, Pilgrims, Pioneers, & Aliens, helps you discover ways to research your ancestors as they migrated from place to place.

▶ **George Morgan's Along Those Lines**
(**www.ancestry.com/library/view/columns/
george/george.asp**): This column started on AOL but
is now available at the Ancestry.com site (Keyword:
Genealogy). George's articles deal with many different
aspects of genealogical research.

▶ **Drew Smith's Digital Computing**
(**www.ancestry.com/library/view/columns/
digital/digital.asp**): Drew's column focuses on
the use of computers and technology in genealogical
research.

▶ **Rhonda McClure's Twigs & Trees**
(**www.genealogy.com**): Rhonda provides information
on various genealogical topics and research strategies in
her column, shown in Figure 7-3.

 **Note**

Rhonda's column moves
around the Genealogy.com
site — check the Home page
for a link.

Figure 7-3. The Twigs & Trees column provides research assistance on a weekly basis.

You can go to the AOL columns identified at the beginning of this list by following these steps:

1. Type the Keyword: **Roots** in the text box on the navigation bar and then click the Go button. The Genealogy Forum window pops up.

2. Double-click the name of a column in the scroll box on the right side of the window. The column appears in the resulting window.

The Joy of Newsletters

If you've ever belonged to a genealogical society or a club of some sort, then you're probably familiar with the concept of a newsletter that you receive several times a year in the mail. Newsletters give you brief updates on news and information about an organization and offer reminders about important upcoming events.

Tip

To find additional online periodicals and columns, try searching a comprehensive genealogical index, such as the Genealogy SiteFinder (`sitefinder.genealogytoolbox.com`), using words like *periodicals*, *columns*, or *e-zines*.

Cross-Reference

We list some comprehensive genealogical indexes in Chapter 4.

Definition

A *newsletter* is a letter-like publication that contains news of interest to members of a particular group of subscribers.

Find It Online

Anyone can access GFNews (www.genealogyforum .com/gfnews/gfnews .html.)

The majority of online newsletters are similar to traditional newsletters in that they focus on particular groups (people who share the same surname, members of a particular family or society, or people who subscribe to a certain service). However, not all online newsletters are e-mailed to subscribers; some on-line newsletters are posted on the Web, where subscribers come and read them.

Checking Out GFNews

The Genealogy Forum on AOL offers a nice selection of newsletter resources. The best known of these resources is the Genealogy Forum News (generally just called *GFNews*), which contains articles organized in specific topics, announcements about the Genealogy Forum, information from special interest groups, lighthearted humor relating to genealogy, letters to the editor, and links to material written by Genealogy Forum columnists. GFNews is a monthly, Web-based newsletter. AOL members can access this newsletter through the Genealogy Forum (by using the following steps), and the general public can find it at www.genealogyforum.com/gfnews/ gfnews.html.

Follow these steps to locate GFNews on AOL:

1. Type the Keyword: **Roots** in the text box on the navigation bar and click the Go button.
2. In the scroll box on the right of the Genealogy Forum window, double-click the link for the current month's GF News.
3. Look over the table of contents for the current issue and click any articles that interest you.

Finding Other Genealogical Newsletters on AOL

You can access other newsletters in the Genealogy Forum's File Libraries Center. For example, you can find the Beyond Beginners Newsletter, the Texas Chat Newsletter, the Weekly Fireside, the Ormsby Village News, and the Genealogy Forum Newsletter. Follow these steps to find a newsletter on AOL:

1. Type the Keyword: **Roots** in the text box on the navigation bar and click the Go button. The Genealogy Forum window pops up.

2. Click the Files button to open the File Libraries Center.

3. Click the Logs, Newsletters and More icon. The Logs, Newsletters and More window appears.

4. Double-click the Newsletters folder.

5. Scroll through the resulting list of newsletters, shown in Figure 7-4, to see what's available.

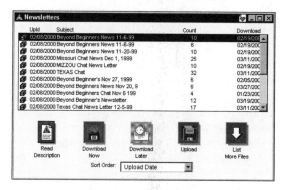

Figure 7-4. The Newsletters window identifies what newsletters are available, as well as allows you to see descriptions or download them.

6. Highlight a newsletter that you're interested in and click Download Now. Clicking this button brings up the Download Manager window.

7. In the Download Manager window, specify the directory on your computer in which you want to save the downloaded file.

8. Type a filename for the newsletter you want to download in the File Name field.

9. Click Save. The file downloads to your computer. Generally, you need to use a word processor to view the file. And you can read it offline.

Tip

You do have other options in this window. If you want to read more information about a newsletter prior to downloading it, click the Read Description button instead of the Download Now button. Or if you want to finish something you're working on before downloading a file, click the Download Later button. If you don't see a newsletter that interests you in the list that first appears, simply click the List More Files button. Additional newsletters pop up at the bottom of the list.

Using Other Online Newsletters

In addition to the newsletters available through AOL, you can find other online newsletters on the Web. Here are a few that are delivered to your virtual doorstep via e-mail:

- ▶ **Eastman's Online Genealogy Newsletter:** Written and distributed weekly by Dick Eastman, this free newsletter covers the latest developments and issues in the genealogical community. In addition to providing information about current happenings, Dick often reviews new books and software, and announces upcoming events. For more information about the newsletter and how to subscribe, visit www.rootscomputing.com.

- ▶ **Missing Links:** Compiled and edited by Julia Case and Myra Vanderpool Gormley, this free weekly newsletter is considered RootsWeb's genealogical journal. It contains articles about how to research, as well as stories about genealogists' successes and challenges. For more information about the newsletter and how to subscribe, check out www.rootsweb.com/~mlnews.

- ▶ **RootsWeb Review:** This free weekly newsletter keeps you abreast of the ongoings at RootsWeb, as well as provides information about how to use the resources at RootsWeb effectively in your research. The *Review* is edited by Julia Case and Myra Vanderpool Gormley. To find out how to subscribe and see back issues, check out www.rootsweb.com/~review.

- ▶ **Ancestry Daily News:** Ancestry.com, AOL's partner in the AOL Families: Genealogy/Family History area (Keyword: **Genealogy**), offers a free newsletter that is distributed on either a daily or weekly basis (you can choose which one to receive when you subscribe at Ancestry.com). It is edited by Juliana Smith, and contains articles on a variety of research-related topics, including several how-to pieces.

Subscribing to the Daily News is a cinch; just follow these steps:

1. Type the Keyword: **Genealogy** in the text box on the navigation bar and click the Go button. The AOL Families: Genealogy/Family History window pops up.

2. Click the Ancestry.com logo near the top-center part of the window. The Ancestry.com@AOL.com page appears.

3. Scroll down the page until you see Sign the Guest Registry, which is Step 2 in the middle column, as shown in Figure 7-5.

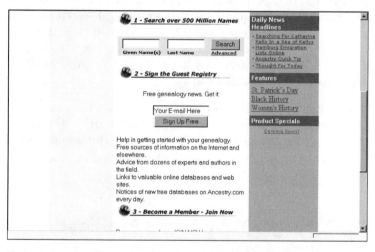

Figure 7-5. Step 2 allows you to subscribe to the Ancestry Daily News newsletter.

4. Enter your e-mail address (*yourscreenname@* **aol.com**) in the Your E-mail Here field and click the Sign Up Free button. You'll now receive the Ancestry Daily News newsletter.

The online newsletters we've just described contain useful information, but you can also find newsletters that pertain specifically to certain surnames or family lines.

Tip

Surname and family-line newsletters are great for learning about other researchers' discoveries that may be relevant to you and your ancestors. They're also wonderful sources of information about when and where the next family reunion will be — so you can plan your next vacation!

Cross-Reference

You can review how to use comprehensive genealogical indexes and genealogy search engines in Chapters 4 and 5.

Tip

Be sure to check one-name studies and family association sites to see if they offer newsletters. (See Chapter 4 for more information.)

Note

We set up AOL News Profiles to notify us any time the words *family history, genealogy,* or *geneology* appear in any news piece. We intentionally misspelled genealogy because you'd be surprised how many times this common misspelling slips through the wires.

Using Search Engines and Indexes to Find Periodicals

In addition to using the resources that we mention earlier and using AOL to find more, don't forget that you can also easily find online periodicals, such as newsletters, journals, e-zines, and columns, by using genealogy-specific search engines and indexes. These search engines and indexes identify Internet resources (including e-mail and Web-based newsletters) and link you directly to them.

You can also find periodicals that specifically cater to a particular surname or family line. To use a genealogical search engine or a comprehensive genealogical index to find such periodicals, simply enter the name you're researching in the search engine or index's search box. You may have to scroll through the results to see if a periodical exists.

When using a comprehensive site, you can click the category in the directory that contains links to periodicals or to surnames beginning with a particular letter. Then scroll through the results page to see if any periodicals are available.

Don't Forget Your News Profiles

Another way to get genealogy news is to set up the AOL News Profiles feature to notify you whenever a genealogy-related story comes across the wire. You can set up a profile to look for a particular word or phrase in articles, announcements, and press releases. Then, like any good news clipping service, each time AOL detects an article, an announcement, or a press release that matches your profile, you receive that information in an e-mail.

The News Profiles service is worth your time because it enables you to keep abreast of issues and developments in the online genealogy community, especially within AOL, Ancestry.com, and Genealogy.com. You may get an occasional story that isn't really related to genealogical or family history research, but this is unavoidable when keywords in your profile have more than one meaning. For example, sometimes we receive stories about a health matter in which the term *family history* is used to describe a chronic condition.

Now that we've convinced you to use News Profiles, we need to tell you how to set up your own profile. Just follow these steps:

1. Type the Keyword: **News Profiles** in the text box on the navigation bar and then click the Go button. The News Profiles window pops up, as shown in Figure 7-6. On the left side, you find a list of instructional topics that you can click for more information about setting up your News Profiles. On the right are two icons — one to create your profiles and one to modify them.

Figure 7-6. The News Profiles window.

2. Click the Create Your News Profiles icon. A new Profile window appears, in which you complete Step 1 of the setup process.
3. In the Create a Title for Your News field, enter a name for this profile.
4. In the Limit the Number of Daily Stories field, enter a number between 1 and 50 for the maximum number of articles you want AOL to forward to you daily, and then click Next button. The profile window, shown in Figure 7-7, comes up, in which you complete Step 2.

Figure 7-7. In Step 2, you enter the word(s) you want AOL to look for in each article.

5. Type the word or words you want AOL to watch for in stories and announcements. Be sure to separate each term with a comma. For example, if you want AOL to watch for articles with the word *genealogy* in them, type **genealogy** in the text box; to watch for articles containing *genealogy* and *family history,* type **genealogy, family history** in the box. Then click Next to move on to the Step 3 window.

6. Enter any words that you require in every article and click Next. The Step 4 window pops up.

7. Enter words that prompt AOL to exclude an article, even if it matches the requirements in Steps 2 and 3, and then click Next. The window containing Step 5 appears.

8. In the left scroll box, highlight a source you want AOL to review when clipping articles for you and then click the Add button. Repeat this step for each source you want to add. (Your choices include the AP International News wire service, Reuters World Service wire, and the AP Entertainment Source, among many others.)

9. When you're done adding sources, click Next. The Step 6 window appears and summarizes the profile you've just created.

10. If everything looks correct, click the Done button.

Staying In the News

If you're not really interested in having the news sent to you, you can opt out of News Profiles and instead use the Genealogy Forum's Genealogy in the News. This page contains information about the latest developments in the genealogical community and press releases. Here's how to find it on AOL:

1. Type the Keyword: **Roots** in the text box on the navigation bar and click the Go button.

2. In the scroll box on the right side of the Genealogy Forum window, double-click Genealogy in the News. The Genealogy in the News page pops up, as shown in Figure 7-8.

Figure 7-8. The Genealogy in the News page.

3. Look over the table of contents and click any articles or press releases that interest you.

Summary

In this chapter, you found out how to find online sources of news and information about the genealogical community. Knowing where to find information about current issues in the genealogical community, as well as the latest developments in genealogical software, will come in quite handy in the next chapter when we discuss choosing a genealogical database.

P A R T

III

STORING YOUR
ANCESTRAL TREASURES

Quick Look

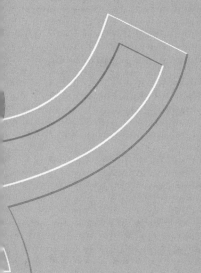

Chapter 8

Choosing Genealogical Database Software

In the preceding chapters, you got a look at some of the ways your computer can be very useful for researching your genealogy. Now, let's talk about another wonderful use for your computer — it is the perfect tool for housing a genealogical database.

Using a genealogical database can be a lot of fun. Entering information is a great way to review what you've collected about a particular person, and to think about what else you want to find out. Generating reports is an efficient and exciting way to involve others in the adventure and plan your future research. Some programs can even help you generate entire Web pages based on your data — much more easily than you may think.

What's a Genealogical Database?

A *database* is a program specifically designed to hold data and make it readily available. A genealogical database takes this simple concept one step further; such programs are specially designed to handle the characteristics of genealogical data and the tasks that go into sharing it. As you collect and verify more and more information about your relatives (both online and offline), you can quickly get swamped with data. Even the most organized paper files can become a jungle when you've got several generations' worth of information to track, use, and keep organized. A genealogical database enables you to manage all this information.

Most genealogical databases enable you to

▶ Store information on many, many people (names, dates, places, facts, and stories)

▶ Store scanned photos and video or audio clips

▶ Keep track of your sources

▶ Share information with others in the form of nice-looking family trees and tidy reports

▶ Create data files so that you can share your findings with others

▶ Focus your plans for further research

System Requirements for a Genealogy Database

Your computer has to meet at least the minimum system requirements before the software can work effectively on it. Otherwise, you may find yourself with all sorts of "interesting" computer complications and crashes. Here's a list of requirements that most programs generally share:

▶ A Pentium processor and Windows 95/98 (for a PC designed to run Windows)

OR

▶ A Power PC processor OS 7.1.2 (or higher) for a Macintosh

AND

Note

If you ever plan to share your research files with other researchers, you should consider a database program that was created especially for genealogy research. Otherwise, you may spend more time trying to adapt a general-purpose database program to meet your needs than you actually spend doing your research, entering new information, and sharing your results. Your computer should work for you — not the other way around.

Definition

A *genealogical database* is a computer program in which you enter, store, and use information about people (usually your relatives).

Tip

Each genealogical database has its own specific system requirements that you should review before purchasing the software. They tell you whether your current computer system has what it takes to run the program.

8

Choosing Genealogical
Database Software

Tip

If you're conducting research and sharing it online — which you probably are if you're reading this book — your computer should have some Internet features, such as Web publishing.

▶ At least 500MB of free (unoccupied) hard drive space

▶ At least 64MB of RAM

▶ A CD-ROM drive

▶ A monitor with at least a VGA display with 256 colors

▶ A mouse

Essential Genealogy Database Features

To be worth your while, genealogy database software should make certain tasks easier for you. Here's where we lay out what we think your software should offer you. The programs we mention in this chapter meet our requirements (and then some). First and foremost, the software shouldn't be overly complicated or difficult to use. But it should also let you

▶ Store a variety of data.

▶ Have some options and features that you can grow into as you continue your genealogical research.

▶ Quickly, easily, and intuitively search the database for information.

▶ Choose from more than one option when you generate and print reports and trees.

The Big Guys

Whether you're new to genealogy or an old pro, chances are good that you've heard of at least a couple of genealogical databases. But there are lots to choose from! Here are some well-known mainstream programs and a quick look at each one.

Definition

*Commercial software programs are generally available through traditional retail channels, including stores that carry computers and on-line shopping services such as AOL Shop Direct. (Keyword: **Shopdirect**).*

Ancestral Quest

Ancestral Quest (see Figure 8-1) is the only commercial genealogical program that is built on a Personal Ancestral File (PAF) database, a popular database format used by the Church of Jesus Christ of Latter-day Saints. (For more information about

PAF, check out the section later in this chapter about freeware and shareware.) While the software has its own colorful history, it's now produced and distributed by The Hope Foundation. You can use Ancestral Quest to

- ▶ Cite sources with its citation features.
- ▶ Create professional-looking trees, charts, and reports.
- ▶ Store information on an unlimited number of people.
- ▶ Import and export your data directly to PAF because the software is (as you might expect) truly PAF-compatible.
- ▶ Create Web pages containing information stored in your database.
- ▶ Use the software's built-in birthday and anniversary calendar.
- ▶ Make use of its ability to handle all Church of Jesus Christ of Latter-day Saints (LDS) events. The program produces LDS charts and reports.
- ▶ Search for a particular individual within your database very easily.
- ▶ Use the multimedia scrapbooking feature.

Tip

If you find yourself collecting a lot of data that already exists in the PAF format — or you intend to share data almost entirely with others who use this format — you may want to choose this software (rather than wrestle with several file formats).

Find It Online

You can read more about Ancestral Quest at www .ancestralquest.com.

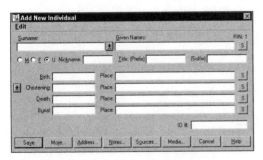

Figure 8-1. The entry screen for Ancestral Quest.

Find It Online

The Family Origins Web site provides detailed information about the product's features. You can find it at www.familyorigins.com.

Family Origins

Another easy-to-use genealogical database program is Family Origins. It's produced by FormalSoft, Inc. and is distributed by Parsons Technology. Typically, you can find Family Origins at electronics and computer stores, or you can order it online from a variety of sources. With Family Origins, you can

▶ Choose either of two interfaces for entering information — a family view or a tree view.

▶ Drag and drop information from one Family Origins file to another.

▶ Store and organize a virtually unlimited number of names and facts.

▶ Use multimedia scrapbook features to store digital photos, sound, and video.

▶ Generate all sorts of trees and reports.

▶ Quickly search your database for a particular individual's information.

▶ Use the correspondence log to track your e-mail and letters to and from other researchers.

▶ Spell-check your narratives with the spell checker.

▶ Organize your sources of information with the Source Manager.

▶ Put information from your database on your own Web page.

Family Tree Maker

Find It Online

You can find many resources in addition to software at Family Tree Maker's Web site (www.familytreemaker.com). You can also find AOL's version of Ultimate Family Tree at AOL ShopDirect. Choose Software⇨Hobby to find it.

Family Tree Maker is one of the best-known commercial programs for creating a genealogy database. Because the software is easy to use, it's a favorite among beginners and experienced family historians. Genealogy.com (formerly part of Broderbund and Mattel) produces and distributes it. Family Tree Maker features

▶ An easy-to-use interface (as shown in Figure 8-2).

▶ A research journal with a to-do list that helps you plan your research.

▶ Unlimited storage of facts. Family Tree Maker actually assigns a unique number to each individual about whom you have data.

▶ A simple interface for entering details about the sources of your information.

▶ Choices that help you produce a variety of trees and reports, including all-in-one family trees (which include everyone in your database) and Family Group Sheets.

▶ A multimedia scrapbook for storing and using photos, sound, and video.

▶ Built-in assistance with creating Web pages and InterneTrees (charts available on the Family Tree Maker Web site).

▶ Desktop publishing (for a professional look) and a spell checker.

▶ Maps you can use to see and illustrate where your relatives lived.

▶ An electronic address book you can use for mailing lists, name tags, and so forth.

Cross-Reference

We walk you through the process of downloading and using a demonstration version of Family Tree Maker in Chapter 9.

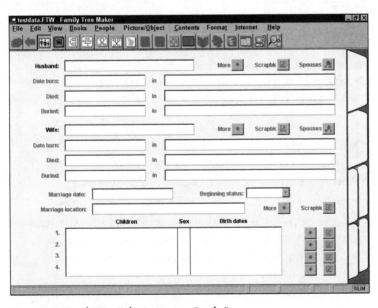

Figure 8-2. Family Tree Maker's signature Family Page.

Generations Family Tree

Another popular genealogical database is Generations Family Tree. Entering information is easy, the screens are simple to use, and the reports are very attractive. Generations Family Tree is

Access Sierra's Web site for its genealogical programs at www.sierra.com/ sierrahome/ familytree.

produced and distributed by SierraHome; you can get it from most electronic and computer stores, as well as online. Generations Family Tree features

▶ An easy-to-use interface called EasyTree

▶ Various options for creating family trees — including ancestor, descendant, hourglass, and timeline trees

▶ Various options for genealogy reports, including Register, NGS Quarterly, Ahnentafel, kinship, LDS, and custom reports

▶ Capabilities for generating Internet Family Trees and reports for the Web

▶ Multimedia scrapbook capabilities

▶ Unique color options that allow you to differentiate between individual boxes, family branches, and generations

▶ A photo and graphics program called Snapshot Express that you can use to edit images

Legacy

Check out www. legacyfamilytree .com for additional information about Legacy software.

Legacy is a genealogical database program produced and distributed by the Millennia Corporation. You can order it online at the Legacy Web site. Legacy's features allow you to

▶ Document your sources easily.

▶ Enter and edit information in either of two easy-to-use interfaces (Family View or Pedigree View; see Figure 8-3).

▶ Store an unlimited number of names and events.

▶ Conduct specialized searches within your database.

▶ Use a pop-up calendar that helps you identify dates (calendars range from 1700 to 2099).

▶ Create multimedia scrapbooks that can include photos and sound files.

▶ Generate a to-do list to help you with your research.

▶ Create a variety of trees and reports.

▶ Create Web pages by using the information contained in your database.

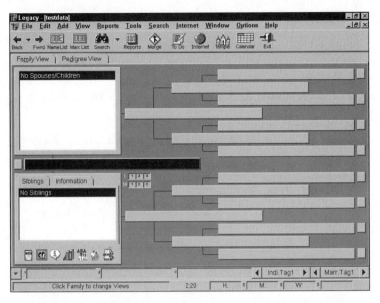

Figure 8-3. Legacy's Pedigree View entry interface.

The Master Genealogist

The Master Genealogist is a favorite among professional genealogical researchers. It's produced and distributed by Wholly Genes Software, and you can order it online directly from the company. The Master Genealogist lets you

> ▶ Transfer custom data with GenBridge, which is a feature that enables you to import information from other databases.

> ▶ Drag and drop information among charts.

> ▶ Store information on an unlimited number of people and an unlimited number of facts per person.

> ▶ Create unique customized trees and reports.

> ▶ Plan your online adventures in search of ancestral information with built-in research aids.

> ▶ Create a family history book with desktop-publishing features.

> ▶ Store information about an unlimited number of sources.

> ▶ Include multimedia files (such as photos and sound) within the database.

Find It Online

For more information about The Master Genealogist, be sure to visit www.whollygenes.com.

8

Choosing Genealogical
Database Software

Reunion

Find It Online

You can find Reunion's Web page at www. LeisterPro.com.

Reunion is the best-known genealogical database for Macintosh computers. It is produced and distributed by Leister Productions, Inc. Its Web site lists stores where you can get a copy of the program. Reunion's easy-to-understand interface lets you

- ▶ Store names and information for an unlimited number of people.
- ▶ Generate trees with information about up to 99 generations.
- ▶ Create a variety of trees and reports, including timeline charts.
- ▶ Create multimedia scrapbooks that support photos, video, and sound.
- ▶ Use its built-in tools to help you create Web pages by using your database.
- ▶ Generate birthday and anniversary lists, as well as mailing lists to use for reunions and newsletters.
- ▶ It has full-GEDCOM (a file that you can share with researchers who are using another type of genealogical database software) export and import functions so you can share information with (and receive information from) computers other than Macs.
- ▶ Use actuarial tables to calculate life expectancies for ancestors.
- ▶ Cite and document sources.

Ultimate Family Tree

Ultimate Family Tree (see Figure 8-4) is produced and distributed by Genealogy.com. It has wonderful source-citation capabilities, as well as a relatively easy-to-use interface. You can order from several sources online (including directly from Genealogy.com) and find it in many electronic and computer superstores. Ultimate Family Tree lets you

- ▶ Quickly enter information with wizards that guide you through the process.
- ▶ View tutorials if you need advice on a feature.
- ▶ Cite sources by using guidance templates.

▶ Create correspondence in 13 different languages by using the Multi-Language Records Requester.

▶ Generate hundreds of reports and trees, as well as books.

▶ Use multimedia scrapbooking to include photos, documents, and maps.

▶ Create your own Web pages by using your genealogical data.

 **Find It Online**

Check out www. ultimatefamilytree .com for more information online about Ultimate Family Tree.

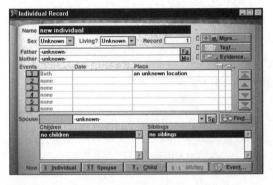

Figure 8-4. Ultimate Family Tree's data entry interface.

Trying Out the Freebies (Where to Find Demos)

Before you spend your hard-earned money on a genealogical database, we strongly recommend that you try out a few to see which features you particularly like and need. You can do this by downloading demonstration (demo) versions of the software — these are free, trial copies meant to allow you to test-drive the program. Some demos limit the number of entries you can make; others have time limitations (for example, you may be able to try a full-featured version of the program for only five days or two weeks).

Here's where to get the demo versions of some of the programs we've identified in this chapter:

▶ Ancestral Quest at www.ancestralquest.com/ download.htm

Continued

Trying Out the Freebies (Where to Find Demos) *(continued)*

▶ Family Origins at `www.familyorigins.com/demos.htm`

▶ Family Tree Maker for Windows at `www.familytreemaker.com/ftwdemos.html`

▶ Legacy at `www.legacyfamilytree.com/Download.asp`

▶ Reunion at `www.leisterpro.com/doc/demo/demo.html`

▶ Ultimate Family Tree at `www.ultimatefamilytree.com/UFT/Nav/demo1.html`

At this time, SierraHome doesn't offer a demo version of Generations Family Tree. And the demo version of The Master Genealogist is actually a tutorial that shows you how the program works, not a functioning version of the program itself.

Definition

Freeware is computer software that you can download from the Internet or get on disk, and use for free.

Definition

Shareware is software marketed directly by its creator that you can test before you purchase it.

Other Options: Freeware and Shareware

A lot of people forget that commercial software isn't the only type of program available when it comes to genealogical databases. Many software packages fall into the categories of *freeware* (software you can download or get on floppy disk and use at no charge) and *shareware* (software you can test first, and then pay a fee to the creator to continue using it). Personal Ancestral File is a good example of freeware; Brother's Keeper is shareware. Here's a little more information about each:

Personal Ancestral File

Personal Ancestral File (PAF) is the genealogical database of the Church of Jesus Christ of Latter-day Saints (LDS). It's offered free on the LDS Web site, along with the FamilySearch Internet Genealogy Service (www.familysearch.com).

▶ You can create trees and reports by using the information in your database.

▶ It has source-citation features.

▶ It has multimedia scrapbooking capabilities to handle photos, video, and sound.

▶ You can select the language in which you want your information displayed.

Brother's Keeper

This is a shareware program by John Steed. You can download a copy of Brother's Keeper from its Web site (ourworld. compuserve.com/homepages/brothers_keeper) and try it before buying it. Then, if you decide to purchase a copy, you can do so online, or by mail or fax.

▶ It can hold up to 1 million names.

▶ It has source citations for events.

▶ You can include photos in your database.

▶ You can generate a variety of trees and reports, as well as a book with an index and a timeline.

▶ You can identify people to split off and include in a new database.

Cross-Reference

For step-by-step instructions on downloading and using a demonstration version of PAF, check out Chapter 9.

Searching for the Perfect Package

When you've compared the features of some of the many available genealogical databases, you can choose a package that's right for you. This section offers pointers on searching and selecting.

Tip

Visit the Web pages for each of the programs we've described to see which program best addresses your research and data-sharing needs.

You may discover that none of the programs you look at are exactly what you're looking for. In that case, you should know your other options. Never fear.

Looking in General

To find additional software options, you can conduct a search of AOL and the Web. Simply type the words **genealogical software** in the text box on the navigation bar; then click the Search button with your mouse. AOL's Web browser opens and returns results that you can use to find other software (see Figure 8-5).

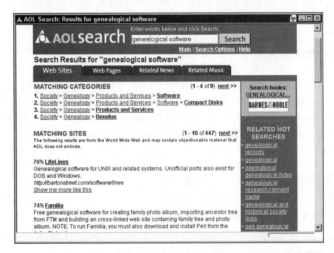

Figure 8-5. The results of a search on the words *genealogical software.*

Another way to find information about software packages is to check out the File Libraries Center in the Genealogy Forum. Here's what you do:

1. Enter the Keyword: **Roots** in the text box on the navigation bar and click the Go button.

2. In the Genealogy Forum window, click the Files button. This brings up the File Libraries Center.

3. Click the icon for Software and Tools. A window pops up with these categories: Genealogy Tips and Resources; Macintosh Software Library; Windows/DOS Files & Utilities; Windows/DOS Programs; Genealogy Clip Art; and Ancestor Photos and Graphics.

4. Click the appropriate category. A list pops up, showing programs available for downloading.

5. Scroll through the list and select any program that you want to download.

Checking Out Reviews

You may see the name of a program that looks intriguing, but still wonder what the software does or how well it performs. Software reviews are the answer when you encounter this dilemma! Follow these steps to find software reviews on AOL:

1. Enter the Keyword: **Roots** in the text box on the navigation bar. The Genealogy Forum window comes up.

2. Click the Search the Forum button.

3. Type **software review** in the search field and click List Articles. This brings up a list of articles that you can then read by double-clicking each entry. Many of the reviews are for older versions of the software we've discussed here, but that area is always open to change.

 Find It Online

To find information about various software packages and see reviews on the Web, you can check out the GenealogySoftware Toolbox at www. genealogysoftware .com. It has information about the companies/individuals that produce the software, lists of features, and reviews by other users.

Using AOL to Get Software

You know you can run out to the store — computer, electronics, office-supply, and even some bookstores — to buy software, but did you know you can download some programs directly through AOL? You can even purchase some software through AOL's online store.

Downloading

Downloading free software with AOL is easy — and it's a good way to try things out before you spend any money. Although not all the programs we've described in this chapter are available for downloading, you can find a few — or find some other programs that weren't on the list and try them out. Here's what you do to download software:

1. Type **Software** in the text box on the navigation bar and click Go. This opens AOL Computing's PC Download Center. In the Download Catalogue on the right side of the window, you can select whether to download shareware or buy software.

2. Click the Shareware tab; then scroll down the list and select Home & Hobby by double-clicking it.

3. Select Family Life (from the categories on the left side of the window) by double-clicking it.

4. Double-click Genealogy in the library list on the right (see Figure 8-6).

5. Scroll through the list of software and make your selection.

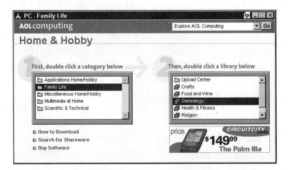

Figure 8-6. You can find downloadable genealogical software in the Family Life category and Genealogy library of the PC Download Center.

Shopping

When you're looking to purchase genealogical software, use the Keyword: **Genealogy Store** to get the Genealogy Forum's

Shopper's Guide. From there, you can click the link for Genealogy Software, select a program you'd like to have more information about, and/or place an order.

Another option for online software shopping is Ancestry.com, which is AOL's partner in the Genealogy/Family History section of AOL Families. While the Shop & Save section of Ancestry.com@AOL Families is not yet up and running, you can see what's available directly from Ancestry.com's online ordering center. All you have to do is type **www.ancestry.com** in the text box on the navigation bar and click the Go button. Click the Shop tab and then follow the directions or wander around in the site to see what's there.

Find It Online

Check the AOL Shopping Channel and AOL Shop Direct if you're interested in purchasing software online.

Follow these steps to use Shop@AOL to find genealogy software:

1. Click the Shopping button on the left side of the AOL Welcome screen. This brings up the Shopping Main window.

2. In the Shopping Search field, type **genealogy software** and click Search. This brings up a Web page with a list of results — products that match the term *genealogy software* (see Figure 8-7).

Figure 8-7. Using the search term *genealogy software* in the Shopping Search brings up a list of potential software matches that you can read about and purchase online.

3. Scroll through the list and click any items that interest you.

4. If you decide to purchase a product, follow any online instructions for doing so.

Summary

This chapter explained what a genealogical database is and looked at examples of several popular commercial programs. It also provided information about freeware and shareware alternatives to commercial programs. And (last but not least) it gave you information about how to find genealogical software and reviews, as well as how to download and purchase software on AOL. In the next chapter, we delve into how to use one or two of these genealogical databases to store your information.

Quick Look

▶ **Do You have a Genealogical Database?**   **page 203**

If you don't yet have a genealogical database (or you don't care for the one you have), we'll show you how to get a free copy of two different programs to see whether one of them can meet your needs. We'll show you how to download a demonstration copy of Family Tree Maker and a full-featured version of Personal Ancestral File.

▶ **Want to Start Your Family Database?**   **page 207**

We'll show you how to create a family file in both of the genealogical databases that we download in this chapter. This way, you can actually test the two programs and play around with their features to see which one you prefer.

▶ **Need Some Reminders?**   **page 214**

Lastly, we're going to remind you about a couple of important features of genealogical databases — including multimedia items in your electronic scrapbook and documenting your sources — using Family Tree Maker and Personal Ancestral File as examples.

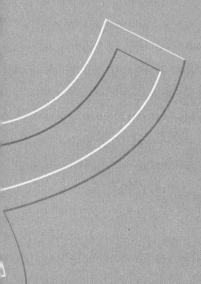

Chapter 9

Creating a Database

Cross-Reference

Chapter 8 has more detailed information about the features of Family Tree Maker and Personal Ancestral File.

The previous chapter explained what a genealogical database is, as well as where to find one. Now it's time to show you how one works. The best way to find out how a genealogical database works is to start working with one yourself. In this chapter, we show you how to download a demonstration version of Family Tree Maker and the full version of Personal Ancestral File. Then we'll try them out, entering information into both databases so you can see how they really work.

Downloading Programs

Downloading means getting an electronic copy of something (software, a picture, a text file) over the Internet. AOL gives you a couple of ways to download files without having to shut down the AOL software:

Definition

Downloading is the process of pulling files off the Internet and loading them onto your computer.

▶ The files you can get directly through AOL are stored in the service's file libraries (also called *resource centers*).

▶ You can get other files by using your AOL Web browser and following the instructions on the individual Web pages from which the files are available. This second method is the one used in this chapter to download copies of the genealogical databases we'll work with.

Family Tree Maker (Trial Version)

Family Tree Maker is one of the most popular genealogical databases for Windows-based computers. It's easy to use, and you can find it in almost any store that carries software. Genealogy.com, the producer of Family Tree Maker, offers a demonstration version of the software that you can download from the Family Tree Maker Web site. Just follow these steps to download a demonstration version:

Note

The popularity of Family Tree Maker makes finding it online and in bricks-and-mortar retailers easy.

1. Enter **www.familytreemaker.com/ftwdemos.html** in the text box on the navigation bar; then click Go. AOL opens a Web browser and takes you to the Family Tree Maker download Web page. The page is divided into two columns: Information about the trial version of the Family Tree Maker software is on the left side, and information about the Family Archive Viewer is on the right side.

2. Click the Get the Trial Version Now link (in the Trial Version 7.0 column on the left, as shown in Figure 9-1). Another Web page describing the trial version of Family Tree Maker appears, offering information about the trial software, instructions on how to buy a copy of Family Tree Maker if you like the trial version, as well as instructions for downloading the trial version.

Note

The Family Archive Viewer is a limited, previous version of Family Tree Maker. It enables you to view reports without using the newest version of Family Tree Maker as your primary genealogical database or owning a full-featured version of the program.

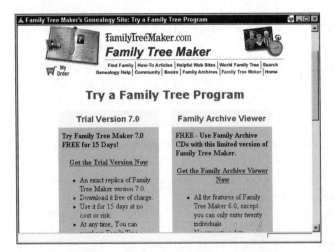

Figure 9-1. The Get the Trial Version Now link is in the left column of the download page.

3. Scroll to the bottom of the Web page and click the Download the Family Tree Maker Trial Version link. Instead of scrolling, you can also click the Download link near the top of the page, which takes you to the download instructions at the bottom of the Web page. Once at the bottom, click the Download the Family Tree Maker Trial Version link. A File Download window opens, asking whether you prefer to run the program from its current location or save it to disk.

4. Select the Save This Program to Disk radio button; then click OK. A Save As dialog box pops up, asking you to choose where you want to save the trial version (see Figure 9-2).

Figure 9-2. Use the Save As dialog box to identify where to save the trial version and what to name it.

5. Choose a directory on your computer in the Save In field at the top.

6. Assign a filename in the File name field.

7. Click Save. A progress window shows the file download-ing to your computer. Upon completion (if you didn't se-lect the Close This Dialog Box when Download Complete check box), you'll get a Download Complete dialog box.

8. If you're ready to begin working with the Family Tree Maker Trial Version, click Open. A Setup window pops up, asking you to close all other applications and run Setup to install the trial version, so you may want to exit AOL before completing the install.

9. Click Setup, and the program starts the Install Wizard, which guides you through the process of installing the Family Tree Maker Trial Version. You have 15 days to evaluate the trial version, after which time your data-bases in Family Tree Maker become inactive.

Personal Ancestral File

Personal Ancestral File (PAF) is software endorsed by and avail-able from the Church of Jesus Christ of Latter-day Saints (LDS). You can get a fully functional copy of the software for free at the LDS Web site. Here's what you do:

1. Type **www.familysearch.org** in the text box on the navigation bar, and then click Go. AOL opens a Web browser window and takes you the FamilySearch Internet Genealogy Service site.

2. Click the Order Family History Resources link on the left side of the screen. The FamilySearch Online Distribution Center page pops up.

3. Click the Software Downloads — Free link; then select Personal Ancestral File 4.0.4 — Multi Language from the list of software (see Figure 9-3).

Note

Personal Ancestral File is the genealogical database en-dorsed by and available from the Church of Jesus Christ of Latter-day Saints.

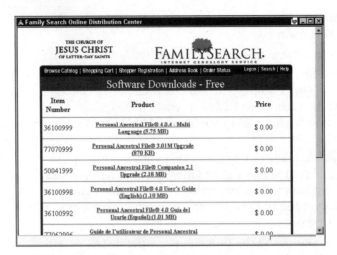

Figure 9-3. The Software Downloads — Free Web page at the LDS site.

4. Click the Proceed button to download a copy from the Web page that describes the product.

5. Read the License Agreement that pops up and then click Continue or Cancel. If you cancel the procedure, the downloading stops. If you click Continue, a Registration page comes up (see Figure 9-4).

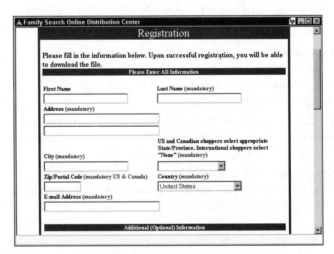

Figure 9-4. Complete this Registration page to finish downloading Personal Ancestral File.

6. Complete the registration form; then click Register. This includes providing your name, street and e-mail addresses, and answering some demographic-type questions. A new window pops up explaining briefly how to download the software.

7. Click the Click Here link to download PAF to your computer. A File Download dialog box opens, asking whether you prefer to run the program from its current location or save it to disk.

8. Select the Save This Program to Disk radio button and click OK. A Save As dialog box pops up, asking you to choose where you want to save the trial version.

9. Choose the directory on your computer in the Save In field at the top, assign a filename in the File Name field, and click Save. A progress window shows the file downloading to your computer. Upon completion, you'll get a Download Complete dialog box.

10. If you're ready to begin working with Personal Ancestral File, click Open. A Setup window pops up, asking you to close all other applications and run Setup to install.

11. Click Setup, and the program starts the Install Wizard, which guides you through the process of installing Personal Ancestral File.

Setting Up a New Database

After you've downloaded and installed one or both of the two genealogical databases we'll work with here, you can begin creating a family database. Creating your family database in a genealogical database program is relatively with both programs.

Creating a New Database in Family Tree Maker (Trial Version)

Creating a new family file in Family Tree Maker is easy. To start a Family File, follow these steps:

1. Double-click the icon for Family Tree Maker to open the program. When you open the Family Tree Maker Trial Version for the first time, an Open Family File window pops up.

2. With the Family File window open, either identify a file
   to import into Family Tree Maker or create a new file:

   • If you're creating a new file, click the New button and
     type in a name for the new file.

   • If you're opening an existing file, type the name of
     the file in the File Name field; then pick the file for-
     mat from the Files of Type drop-down list and click
     Open.

   A New Family File window comes up.

3. Provide a name for your new family file in the File Name
   field; make sure the Files of Type field is set to Family
   Tree Maker for Windows. You can use your name, just
   your surname, or whatever you choose.

4. Click Save.

Now your Family File is started. Next, you'll need to enter information about the members of your family. Begin by providing
information about yourself in the Start Your Family Tree window (see Figure 9-5) that pops up after you create the file.

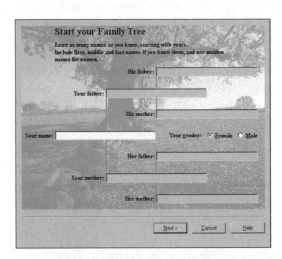

Figure 9-5. Start creating your Family Tree Maker database by completing the Start
Your Family Tree window.

To start your family tree from the Start Your Family Tree Window, follow these steps:

1. In the Your Name field, enter your full name.

2. Click the appropriate gender for yourself.

3. Tab to the Your Father field and enter his full name.

4. Tab to the Your Mother field and enter her full name.

5. Tab to each of your grandparents' fields and provide their names.

6. After you've completed all the fields in the Start Your Family Tree window, click the Next button.

7. When the Births window appears, enter birth dates and places for everyone you identified in the Start Your Family Tree window; then click Next.

8. When the Deaths window appears, enter death dates and places for everyone you identified in the Start Your Family Tree window; then click Next.

9. A FamilyFinder Search window pops up. Read over the FamilyFinder Search explanation and decide whether you want to do this. Indicate whether you want to run an online FamilyFinder Search, a CD-based search, or no search at this time. Click Finish.

10. A dialog box comes up, stating that you can run a FamilyFinder Search at any time by clicking the appropriate icon on the toolbar. Click OK.

11. Your Family Page appears (as shown in Figure 9-6), showing some of the information that you provided in the Start Your Family Tree and subsequent wizard windows. Complete any empty fields on your Family Page.

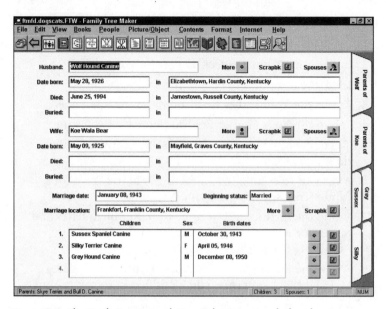

Figure 9-6. The Family Page is Family Tree Maker's signature look and an easy-to-use interface.

For more information about using specific features of Family Tree Maker, we recommend *Family Tree Maker For Dummies*, which is available from IDG Books Worldwide, Inc.

You can navigate through the Family Page by using the Tab key or clicking fields. There are spaces for information about your spouse and marriage (if applicable) and children (if applicable). You can also click icons that lead you to additional pages where you can enter more information about yourself and your spouse — they include a More icon, a Scrapbook icon, and a Spouses icon. Use the More icon to get to pages where you can enter facts about yourself, addresses, medical information, lineage data, and notes. The Scrapbook icon takes you to the multimedia scrapbook feature where you can attach photos, video clips, and sound files. And you use the Spouses icon if you've had multiple marriages.

To get to other individuals' Family Pages, you can click the tabs that run down the right side of the screen, or you can select a person's name from the Index of Individuals (click the icon on the toolbar or use the View pull-down menu).

Personal Ancestral File

The data-entry interface in Personal Ancestral File (PAF) is simple and easy to use (as shown in Figure 9-7).

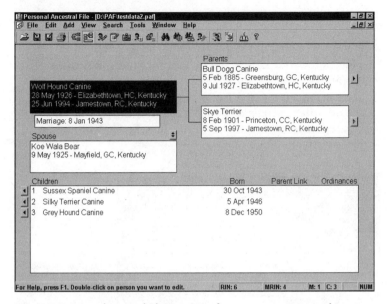

Figure 9-7. Personal Ancestral File's entry interface is easy to navigate and use.

Starting a PAF Database

Follow these steps to create a PAF database file.

1. Double-click the PAF icon to open the program.

2. When you first open PAF, you're greeted with a Welcome to Personal Ancestral File window. You can select whether to search all drives for PAF files, open an existing database, create a new file, or close the window. You can also designate whether to use Church of Jesus Christ of Latter-day Saints formatted information on the screens and reports.

3. When you click New to create a new file, the Create New Family File appears, which enables you to designate where your computer should store your family file; here's where you also assign a filename and file type. Using the Save In pull-down box, select the directory in which you want your file stored.

4. In the File Name field, give your family file a name.

5. Double-check the Save As Type field to ensure that you're creating a PAF file. When you're satisfied that you are doing so, click Save.

A Preferences window (see Figure 9-8) pops up with the Prepared By tab open, where you can enter information about yourself as the preparer of the database. It has fields for your names (given and surname), address, country, phone number, Ancestral File Number, and e-mail address. There are other tabs where you can designate other preferences for your family file — they are categorized as General, File, InfoBox, Fonts, Multimedia, Formats, and Folders.

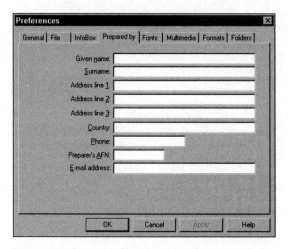

Figure 9-8. The Prepared by tab in the Preferences window.

6. After you complete the Prepared By tab of the Preferences window (if you choose to do so), as well as any other tabs, click OK. The Preferences window closes — and your family file or database has begun.

For more specific information about using PAF, check out the Getting Started Guide and the Feedback and Frequently Asked Questions under the Help pull-down menu.

Putting Specific Info into Your PAF Database

Now you see the main data-entry screen, where you begin providing specific information about individuals. Follow these steps to enter information.

1. Double-click the field for the person about whom you want to enter information. If you're just starting out, double-click the main individual's box.

The Add Individual window (shown in Figure 9-9) comes up; here you can provide all sorts of information about the person. There are fields for each individual's name, gender, life events (including birth, christening, death, and burial), LDS ordinances, and other information. Source icons identify the name and each life event and LDS ordinance that you can click to enter source citations. On the right side of the window, there are four icons — one takes you to a window where you can enter notes, one enables you to view all sources, another allows you to enter address book information, and the final one enables you to attach multimedia files.

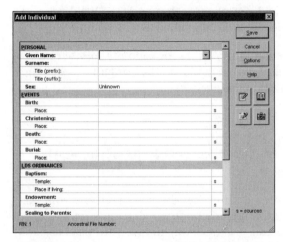

Figure 9-9. The Add Individual window has fields for names and facts about the individual.

2. After you've completed any of the Add Individual fields for which you have information, click Save.

3. Double-click the Spouse field (if appropriate) and complete the Add Individual window for the spouse. Then click Save.

4. When you click Save for the Spouse, a Marriage window pops up where you can provide information about the marriage.

5. Double-click the Children field (as appropriate); a dialog box appears, asking whether you want to Add New Individual or Select Existing Individual.

6. Click Add New Individual to create an entry for your child. Provide the information and click Save.

   After you click Save, another dialog box appears, asking whether you want to add another child for the main individual. If you have other children to add, click Yes. If not, click No.

7. Double-clicking the top box to the right of the main individual's name brings up a dialog box asking whether you want to add a father for that person. Click Yes; then complete the Add Individual box.

8. Double-clicking the lower box to the right of the main individual's name brings up a dialog box asking whether you want to add a mother for that person. Click Yes; then complete the Add Individual box.

To navigate to the data-entry pages for each of the other individuals on this page (spouse, child, mother, or father), click the little arrow icons next to the names.

Enhancing Your File with Multimedia

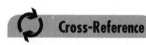

Cross-Reference

Chapter 10 includes detailed information about using photos, video, and audio in your genealogical files.

In addition to written information about yourself and your relatives, you may want to include photos, video clips, or sound files. Using such media is a great way to give your database a personal feel — others will be able to put a face or voice with a name.

The basic technique of adding multimedia works like this:

1. From the Family Tree Maker Family Page for the individual for whom you want to include a photo, a video, or an audio file, click the Scrapbook icon next to the person's name.

2. A screen that is filled with lots of little numbered boxes appears. To use the Picture/Object pull-down menu to attach an item to the scrapbook, click the down-arrow icon in the lower-right corner of the box in which you

want to attach a media file. The More About
Picture/Object window (see Figure 9-10) pops up, in
which you can provide information about the object —
including a caption, category of item, date of origin, type
of item, and description. You can also provide preferences about printing, whether to play it in a scrapbook
slide show, and whether the item is on a PhotoCD.

3. When you've provided the needed information,
   click OK.

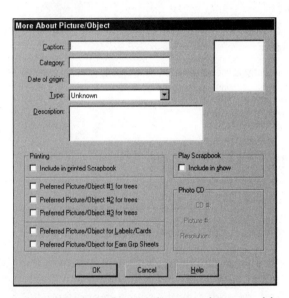

Figure 9-10. Use Family Tree Maker's More About Picture/Object window to enter captions and other information about a scrapbook item.

To include a multimedia file (photo, video, or sound) for an individual using PAF, all you have to do is click the camera icon in
the Add/Edit Individual window. This brings up a Multimedia
Collection window where you can identify media items and
provide captions (as shown in Figure 9-11). Simply click the
Add button and walk through the fields providing information
such as the type of item, the filename under which the item is
stored on your computer, a caption, and a description.

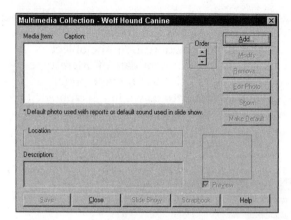

Figure 9-11. The PAF Multimedia Collection window allows you to identify the item's filename and provide information about the item.

Don't Forget to Cite Your Sources!

Tip

Get into the habit of citing your sources as you enter information about individuals in your database; it saves lots of work later.

Definition

Citing sources is another way to say documenting your research findings — a way of putting "here's where I found this" in writing and giving credit where it's due.

As you're entering information about your family into your database, it's important that you cite the sources of that information. Doing so is always a good idea, for at least three reasons:

▶ It provides you and others with a reference to return to if a question arises about some of your findings.

▶ It validates your research as being sound, careful, and complete.

▶ It's really easy to do with Family Tree Maker and PAF.

In Family Tree Maker, highlight the name of the person or the event you want to provide a source citation for; then select Source from the View pull-down menu. This brings up the Source Citation window (see Figure 9-12) where you can enter information about the source. It includes a title of source, citation page, citation text, and footnote. The title of source leads back to another window called Master Source Information, where you can enter the details about the actual source (much like a bibliographic entry).

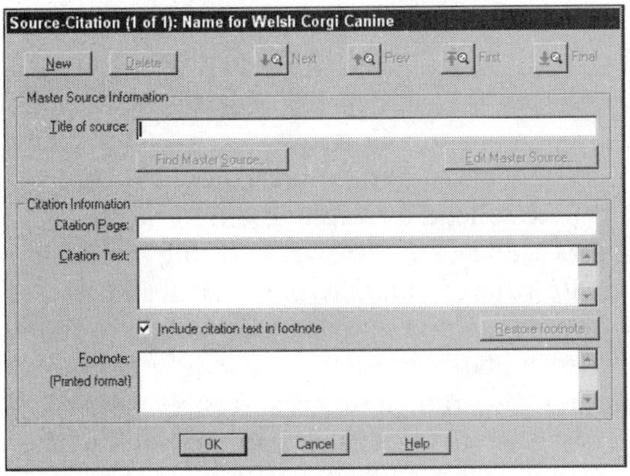

Figure 9-12. Family Tree Maker's Source Citation window.

In PAF, you just click the little S icon next to the name or event in the Add/Edit Individual window. This brings up a Select Source window where you can choose from a list of sources you've already entered or create a new source. The Edit Source window (see Figure 9-13) includes fields for the title, the author, publication information, a call number, actual text (quote), comments, and a sample footnote. There are also boxes for designating whether to italicize the title in your reports and print the publication information in parentheses. You can also identify the repository from which you received your information.

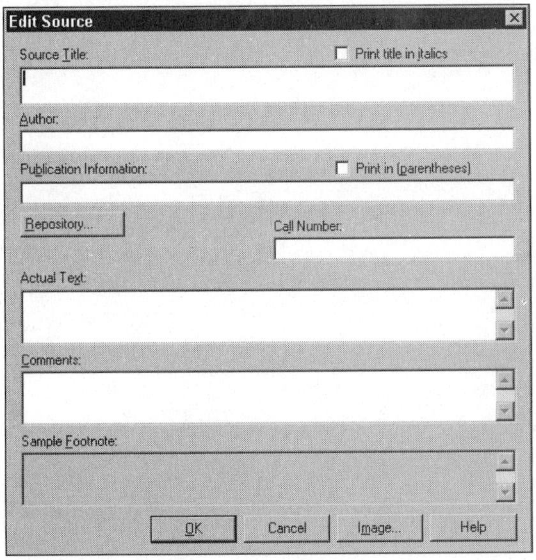

Figure 9-13. PAF's Edit Source window.

Summary

This chapter had a lot of steps to follow, but every one of them gets you closer to creating a gold mine of genealogical data. We've covered how to download a couple of different genealogical databases, as well as how to start entering information into them to create your own family files. And let's not forget that we touched on including multimedia objects and citing sources so your descendants and fellow researchers have a firm foundation for later research. Acting responsibly with source information can become a valuable habit as you enter your findings into your database. And now that you've begun creating your database, it's time to start generating some family trees and reports. That's the goal of the next chapter; we hope you'll keep reading while you're on a roll.

Quick Look

Chapter 10

Discovering Computer Companions

IN THIS CHAPTER

Discovering utilities

Touching up those old photographs

Using your word processor to sum up your research

Storing your electronic treasures

You're likely to run across many treasures while exploring your ancestors' lives. These treasures can come in many different forms, from family stories to pictures of your great-grandfather. At some point, you may want to use these treasures in a way that is beyond the capabilities of your computer or genealogical software. In this chapter, we discuss ways to extend the capabilities of your current equipment.

Benefiting from Utilities

At some point in researching your genealogy, you may want to use your findings in a way that your genealogical software just can't handle or doesn't handle the way that you want. For example, you may want to generate a certain kind of chart or report, place your data online, or even write a book for publication. Fortunately, other researchers have had similar experiences and have done something about it by creating utilities.

Types of Utilities

Utilities are usually small programs that perform one specific function rather than multiple functions (such as those performed by a genealogical database). Some utilities are programs that you add on to your existing software, and some can do the job by themselves. We discuss some general types of utilities that you're likely to encounter in the following few sections.

Data Conversion Utilities

Data conversion utilities usually convert the information in your genealogical database to some other file format. A good example of a data conversion utility is one that converts a file from your genealogical database into HTML so that you can place it on the Web. Here are some examples of data conversion utilities:

▶ **GED2HTML** (`www.gendex.com/ged2html`): This utility converts the contents of a GEDCOM file (a standard file produced by your genealogical database) into HTML. This is a useful utility if you want to place your database on the Web for other genealogists to see (see Figure 10-1).

▶ **GEDClean** (`www.raynorshyn.com/gedclean`): Before you place information from your database online, it's a good idea to strip out any information about living individuals. GEDClean helps you clean your file of any personal information about living people and can even take out the names of living family members if you desire.

Note

While genealogical software programs perform many functions, utilities (used either alone or added to existing software), tend to perform specific functions. You can search for utilities online that perform particular tasks related to your research.

10

Discovering Computer Companions

Definition

HTML (which stands for *Hyper Text Markup Language*) is a computer language that Web browsers use to interpret text and display it graphically.

Cross-Reference

We discuss the GEDCOM file format in more detail in Chapter 11.

Tip

You can use GEDClean to privatize data files that contain personal information about living relatives. Then, if you'd like to post the data file to a Web page, you can use GED2HTML to convert the file to HTML format.

Note

The Soundex system is made up of a letter followed by three numerals. The code created by the Soundex calculator allows you to find names of people in the Soundex index who were enumerated in the United States censuses between 1880 and 1920.

Find It Online

You'll find the downloadable Soundex calculator in the Software and Tools section of the Files Library Center in the Genealogy Forum (Keyword: **Roots**). Once you're at the Software and Tools section, select Windows/DOS Files & Utilities to find the calculator.

Find It Online

Look under Windows/DOS Programs in the Software and Tools section of the Genealogy Forum's Files Library Center to find the Census Research Tool. You can get to the Genealogy Forum using the Keyword: **Roots**.

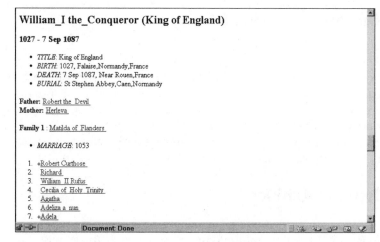

Figure 10-1. An HTML page resulting from the GED2HTML conversion of a GEDCOM file.

Research Utilities

You can use a variety of research utilities to help you accomplish certain research goals. For example, these utilities may help you organize your research or assist you in using certain kind of records. Here are a few research utilities that we recommend:

▶ **Soundex Calculator (Genealogy Forum's Files Library Center):** This utility (shown in Figure 10-2) converts surnames into their Soundex (an alpha-numeric code that represents how a name is pronounced) equivalents. The calculator can convert a single name or a list of names into three different Soundex types.

▶ **Census Research Tool (Genealogy Forum's Files Library Center):** This research utility allows you to enter information from a census microfilm into the utility to produce a printable report.

Figure 10-2. The Soundex Calculator conversion of the surname Helm.

Publishing Utilities

If you decide to write a book or an article about your genealogy research, a few utilities can shorten the amount of time it
takes to complete the project. Here are a few publishing utilities that provide shortcuts for very time-intensive tasks:

> ▶ **GenIndex (the Genealogy Forum's Files Library
> Center):** This utility creates name indexes that you can
> use in the genealogical books that you write.

> ▶ **Family Atlas (`www.parsonstech.com/software/
> famatlas.html`):** This utility enables you to add maps
> to your books, showing migration patterns and the loca-
> tions at which special events occurred in your family
> history (see Figure 10-3). It uses a GEDCOM file that you
> export from your genealogical software into Family Atlas
> to create the maps.

Find It Online

The GenIndex is included in
the Windows/DOS Files &
Utilities, which you can get to
by selecting the Software and
Tools section of the Files
Library Center.

Find It Online

Find out more about Family
Atlas and how to order it at
`www.parsonstech.com/
software/famatlas
.html`.

10

Discovering Computer Companions

 **Find It Online**

Go to AOL's Computing Download Center (Keyword: **Download Center**), select the Desktop Publishing category then the Desktop Publishing Programs library. You'll see SnagIt on the list of programs and utilities from which you can choose.

▶ **SnagIt (AOL Computing Download Center):** This utility enables you to capture a picture of a graphic that is displayed on your computer screen. You can save the graphic in a graphic file format and then place it into your word processor to use it for your book or article.

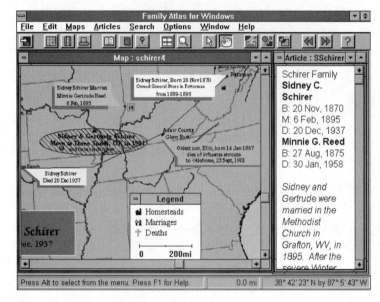

Figure 10-3. A map created by Family Atlas.

Report and Chart Utilities

Researchers are constantly finding new and exciting ways to display information. These innovators usually create utilities that work directly with your genealogical software or with a file that your software can produce. Here are some research and chart utilities that you may want to check out:

▶ **Genelines (www.progenysoftware.com):** This utility displays a timeline of significant events that occurred during your ancestors' lifetimes, thus providing a historical context for your research findings. (See Figure 10-4.)

▶ **Genealogy Charts & Forms (www.dhc.net/ ~design/desig1-5.htm):** You can print over 420 different pre-defined charts and forms with this software.

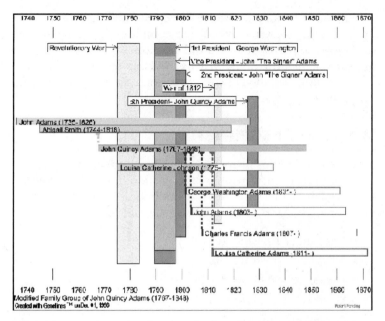

Figure 10-4. A report on the John Adams family produced by Genelines.

Computer Utilities

Although not related specifically to genealogy, you may be interested in other programs that help you maintain, protect, and share your computer files. These types of utilities include file compression programs (which reduce the size of your file or group of files so that you can share them with others) and antivirus programs (which prevent your computer from executing a program that could damage your files). Here are some examples:

▶ **WinZip (the Genealogy Forum's Files Library Center and AOL Computing Download Center):** This utility is a compression program that reduces the size of one file or a group of files. To find out more about file and disk compression options, check out the section later in this chapter that covers storage options.

▶ **PC-cillin (AOL Computing Download Center):** This shareware program searches for viruses on your computer.

Find It Online

You can download a copy of Genelines from the Software and Tools section of the Genealogy Forum's Files Library Center. Simply visit the list of Windows/DOS Programs to find out more about Genelines, and download/purchase a copy.

Find It Online

You can find WinZip in the Software and Tools section of the Files Library Center in the Genealogy Forum (Keyword: **Roots**). Once you're at the Software and Tools section, select Windows/DOS Files & Utilities to get to the list containing WinZip.

10

Discovering Computer Companions

Find It Online

Go to AOL's Computing Download Center (Keyword: **Download Center**) and select the Utilities & Tools catalogue. From there, choose the File Utilities category then the Anti-Virus & Security library. You'll see PC-cillin on the list of programs and utilities from which you can choose.

Caution

Before using any utility that you download, make sure that you run a virus check on it first. That way you don't have to worry about losing or damaging any data stored on your computer.

Tip

Keyword: **Virus** takes you to AOL's Anti-Virus Center, which can give you information about virus hoaxes. You can also update your current antivirus software using this important resource.

Tip

Another place you can find general utilities is the AOL Computing Download Center (Keyword: **Download Center**). It offers 14 catalogues of programs available for downloading – some of these catalogues include Desktop Publishing, Graphics, Internet Tools, Utilities & Tools, and Web Publishing.

When you're looking for utilities, keep in mind that some developers create programs only for the computer operating systems that they use personally. So, if the developer only uses Macintosh, then the utility may be available only for Macintosh users — until someone creates a version that works with another operating system.

Where to Find Utilities

You can find utilities many different places online. A good starting point is the Software and Tools section in the Genealogy Forum's Files Library Center. You can find utilities and other electronic assistants in the following categories:

- ▶ Genealogy Tips and Resources
- ▶ Macintosh Software Library
- ▶ Windows/DOS Files & Utilities
- ▶ Windows/DOS Programs
- ▶ Genealogy Clip Art
- ▶ Ancestor Photos and Graphics

To find a utility in the Genealogy Forum, follow these steps:

1. Type the Keyword: **Roots** in the text box on the navigation bar. This launches the Genealogy Forum window.

2. Click the Files button to go to the Genealogy Forum's Files Library Center.

3. Click the Software and Tools icon on the left side of the window. This brings up the Software and Tools window.

4. Select a platform for the computer that you have. For example, click the Windows/DOS Files & Utilities option if you're looking for a utility for your Windows computer (see Figure 10-5).

5. Double-click a utility that looks interesting to see a description of the function it performs.

6. Click the Download button if you decide that the utility meets your needs.

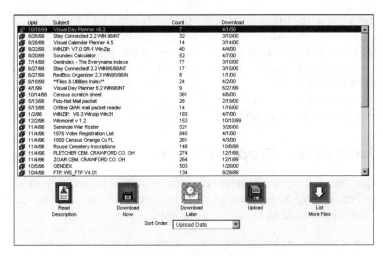

Figure 10-5. The Windows/DOS Files & Utilities library.

You can also find links to utilities on comprehensive genealogy index sites and on sites dedicated to genealogical software such as GenealogySoftware.com (www.genealogysoftware.com).

Using Graphics Software

Photographs and scanned images are often a genealogist's most treasured objects. However, such images (especially if they are old) often are not as clear and unblemished as you would like them to be. In order to make them look better, you can use graphics software to clean up and repair the ditigized versions of pictures and other images.

How Graphics Software Works

Most of the graphics software packages available on the market work in the same general way. You load the software on your computer and then import the graphic or photograph with which you want to work. Typically, you can import a graphic by loading an already existing image file into the program, or you

Tip

If you think a utility might be useful but you're unable to find it online, try posting a message to the soc .genealogy.computing newsgroup to see if anyone is aware of a program that can perform that function.

10

Discovering Computer Companions

can scan a photograph or other image directly into the program. After the image is imported into the program, you use a set of tools to perform certain actions on the image — like cropping, resizing, cleaning up, and so on. After you're satisfied with how the image looks, save it to your hard drive. You can then import the saved image into a genealogical database (if it supports importing pictures) to use in your charts and reports.

Tools of the Graphics Trade

Graphics software allows you to get rid of an image's imperfections. It can also help you to highlight important details of a photograph.

Cropping a picture may make its file size smaller, which is great if you want to share the image on the Internet or add it to a Web page. The smaller the file size, the less time it takes to appear on another person's computer screen.

Graphics software programs have their own bells and whistles, but most have some tools in common. Here are some of the capabilities shared by graphics programs:

▶ **Cropping:** Every graphics program allows you to *crop* (or cut) part of an image out of a larger photograph. Cropping is useful when you want to focus on a specific individual or object in the image, or you want to reduce the size of the background.

▶ **Paint:** You use the Paint tool to add a specific color to your image, just as if you were using a paintbrush on the image. Normally, you select a color from a palette (a group of colors).

▶ **Resize or resample:** You can change the overall size of an image by using the resize or resample tool. Usually, you can increase or decrease the size by a certain percentage.

▶ **Type:** If you want to add text to an image, you can use the Type tool. This tool uses the fonts that are already installed on your computer to add words to images. You can usually change the font color by selecting a color from the palette.

▶ **Paint Bucket:** Sometimes you may want to paint an entire area a single color, but you don't want to take the time to brush it on with the Paint tool. The Paint Bucket fills in a particular area of the image with the color that you designate from the color palette.

▶ **Rotate:** The Rotate tool turns your image a specified amount (such as 90 degrees) clockwise or counterclockwise. This tool enables you to fix photographs that are crooked (taken on an angle) or to turn an image on its side.

▶ **Color balance:** In some instances, you may want to correct the amount of a certain color in a photograph. The color balance function allows you to adjust the amount of certain colors, such as red, green, and blue, to enhance the color of your image.

▶ **Brightness/contrast:** Sometimes images are too dark or too faded to be useful. You can adjust the brightness and contrast of the image so that the image quality is better for viewing or printing.

▶ **Filters:** You can use a number of tools to give images a particular look. For example, you may be able to use filters to blur or sharpen an image, turn your image into a mosaic, or even rid your images of red eye.

▶ **Special effects:** Some programs come with special effects that you can use on your images. For example, you may be able to add a shadow around your image, bevel the image (make it look like a button), or add a halo effect or glow around your image.

Finding Graphics Programs

Both commercial and shareware graphic programs are available. You can usually find commercial products in any store that carries computer software. Two of the more popular commercial graphics programs are Adobe Photoshop (Keyword: **Photoshop**), which we used to display the census record shown in Figure 10-6, and CorelDRAW (Keyword: **CorelDRAW**).

You can download shareware graphics programs from online sources and pay a small fee to license the product. One of the popular shareware programs is Paint Shop Pro, which you can download in the Genealogy Forum's File Libraries Center or in the AOL Computing Download Center.

Caution

Make sure that you let other people know when you share images that you have manipulated the images with graphics software. That way they know there is something different about the image from the original photograph.

10

Discovering Computer Companions

Tip

Commercial graphics programs can be expensive. Before running out and buying expensive software you may not use often, you may want to experiment with a shareware program first. That way you know what features to look for in a commercial product. You can also try to find a demonstration version of commercial products to see if they have all of the features that you would like to have in a graphics program.

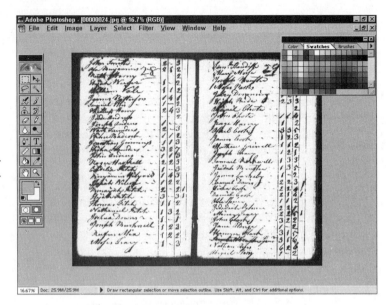

Figure 10-6. Adobe Photoshop with a census record image displayed.

Making the Most of Your Word Processor

Because genealogical research is an ongoing process, it's a good idea to set some intermediate goals so that you feel a sense of accomplishment for the time you've invested. Consider setting a goal to write a family history book, an article, or a newsletter.

Tip

Try to set realistic goals for reporting your research findings. For example, if you have a family gathering coming up in a few months, don't expect to have your family's entire history ready to present. You may instead want to prepare a short newsletter about one line of the family, promising another installment the next time everyone's gathered together.

Although genealogical databases have many useful features, they aren't great at everything. So, you may need another software program that is more conducive to writing. A word processor fits the bill.

Word processors come with many different features. Small word processors let you type and print text, while others allow you to link information between programs (and even the Internet). Many of these programs also have special features that automatically index text, compile Tables of Contents, and embed art elements.

Using a word processor to complete your family history allows you more flexibility in creating a book, article, report, or newsletter. After you type text into a word processor, you can import images to give the document a good look and feel.

If you feel comfortable with the contents of your research document, you can then submit it to a publisher (who usually requires that it be in a standard word processor file such as Microsoft Word or Corel WordPerfect).

For tips on how to use word processors to their fullest, see the AOL Computing Word Processing Center (Keyword: **Text Tools**) and the AOL Computing Desktop Publishing area (Keyword: **Desktop Publishing**).

Experimenting with Methods of Storage

When you purchased your computer, you probably never thought that you would run out of hard drive space. Well, after a few months of researching your genealogy and collecting records, photographs, and digitized images, all of a sudden you have a storage problem. Fortunately, some products are now available to help you cope with this problem.

Compression

By making more efficient use of the space that you already have, you can avoid spending money on more equipment (such as a new computer or an additional hard drive). Compression is one way to maximize your space. This involves making your current files more compact so that they don't take up as much space on your hard drive. Here are two ways that you can compress your files:

> ▶ **Use a compression program to create an archive file that shrinks the size of your files.** This is a particularly good strategy if you won't be using files for an extended period of time. When you need to use the files, you must *extract* (or uncompress) your original files from the archive.

Your genealogical database is likely to have a book report feature. However, the report you create is sometimes not very attractive because you can't position text and other elements exactly where you want them.

A word processor may have come with your computer, or you may have to buy it separately.

▶ **Compress your hard drive.** Some operating systems have a built-in function that automatically compresses your files for optimum storage. Because this feature is built in to the operating system, you don't have to extract the files when you want to use them; you just use them the same way that you always have. When using disk compression, you may notice slightly slower access times when loading databases and other large files, but it is probably worth the space savings.

Additional Hard Drives

Find It Online

To find disk compression utilities or any other kind of utility for your hard drive, check out the AOL Computing Download Center (Keyword: **Download Center**).

If you need to access information quickly and routinely, consider buying a second hard drive. Hard drives can be internal or external and come in a variety of sizes. Also, you need to make sure that the hard drive that you select is compatible with your *controller* (the piece of hardware that connects the hard drive to your computer). The best way to do this is to look at the documentation that originally came with your computer. For reviews on different types of hard drives, take a look at the hardware reviews in the CNET Consumer's Guide in the AOL Computing Section (Keyword: **Computing**) under More⇨ Storage⇨Hard Disks (see Figure 10-7).

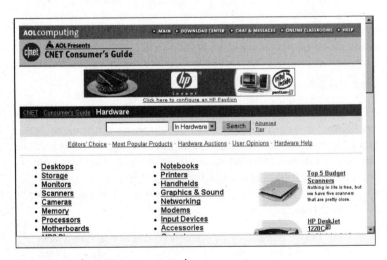

Figure 10-7. The CNET Consumer's Guide.

Removable Cartridge Drives

A popular method of storage over the past few years has been
the removable cartridge drive. In particular, the Iomega Zip 100
and Zip 250 Drives (Keyword: **Iomega**) have brought this type
of drive to the forefront. The drive itself can be mounted inside
your computer or attached externally by using your computer's
parallel port (where your printer is usually connected) or USB
port (found on newer computers, the Universal Standard Bus allows you to just plug in the hardware, which is then automatically recognized by the operating system). When you want to
save some information to the drive, you pop in a cartridge (or
in the case of Zip drives, a Zip disk), which can be removed and
transported just like a floppy disk. When that cartridge is full,
just slide another one into the drive. The media for these types
of drives can store anywhere from 100MB (megabytes) up to
2GB (gigabytes). You can also find reviews of removable cartridge drives in the CNET Consumer's Guide in the AOL
Computing Section (Keyword: **Computing**) under More⇨
Storage⇨Other Storage⇨Removable Cartridge Drives.

CD-R/CD-RW Drives

Removable cartridge drives are magnetic storage devices. As
such, they are vulnerable to damage over time. For a more permanent solution, take a look at Writable CD-ROM drives.
Writable CD-ROM drives come in two versions: CD-R drives,
which allow you to write to a CD once, and CD-RW drives,
which allow you to write and re-write to the same CD-ROM.
After you write to a CD-ROM, you can view the contents by using any CD-ROM drive (it does not have to be another Writable
CD-ROM). Writable CD-ROMs can store up to 650MB of information. When shopping for a Writable CD-ROM, consider the
speed at which it writes and make sure that it supports several
different CD-ROM standards including CD-ROM, CD-R, audio
CD, and Photo CD. You can find CD-R/CD-RW reviews in the
CNET Consumer's Guide in the AOL Computing Section
(Keyword: **Computing**) under More⇨Storage⇨CD-R/CD-RW
Drives.

DVD-RAM Drives

A newer type of drive, DVD-RAM is similar to a CD-RW drive. DVD-RAMs are rewritable and a double-sided disk can store up to 5.2GB of information. The difference is that you can only read a DVD-RAM disk in a DVD-RAM drive. Right now you can't read a DVD-RAM in a DVD-ROM drive (the successor to the CD-ROM drive). The best use of DVD-RAM drives is for long-term storage. For more on DVD-RAM drives, see the CNET Consumer's Guide in the AOL Computing Section (Keyword: **Computing**) under More⇨Storage⇨Options⇨DVD-RAM Drives.

Tape Storage

For files that you'll rarely access or for backing up important files, tape storage may be the answer. A variety of tape drives are available, which can store up to 70GB of information. Most of these drives serve as backup devices for computers and retrieving information from them is not the quickest process. However, if a file is ever corrupted on your computer, then they are worthwhile investments. Tape drives are reviewed in the CNET Consumer's Guide in the AOL Computing Section (Keyword: **Computing**) under More⇨Storage⇨Other Storage⇨Tape Drives.

Summary

Over the course of this chapter, we examined how you can use utilities to make your job as a genealogist a lot easier, the benefits of using graphics software to improve your digitized images, where word processors come in handy writing family histories, and what types of equipment might help you store all of your valuable research information. Now that you have your information in your genealogical database and stored where you can get to it, you're ready to find out how to share it. Chapter 11 looks at how to create reports with your genealogical software to share with other researchers.

P A R T

IV

FUN WAYS TO SHARE
YOUR HISTORY

Quick Look

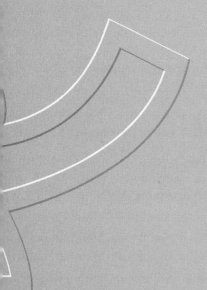

Chapter 11

Reporting Your Findings

Sharing the information that you discover on your genealogical journey can be a fulfilling experience. Often the reports and charts that you create can assist others who are researching the same family lines as you, or compel others to provide you with information that you're missing. In this chapter, we look at some of the standard report types used in genealogy, discuss ways to generate reports from two popular genealogical databases, and show you how to create and use GEDCOM files from genealogical databases.

Recognizing Standard Reports on Sight

Over the years, the genealogical community has created some standard ways of viewing genealogical data, which are called reports (or charts). Standard reports are useful because they allow researchers to find the information they're looking for quickly. Because researchers are already familiar with the formats, they can easily search standard reports by using keywords and names. The following sections take a look at some of the most common standard reports that you'll encounter.

Pedigree Chart

Probably the most familiar of the genealogical reports is the pedigree or ancestor chart (shown in Figure 11-1) because it contains many of the details commonly found in family trees. Pedigree charts show only the direct ancestors of an individual — parents, grandparents, great-grandparents, and so on. They don't show brothers, sisters, cousins, aunts, uncles, nieces, or nephews.

The pedigree chart usually begins with a single box for the individual who is the subject of the report. Two lines are extended from this box, one to the subject's father and the other to the subjects's mother. Then two lines extend from the subject's father to his father and mother, and so on, going back through the generations.

Definition

A pedigree chart displays the ancestry of a particular person.

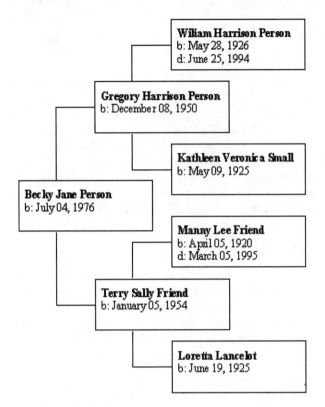

Figure 11-1. A three-generation pedigree chart.

A pedigree chart is a good reference tool to use when you're going on research trips, when you want to illustrate the relationship of your ancestors in a book or article, or when you want to share some basic information about your research with another genealogist.

Descendant Chart

After you've researched your family history back three or four generations (or more), you may want to produce a report that shows all the descendants from a particular ancestor. The descendant chart, shown in Figure 11-2, fits this bill. This chart shows all the descendants of an individual, including the siblings of those descendants.

The top box of the report represents the individual who is the subject of the report, and sometimes a spouse is also represented (refer to Figure 11-2). The lines below the box of the subject lead to each of his or her children. Additional lines drawn from each of the children represent another generation, and so on.

Definition

A descendant chart represents a person's lineage, displaying all of his or her descendants.

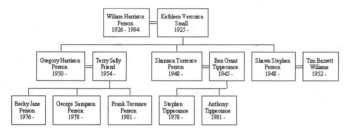

Figure 11-2. A three-generation descendant chart.

You can use descendant charts for a quick reference on research trips and for illustrations of family relationships in books and articles.

Family Group Sheet

If you want to concentrate on the details of a specific family unit, the Family Group Sheet (also called a Family Group Record) is a good report to use. These reports are handy on research trips if you're looking for information on several members of the same family. Family Group Sheets are also good reports to share with other researchers because much of the critical information that other researchers need to know is arranged concisely on them.

Tip

It's fun to create large descendant charts for family reunions, birthdays, anniversaries, or other special family occasions.

The Family Group Sheet typically contains the following information on each person in the nuclear family:

> ▶ **Father:** The information on the father can include the dates and places for his birth, baptism/christening, marriage, death, and burial; the names of his parents and any other wives; residences; occupation; religion; and military service.

- ▶ **Mother:** The mother's information can include the dates and places for her birth, baptism/christening, marriage, death, and burial; and the names of her parents and any other husbands.
- ▶ **Children:** Information on the children can include the child's name; sex; places and dates of birth, marriage, and death; and spouse's name.

The information that appears on a Family Group Sheet depends on the manufacturer of the sheet or the genealogical database that created the report. For example, the Family Group Sheet shown in Figure 11-3 contains just a portion of the information that we mention in the preceding list.

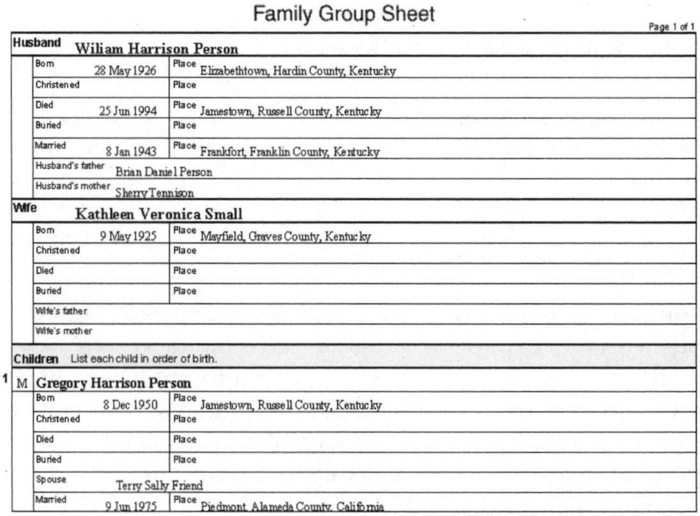

Family Group Sheet

Page 1 of 1

Husband	**Wiliam Harrison Person**		
Born	28 May 1926	Place	Elizabethtown, Hardin County, Kentucky
Christened		Place	
Died	25 Jun 1994	Place	Jamestown, Russell County, Kentucky
Buried		Place	
Married	8 Jan 1943	Place	Frankfort, Franklin County, Kentucky
Husband's father	Brian Daniel Person		
Husband's mother	Sherry Tennison		
Wife	**Kathleen Veronica Small**		
Born	9 May 1925	Place	Mayfield, Graves County, Kentucky
Christened		Place	
Died		Place	
Buried		Place	
Wife's father			
Wife's mother			
Children	List each child in order of birth.		
1 M	**Gregory Harrison Person**		
Born	8 Dec 1950	Place	Jamestown, Russell County, Kentucky
Christened		Place	
Died		Place	
Buried		Place	
Spouse	Terry Sally Friend		
Married	9 Jun 1975	Place	Piedmont, Alameda County, California

Figure 11-3. Personal Ancestral File's Family Group Sheet.

Reporting by the Numbers

Pedigree charts, descendant charts, and Family Group Sheets work well when you're dealing with only a few generations of individuals. However, when you've completed enough research, you may find that they aren't adequate to keep track of all your ancestors. If you decide to write a book or an article that covers ten generations, for example, these reports may become completely unmanageable — not to mention the frustrating problem of keeping descendants who have the same name straight.

To solve these two problems, genealogists use textual reports that allow you to list several generations compactly. They also use numbering systems to help you keep track of the eight John Smiths in your family line.

Numbering systems allow you to assign a unique number to each individual who appears in a report. This number is used to distinguish one person from another. You can also incorporate the number in your filing system to keep track of the paper copies of records that you compile on individuals. Many different numbering systems are used by genealogists, but we take a look at the most popular three: Ahnentafel, Register, and Modified Register.

Ahnentafel

The Ahnentafel numbering system (also called Sosa-Stradonitz) gets its name from the German words meaning "ancestor table." A Spanish genealogist named Jerome de Sosa introduced this numbering system in 1676, and it became popular in 1896 when it was used by Stephan Kekule von Stradonitz (hence the name Sosa-Stradonitz). This numbering system is based on a mathematical relationship between parents and their children, as shown in Figure 11-4. Here is how it works:

Tip

The Ahnentafel numbering system is used when creating a report on your ancestors.

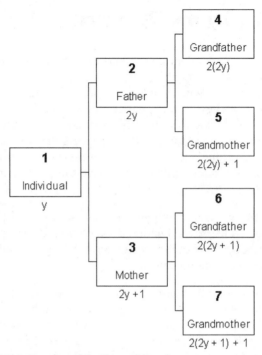

Figure 11-4. An outline of the Ahnentafel number system as used in a pedigree chart.

▶ The subject of the report is assigned a particular number: y.

▶ The subject's father is assigned the number that is double the subject's number: 2y.

▶ The subject's mother is assigned a number that is double the child's number plus one: 2y + 1.

▶ The father's father is assigned the number that is double the father's number: 2(2y).

The father's mother is assigned the number that is double the father's number plus one: 2(2y) + 1.

▶ The mother's father is assigned a number that is double the mother's number: 2(2y + 1).

The mother's mother is assigned a number that is double the mother's number plus one: 2(2y + 1) + 1.

▶ And so forth through the ancestors.

The Ahnentafel numbering system is used in reports showing the ancestors of a particular individual. Figure 11-5 shows an example of the numbering system used in a report on the ancestors of William Harrison Person.

Generation No. 1

1. WILLIAM HARRISON[4] PERSON *(BRIAN DANIEL[3], WALTER CAMPBELL[2], WELSH CORGI[1] CANINE)* was born May 28, 1926 in Elizabethtown, Hardin County, Kentucky, and died June 25, 1994 in Jamestown, Russell County, Kentucky. He married KATHLEEN VERONICA SMALL January 08, 1943 in Frankfort, Franklin County, Kentucky. She was born May 09, 1925 in Mayfield, Graves County, Kentucky.

Children of WILLIAM PERSON and KATHLEEN SMALL are:
2.   i.   GREGORY HARRISON[5] PERSON, b. December 08, 1950, Jamestown, Russell County, Kentucky.
3.   ii.   SHANNON TORRENCE PERSON, b. April 05, 1948, Elizabethtown, Hardin County, Kentucky.
       iii.   SHAWN STEPHEN PERSON, b. April 05, 1948, Elizabethtown, Hardin County, Kentucky, m. TIM BARRETT WILIAMS, January 01, 1980, Red Wing, Goodhue County, Minnesota; b. June 07, 1952, Charlotte, Eaton County, Michigan.

Generation No. 2

2. GREGORY HARRISON[5] PERSON *(WILLIAM HARRISON[4], BRIAN DANIEL[3], WALTER CAMPBELL[2], WELSH CORGI[1] CANINE)* was born December 08, 1950 in Jamestown, Russell County, Kentucky. He married TERRY SALLY FRIEND June 09, 1975 in Piedmont, Alameda County, California, daughter of MANNY FRIEND and LORETTA LANCELOT. She was born January 05, 1954 in Battle Mountain, Lander County, Nevada.

Children of GREGORY PERSON and TERRY FRIEND are:
    i.   BECKY JANE[6] PERSON, b. July 04, 1976.
    ii.   GEORGE SAMPSON PERSON, b. May 18, 1978.
    iii.   FRANK TERRANCE PERSON, b. September 01, 1981.

3. SHANNON TORRENCE[5] PERSON *(WILLIAM HARRISON[4], BRIAN DANIEL[3], WALTER CAMPBELL[2], WELSH CORGI[1] CANINE)* was born April 05, 1948 in Elizabethtown, Hardin County, Kentucky. She married BEN GRANT TIPPECANOE November 30, 1973 in Elizabethtown, Hardin County, Kentucky. He was born October 08, 1945 in La Plata, Charles County, Maryland.

Figure 11-5. An Ahnentafel report.

If you go back several generations, the Ahnentafel numbering system may be tedious to calculate. Fortunately, several genealogical databases can automatically calculate the number for each individual.

Register System

Another popular numbering system is the Register system. The Register system is the official numbering system of the *New England Historical and Genealogical Register,* a publication of the New England Historic Genealogical Society. The Register system is used in descendant reports.

The subject of a descendant report is the person from whom all the other people in the report are descended — usually the original immigrant (or *progenitor*).

Tip

The Register system is used to show the descendants of a person.

Here's how the numbering system works:

▶ The subject is assigned the Arabic number 1.

▶ The individual's children, represented by the second row in Figure 11-6, are assigned small Roman numerals representing the order in which they were born. The first child is (i), the second is (ii), and so forth.

▶ The subject's children who have children of their own are also assigned the next Arabic numbers in the series.

▶ The subject's grandchildren, represented in the third row of Figure 11-6, are assigned small Roman numerals just as their parents were; they are also assigned the next Arabic number in sequence if they have descendants.

▶ This process continues until all the subject's descendants are represented.

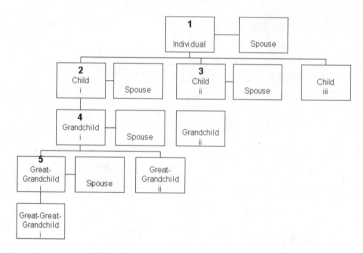

Figure 11-6. An outline of the Register system in a descendant chart.

If you use the Register system, as shown in Figure 11-7, remember that if an individual does not have descendants (children), then he or she should be excluded from the remainder of the report.

Generation No. 1

1. William Harrison⁴Person (Brian Daniel³, Walter Campbell², Welsh Corgi¹ Canine) was born May 28, 1926 in Elizabethtown, Hardin County, Kentucky, and died June 25, 1994 in Jamestown, Russell County, Kentucky. He married **Kathleen Veronica Small** January 08, 1943 in Frankfort, Franklin County, Kentucky. She was born May 09, 1925 in Mayfield, Graves County, Kentucky.

Children of William Person and Kathleen Small are:
+   2   i.   Gregory Harrison⁵ Person, born December 08, 1950 in Jamestown, Russell County, Kentucky.
+   3   ii.   Shannon Torrence Person, born April 05, 1948 in Elizabethtown, Hardin County, Kentucky.
    4   iii.   Shawn Stephen Person, born April 05, 1948 in Elizabethtown, Hardin County, Kentucky. He met Tim Barrett Wiliams January 01, 1980 in Red Wing, Goodhue County, Minnesota; born June 07, 1952 in Charlotte, Eaton County, Michigan.

Generation No. 2

2. Gregory Harrison⁵ Person (William Harrison⁴, Brian Daniel³, Walter Campbell², Welsh Corgi¹ Canine) was born December 08, 1950 in Jamestown, Russell County, Kentucky. He married **Terry Sally Friend** June 09, 1975 in Piedmont, Alameda County, California, daughter of Manny Friend and Loretta Lancelot. She was born January 05, 1954 in Battle Mountain, Lander County, Nevada.

Children of Gregory Person and Terry Friend are:
    5   i.   Becky Jane⁶ Person, born July 04, 1976.
    6   ii.   George Sampson Person, born May 18, 1978.
    7   iii.   Frank Terrance Person, born September 01, 1981.

3. Shannon Torrence⁵ Person (William Harrison⁴, Brian Daniel³, Walter Campbell², Welsh Corgi¹ Canine) was born April 05, 1948 in Elizabethtown, Hardin County, Kentucky. She married **Ben Grant Tippecanoe** November 30, 1973 in Elizabethtown, Hardin County, Kentucky. He was born October 08, 1945 in La Plata, Charles County, Maryland.

Figure 11-7. A descendant report numbered with the Register system.

As the first person who immigrated (called a progenitor) is assigned the Arabic number 1, you may be wondering how the ancestors (those from the mother county) of the original immigrant are numbered. "Number" these ancestors by using letters. For example, the father of the original immigrant would be assigned the letter A, the grandfather of the immigrant would be assigned B, and so on.

Modified Register System

The Modified Register system is the official system of the National Genealogical Society for its publications. (You may hear it referred to as the National Genealogical Society Quarterly (NGSQ) system or Record system). It is similar to the Register system with one major difference: Every person receives an Arabic numeral regardless of whether he or she has offspring (see Figure 11-8). Also, those individuals with offspring (and who have their own entries) are designated with the plus (+) sign.

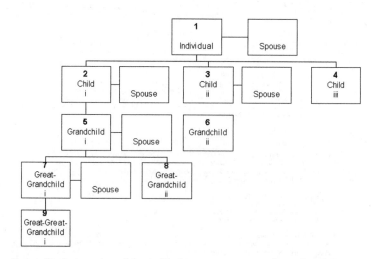

Figure 11-8. An outline of the Modified Register system in a descendant chart.

As with the Register system, individuals without descendants are excluded from the rest of the report.

Generating Reports with Your Genealogical Database

In the past, genealogists would sit in front of a typewriter and meticulously type their ancestors' names on preprinted forms. Or, if they didn't use preprinted forms, they'd pull out their rulers and design their own forms and charts. All this additional work can take precious time away from research.

Cross-Reference

We provide you with information about choosing database software in Chapter 8.

Today, you can create a report instantly by using your genealogical database software (as long as you've taken the time to enter the information into the database). To show you how easy it is, we take you through the process of creating a report in two popular of genealogical software programs: Personal Ancestral File and Family Tree Maker.

Personal Ancestral File

Personal Ancestral File, commonly called PAF, is the genealogical database distributed by the LDS Church. You can download
a full working copy of Personal Ancestral File Version 4.0 from
the FamilySearch Internet site (`www.familysearch.org`). After
you install the software and create some records of your ancestors, you're ready to create a report. Here's how:

For details on downloading
and installing Personal
Ancestral File with AOL, see
Chapter 9.

1. Start the Personal Ancestral File program by double-
   clicking the program icon or by choosing it from the
   Start menu. After the program launches, you see either
   the Family View or the Pedigree View.

You can find more information on Personal Ancestral
File on the FamilySearch
Internet site at www
.familysearch.org.

2. In either view, find the individual that you want to be
   the subject of the report and click the box containing
   that person's name.

3. Choose File⇨Print Reports. The Reports and Charts dialog box appears, as shown in Figure 11-9, with several
   tabs listing the various report types that you can create.

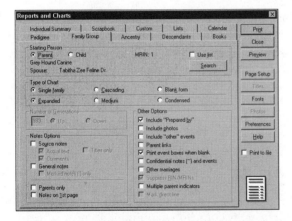

Figure 11-9. The Reports and Charts dialog box in Personal Ancestral File.

4. Click the tab for the type of report that you want to
   create.

5. Each tab has a list of options that you can select to control how your report will look. Set these options to your
   desired settings.

6. Click the Preview button to see how the report will
   look before you print it. The Print Preview window
   launches, as shown in Figure 11-10.

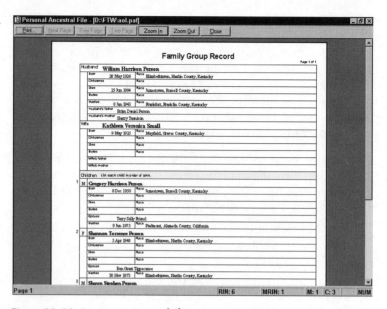

Figure 11-10. Preview your report before printing it in PAF.

7. Use the Zoom and Page buttons to ensure that the report contains the data that you want.

8. When you're ready to print the report, just click the Print button. To change a setting on the report before printing it, click the Close button. If you choose to print the report, the Print dialog box appears. Select the number of copies you want to print and then click the OK button.

Family Tree Maker

Family Tree Maker is a popular commercial genealogical database created by Genealogy.com. You can find it at most stores that carry software, and online through the Shop@AOL area (Keyword: **Computing Shop**).

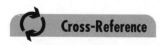

After you install Family Tree Maker and enter some information in the database, creating reports is easy. Here is an example of how to create a pedigree chart (known in Family Tree Maker as an Ancestor tree):

1. Launch the Family Tree Maker program by double-clicking the program icon or by choosing it from the Start menu.

2 Open the Family Page of the person who is the focus of the Ancestor tree and click in the field where his or her name appears. You can open the Family Page by clicking the tabs on the right side of the screen or by choosing View⇨Index of Individuals.

3. Choose View⇨Ancestor Tree or click the Ancestor Tree button. If you're looking at the default toolbar, the Ancestor Tree button is the 5th button from the left and the 15th from the right. A drop-down menu appears, from which you can select the type of format for the chart.

4. Choose a format for your tree. Your choices are Fan, Standard, and Vertical. After you choose a format, Family Tree Maker generates the report and displays it on-screen, as shown in Figure 11-11.

Tip

You can find AOL's version of another genealogy program, Ultimate Family tree, at Keyword: **AOL Shop Direct**.

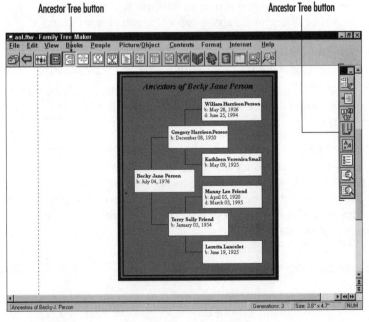

Figure 11-11. An Ancestor tree report in Family Tree Maker.

5. You can customize your Ancestor tree by using the series of eight buttons that appear on the side toolbar.

11

Reporting Your Findings

Tip

For more tips on using Family Tree Maker, check out our book *Family Tree Maker For Dummies* (IDG Books Worldwide, Inc.).

6. Verify that the chart includes the information that you want.

7. Print your completed report by choosing File⇨Print Ancestor Tree.

For more on customizing your charts, choose Help⇨Contents or consult your Family Tree Maker User's Manual.

Speaking about GEDCOM

As soon as you start using genealogical databases, you're likely to run into the acronym GEDCOM. GEDCOM, which stands for GEnealogical Data COMmunication, is a text file format that allows genealogists to transfer information between different genealogical software. Here are a couple of situations in which GEDCOM can save the day:

▶ When you send a report to another researcher who is using different database software, you can save your database file as a GEDCOM file, and, provided that the other researcher has a program that supports GEDCOM, you can share the information without any problem.

▶ If you want to post your research for a large group of researchers to see, you can save it as a GEDCOM file so that it is easily accessible.

The GEDCOM file format was developed by the LDS Church and was first introduced in 1987. The first two versions of GEDCOM were released for public discussion only and were not meant to serve as the standard. With the introduction of its fifth version, GEDCOM was accepted by the genealogical community as a standard.

Importing GEDCOM Files

Importing a GEDCOM file can cut down on the time you spend typing information in your database. You can import a GEDCOM file into your genealogical database (as a new database file) and then save that data in the file format for your own database.

Figure 11-12 shows the contents of a GEDCOM file. The tags on each line tell your genealogical database software where to place the information on that line within the fields of your database. You can view the contents of a GEDCOM file by using any word processing program or text editor.

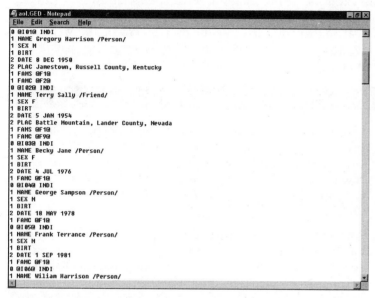

```
aol.GED - Notepad
File  Edit  Search  Help
0 @I01@ INDI
1 NAME Gregory Harrison /Person/
1 SEX M
1 BIRT
2 DATE 8 DEC 1950
2 PLAC Jamestown, Russell County, Kentucky
1 FAMS @F1@
1 FAMC @F2@
0 @I02@ INDI
1 NAME Terry Sally /Friend/
1 SEX F
1 BIRT
2 DATE 5 JAN 1954
2 PLAC Battle Mountain, Lander County, Nevada
1 FAMS @F1@
1 FAMC @F9@
0 @I03@ INDI
1 NAME Becky Jane /Person/
1 SEX F
1 BIRT
2 DATE 4 JUL 1976
1 FAMC @F1@
0 @I04@ INDI
1 NAME George Sampson /Person/
1 SEX M
1 BIRT
2 DATE 18 MAY 1978
1 FAMC @F1@
0 @I05@ INDI
1 NAME Frank Terrance /Person/
1 SEX M
1 BIRT
2 DATE 1 SEP 1981
1 FAMC @F1@
0 @I06@ INDI
1 NAME Wiliam Harrison /Person/
```

Figure 11-12. The text of a GEDCOM file.

Converting Data to a GEDCOM File

To convert the data in your genealogical database to a GEDCOM file, follow the instructions provided in your software's manual or Help menu. You can create the GEDCOM file relatively easily; most software guides you through the process with a series of prompts or dialog boxes. If you're using Personal Ancestral File, you can export your file by choosing File⇨Export. In Family Tree Maker, choose File⇨Copy/Export Family File.

Caution

We recommend that you never import another researcher's information into your personal database file. Always create a new database file and import the GEDCOM file into it. Then if you want to include some of that information in your personal database file, you can merge the records or copy them between the databases.

Tip

If you make any changes to a GEDCOM file, make sure that you save it as a text document with a .ged extension. If you do not save it as a text file, a genealogical database will not be able to import it properly.

11

Reporting Your Findings

Caution

You should always privatize your GEDCOM file before sharing it with a fellow researcher. Create a copy of the file that you want to export, and then review the document and delete information about living individuals. (Always be sure to copy your original file and then privatize the copy, of course!) That way you can avoid any bad feelings from your living relatives, and you can guarantee that their private information isn't shared with the genealogical community.

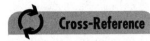

For information on a GED-COM to HTML converter called GED2HTML, see Chapter 10.

Sharing GEDCOM Files on the Web

In addition to creating GEDCOM files to exchange with individual researchers, you can generate GEDCOM files to submit to larger cooperatives that make the data from many GEDCOM files available to thousands of researchers worldwide via the Web and e-mail. You can also convert your GEDCOM file to HTML so that you can place the data directly on the Web for others to access. Software utilities are available that make it a snap to convert your GEDCOM file to HTML.

Gotta Have a Color Printer!

If you want to spice up your charts and reports, consider printing them with a color printer. Although color printers used to be too expensive for most genealogists (and other regular people), today you can pick up a color printer that does a pretty good job with graphics for just a few hundred dollars.

Adding color to your charts and reports can often highlight family relationships. For example, if you want to create a descendant chart (which shows all the descendants of an ancestor) for your grandmother's 90th birthday party, you can use different colors to highlight various family lines and to clearly demonstrate your grandmother's direct line.

Probably the most common type of color printer is a color inkjet printer. These printers are economical and now have improved printing capabilities. Manufacturers of color inkjet printers include Epson, Hewlett-Packard, Canon, Lexmark, Xerox, and NEC.

If you don't happen to own a color printer and don't really want to buy one, you may be able to use one at your local copy shop so that you can print a color chart for a special occasion that's coming.

For more on printers, see the CNET Consumer's Guide in the AOL Computing area (Keyword: **Computing**) or AOL Print Central (Keyword: **Print Central**). You can also use Keyword: **Shop Direct.** Choose the Hardware link and then the Printers link to see printers that AOL experts have tested and approved.

Summary

In this chapter, we looked at ways to share the information that you find researching. We discussed the different types of standard genealogical reports, numbering systems, creating reports in genealogical software, and the merits of using GEDCOM files. In Chapter 12, we take information sharing a step further by discussing how to create your own Web page so you can share your information with the world.

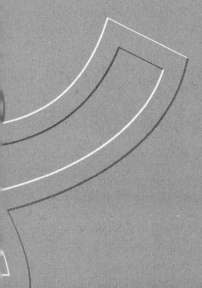

Quick Look

Chapter 12

Creating Your Own Web Page

The advent of the Web significantly changed how genealogists communicate and share information. Now, instead of sending another researcher a handwritten letter attached to poor-quality photocopies, you can direct that researcher to a Web page that displays the contents of your genealogical database and photos of your ancestors. In this chapter, we look at why you should consider creating a Web page, and we show you how to get started when you're ready to take the leap and build your own. We also show you some nifty tools that can make building a Web page easier than you may think and show you where you can locate space online to house your pages.

Why Place My Information on a Web Page?

You're not alone if you're wondering why you would want to place information on a Web site of your own. Many genealogists are asking this question. Well, we think can think of several reasons:

▶ **Advertise your research subject.** A Web page allows you to advertise the families you're researching. If you notify comprehensive genealogical index sites and search engines that your Web page exists, others with the same research interests will be able to find you more easily.

▶ **Share your tricks and helpful hints.** Information about the research process can help other researchers who are struggling to find their ancestors.

▶ **Feel the power that comes with accomplishment.** Building a Web site is an ongoing project, but when you complete the first phase of your own site and it goes online, you're sure to feel a rush of accomplishment. After all, you've created something that displays your research.

▶ **Make fast, easy updates — by design.** Any details that you place online can be quickly and easily updated. If you publish your research in some other format (such as in a magazine, a journal, or a book), you know that correcting errors and making updates in those venues can take quite a bit of time.

▶ **Start a group.** You can put together informal research groups that can share information through a Web site.

Whatever the reason, sharing information online is an important part of the research process. Your can use your own Web site as a tool that leads to even larger personal discoveries.

Tip

Because a Web site is a work in progress, you can always update it as you gather more data about your ancestors. Make building the first phase of a Web page one of the short-term goals of your genealogical research project.

Tip

After you post your Web page, consider sending out a message announcing it to related mailing lists and message boards. For example, if your Web page has information about ancestors with the surname Helm, you may want to post a message about it to the Helm Mailing List.

Note

You can share information on the Web in a variety of ways. Don't forget about using bulletin boards, chat rooms, newsgroups, and mailing lists to share your research results and tips online.

12

Creating Your Own Web Page

Just What Is HTML?

Caution

Remember not to share information about living persons on your Web page without their expressed permission (this includes photos) so that you don't infringe on their right to privacy.

Definition

HTML, or HyperText Markup Language, is a code that enables Web browsers to translate text documents into graphical images and text.

Tip

The Learning HTML Basics tutorial is a good resource to come back to if you need a refresher course or want to use a new feature in HTML.

Find It Online

Take an online HTML course through AOL by using Keyword: **Build Your Web Page**.

HyperText Markup Language (HTML) is a code in which text documents are written so that Web browsers can read and interpret those documents. When a Web browser sees HTML, it converts the code into graphical images and text that you can see on your computer screen. Normally, you use an HTML editor, a text editor, or a word processor to create an HTML page. HTML is a relatively easy language to learn on your own by using books and other pages as examples. But if you don't want to teach yourself, you may want to look into classes at a local college or attend a seminar where HTML is being taught.

Another option is to attend a virtual class on HTML through the Build Your Web Page (Keyword: **Build Your Web Page**) area of AOL Computing. Build Your Web Page is divided into two sections: The Basics, and Advanced Web Publishing, as shown in Figure 12-1.

The Basics section contains tools to help you build your Web page, clipart for decorating your pages, and a tutorial that helps you learn HTML basics. The Learning HTML Basics tutorial is self-paced so you can learn on your own schedule and at your own convenience.

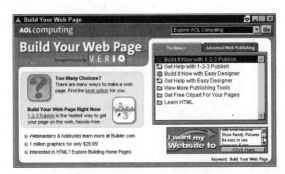

Figure 12-1. The Build Your Web Page window.

Knowing HTML

When you see HTML for the first time, you may be intimidated — but try not to be. We show you an example of the HTML for a simple Web page and walk you through some helpful hints that show you how to use HTML. Any command that you see that is enclosed by brackets, such as <HTML>, is called a tag. Tags are what make your finished Web page look the way you want it to look.

Basically, tags tell your Web browser how to display the information on-screen. For example, take a look at the following line:

```
<TITLE>Your Official America Online Guide to
Genealogy Online</TITLE>
```
What does this tell you? Glad you asked:

▶ The <TITLE> tag tells your browser to treat the text that follows as a title. Your browser then knows to display this text in the title bar at the top of your browser window.

▶ The second tag </TITLE> tells the browser to stop displaying any further text as a title.

Here's an example of an HTML listing so that you can get used to seeing it:

```
<HTML>
<HEAD>
<TITLE>Your Official America Online Guide to
Genealogy Online</TITLE>
</HEAD>
<BODY BGCOLOR = "White" ALINK = "Blue" VLINK =
"Gray">
<H1>
<FONT COLOR = "Green">
<CENTER>Your Official America Online Guide to
Genealogy Online</CENTER>
</FONT>
</H1>
Welcome to Your Official America Online Guide to
Genealogy Online Web Page.<P>
We'll use this page to learn about the following
items:
<UL>
<LI>HTML tags
<LI>Constructing a Web page
<LI>Viewing a Web page
```

Note

The words that are positioned between the angle brackets — such as <HTML> — are known as tags. Tags are the basic building blocks for HTML.

Tip

You can think of tags as on and off switches — where < > means *on* (the beginning of a certain format or style) and </ > means *off* (the end of that format or style).

Definition

BGCOLOR designates the color to use in the background of your Web page. ALINK and VLINK identify the colors of active links (those that you can click to go to other pages) and visited links (those links that you've already clicked to visit other pages).

Tip

Use quotes to offset elements like colors, font sizes, and URLs in HTML.

Definition

A URL (Uniform Resource Locator) is a way of addressing Internet resources, including Web pages.

12

Creating Your Own Web Page

Definition

UL stands for Unordered List; LI stands for List Item. </UL> signifies the end of the list, and <P> indicates a paragraph break.

```
</UL>
<P>
For links to great genealogy sites see the
<A HREF =
"http://www.genealogytoolbox.com">Genealogy
Toolbox</A> Web site.
</BODY>
</HTML>
```

Figure 12-2 shows what this page looks like when it's displayed in a browser.

> **AOL Guide to Online Genealogy**
>
> Welcome to the AOL Guide to Online Genealogy Web Page.
>
> We'll use this page to learn about the following items:
>
> - HTML tags
> - Constructing a Web page
> - Viewing a Web page
>
> For links to great genealogy sites see the Genealogy Toolbox Web site.

Figure 12-2. Our sample page displayed in a Web browser.

A Few Good Tags

Although we wish we could teach you *everything* you need to know about HTML, doing so is beyond the scope of this book. However, we do want to provide you with a few tags that you may find useful in creating your genealogical Web page on AOL. Check out Table 12-1 for some HTML tags that can help you in your Web page creations.

Table 12-1. *Useful HTML Tags*

Tag	Meaning	Browser Reactions
<HTML>	HTML	The browser displays the page in HTML. End the coding with </HTML>.
<HEAD>	Head element	The browser knows that the following text is contained in the header of the document. The ending tag is </HEAD>.
<TITLE>	Title	The text appears in the title bar of the browser. End the title text with </TITLE>.
<BODY>	Body	The text is displayed in the body or main part of the document. Use </BODY> at the end of the body text.
<H1>	Heading	A size one heading is displayed. Headings can come in six sizes, with <H1> being the largest and <H6> being the smallest. End special sizing by using </H1>.
<CENTER>	Center	Text is centered on the page or within a table cell or column. Turn off centering with </CENTER>.
<B>	Bold	Text is bolded between the <B> and </B>.
<I>	Italic	Text is italicized between the <I> and </I>.
<U>	Underline	Text is underlined between the <U> and </U>.
<A HREF = " ">	Hypertext link	The text is a link to another page. The code is ended with </A>.

Continued

Table 12-1. *Useful HTML Tags* (continued)

Tag	Meaning	Browser Reactions
`<FONT COLOR = " ">`	Font color	Sets the font on the page to a particular color. Using `</FONT>` changes the remaining text to the default color.
`<FONT SIZE = " ">`	Font size	Sets the font on the page to a particular size. `</FONT>` ends the special font size.
`<FONT FACE = " ">`	Font face	Sets the font on the page to a particular face (such as Arial or Times New Roman). `</FONT>` reverts the font to the default.
`<OL>`	Ordered list	Displays the items that follow as a numbered list. At the end of your list, use `</OL>` to return to normal formatting.
`<UL>`	Unordered list	Displays the items that follows as a bulleted list. At the end of your list, use `</UL>` to return to normal formatting.

Not all tags in HTML require both on and off tags. Table 12-2 lists useful tags that require only a single tag.

Table 12-2. *Useful Single HTML Tags*

Tag	Meaning	Browser Reactions
`<P>`	Paragraph break	Inserts a line and begins a new paragraph.
` `	Line break	Ends the current line and begins the next line of text.
`<LI>`	List item	Begins an item on a new line in a list.
`<IMG SRC = " ">`	Image source	Inserts a graphic into the document.

Tag	Meaning	Browser Reactions
<HR>	Horizontal rule	Inserts a line horizontally across the page.
<BODY BGCOLOR = " ">	Body background	Sets the background of the document to the specified color.
<ALINK COLOR = " ">	Active link color	Sets the color of each link to the specified color until the link is clicked.
<VLINK COLOR = " ">	Visited link color	Sets the color of each link that has been previously clicked.

Although HTML may seem intimidating at first, once you begin using tags on a regular basis, you won't have a hard time remembering them. The tags that we list in this section should be sufficient to get you started.

The Ease of Using an HTML Editor

If you don't have the time to memorize tags or you just want an easier way to create HTML, consider using an HTML editor. An *HTML editor* is a program that helps you write HTML by inserting the on and off tags when necessary, and providing buttons or menus that allow you to insert tags. These editors can be programs that are installed on your machine, or they can be online applications.

AOL provides the following online HTML editors that you can use to post a Web page:

▶ **1-2-3 Publish:** Using this editor is the easiest way to create a Web page, but it is also offers the least flexibility and few features. To create a Web page, just fill in the blanks by using one of the editor's templates.

▶ **Easy Designer:** This editor allows you greater flexibility than 1-2-3 Publish. You can use a ready-made template or begin with a blank page. Easy Designer includes features such as drag-and-drop capabilities, the ability to add multiple pictures to a page, and personal chat rooms.

Tip

For more detailed information about writing HTML, we recommend *HTML For Dummies,* published by IDG Books Worldwide, Inc.

Definition

An HTML editor is a program that automatically inserts HTML tags for you.

12

If you prefer not to use either of these online editors, you can always download an editor program and write your own HTML and then upload your page to the AOL Hometown area (which we cover in "Finding Prime Real Estate at AOL Hometown," later in this chapter).

Using 1-2-3 Publish

Definition

A template is a form that allows you to plug information into pre-established areas to create a finished document. When you use a template to create a Web page, you just follow the directions and voilà — instant Web page.

Find It Online

Use the Keyword: **Build Your Web Page** to get to AOL's HTML editors.

If you're new to creating Web pages, then 1-2-3 Publish is a good way to create a page quickly. All you have to do is choose some templates and answer questions to generate a Web page. Here's how:

1. Type the Keyword: **Build Your Web Page** in the text box on the navigation bar and click the Go button. This launches the AOL Computing Build Your Web Page window.

2. On the Basics tab, double-click Build It Now with 1-2-3 Publish. This brings up the 1-2-3 Publish home page.

3. Click the Click Here link in the first paragraph. A new page is displayed, as shown in Figure 12-3, which contains a series of seven steps.

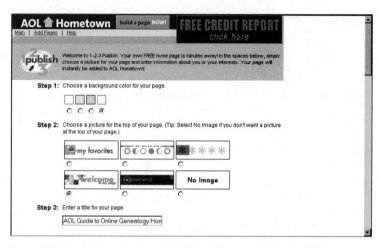

Figure 12-3. Complete a few steps to build a Web page with 1-2-3 Publish.

4. Complete each step by selecting the appropriate radio button or by typing text into the text box.

5. After you've completed the steps, click the Preview My Page button to see what your page will look like.

6. If you're happy with the way things look, click the Save button. If not, click the Modify button.

When you save your page, it's uploaded to the AOL Hometown area. A confirmation page appears, showing you the URL for your new home page (and the URL is also e-mailed to you). Figure 12-4 shows a sample page created with 1-2-3 Publish.

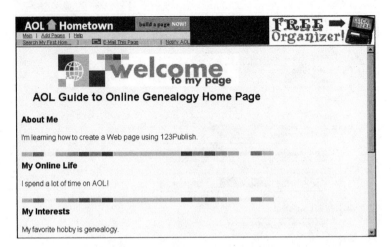

Figure 12-4. A sample Web page created with 1-2-3 Publish.

Using AOL's Web page templates makes it easy and fast to get your genealogical information posted on the Internet.

Consider creating a separate Web page for each of the major family lines you're researching.

After you create your first Web page, you can select from a group of templates to build additional pages for your site. Here are two templates that you may find useful:

▶ **Our Genealogy Page:** This template is a good option if you want to share your family tree or links to other good genealogy Web sites.

▶ **Our Family Page:** This template is great if you're planning a family reunion or want to create a site especially for your family line or surname.

To add pages based on templates, click the link for the template you want to use (such as the Our Genealogy Page link) and then complete the steps just like you did for the first page. Click the Preview My Page button and then the Save button. You have just added a second page to your Web site.

If you have the time, you may want to create a separate genealogy page for each of the major families you're researching. Of course, if you decide that you want more features than the Our Genealogy Page template offers, then you may want to check out the Easy Designer editor, which we discuss in the next section.

Using Easy Designer

Easy Designer takes creating a Web page one step further. You don't have to be an expert in HTML to take advantage of Easy Designer for

- ▶ Dragging and dropping objects (such as pictures) on a page
- ▶ Adding multiple pictures to a page
- ▶ Adding clipart (from thousands of pieces available through AOL) to decorate your pages
- ▶ Adding your own HTML to create sound clips, banners, and a guest book (a place where people can comment on your Web page)

You can create a brand new site with Easy Designer, or you can edit an existing site. For instance, if you created a site with 1-2-3 Publish and want to add more functionality to it, you can use Easy Designer to do so.

Or if you want to start from scratch, follow these steps:

1. Type the Keyword: **Build Your Web Page** in the text box on the navigation bar and click the Go button. This launches the AOL Computing Build Your Web Page window.

2. On the Basics tab, double-click Build It Now with Easy Designer. This brings up the Easy Designer home page.

3. In the yellow Start Here box, click the Create a New Page link. This brings up a page that prepares the Easy Designer environment. While you are waiting for it to complete its tasks, you can play a matching game.

4. When the message Easy Designer is Ready! appears at the top of the page, click the blue Click to Get Started button. This launches the Select a Template window in Easy Designer.

5. Select a category in the Step 1A box on the left by clicking it. For example, if you want to construct a genealogy page, click the Your Family Matters category, as shown in Figure 12-5. When you click a category in the left box, a list of topics appears in the Step 1B box on the right.

Don't be alarmed when you see the dialog box warning you that an Applet window is opening. This simply means that a new window containing snippets of programs (called applets) is about to open.

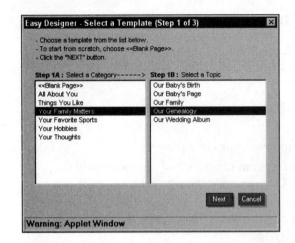

Figure 12-5. Select your template category and topic in the left and right boxes, respectively.

6. Select a topic in the Step 1B box and click the Next button. For example, if you're creating a genealogy page, click Our Genealogy. The Select Your Layout window appears, displaying five layouts.

7. Click the layout that you want for your page and then click the Next button. The Select a Color Style window appears.

8. Select a color style in the Color Styles Name list box. The Color Style Preview pane on the right shows you what this style would look like on your page. If you don't like any of the standard choices, click the Customize button to select you own colors. Click the OK button when you're satisfied with your color selection. The Getting Started window appears, which offers advice on using the template that you selected.

9. Click the Let's Go button. The window disappears, leaving you in the Easy Designer design page, shown in Figure 12-6.

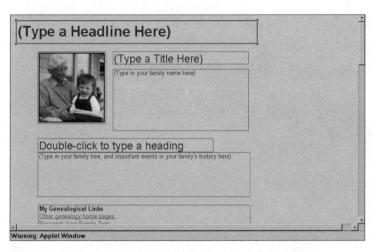

Figure 12-6. Your Easy Designer template ready for your customization.

10. Double-click any text box to alter the text. If you need to, you can adjust the size of the boxes to ensure that they don't overlap.

11. Double-click the picture and then select an image from the AOL image library or click the Upload button to place your own image on the page. Click OK when you're done.

12. Use the toolbar at the top of the page to drag and drop pictures and text boxes on the screen.

13. When you're happy with the way the page looks, click the Save button on the Easy Designer toolbar. The Save Your Page window appears.

14. Enter the title of your page in the first text box, and enter a name for the file to be saved as in the second text box. Then click the Save button. (You can preview the page before saving it by clicking the Preview button.)

When you save the page, it's uploaded to the AOL Hometown area. A confirmation page shows you the URL for your new page (and the URL is e-mailed to you as well). Figure 12-7 shows a sample page created in Easy Designer.

Tip

To see lists of HTML editors (divided into these categories: Shareware, Commercial Software, and Macintosh Tools), go to Keyword: **Publishing Tools**.

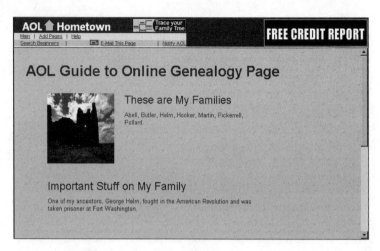

Figure 12-7. A Web page created in Easy Designer.

The Easy Designer software allows you more flexibility than 1-2-3 Publish, but if you want even more control over how your page looks, you may want to use a different HTML editor. For example, you can't add any special code (such as JavaScript) with Easy Designer.

Don't worry. If you dare to be different, you can find other HTML editors that give you what you need. To find an HTML editor, click the Advanced Web Publishing tab of the Build Your Web Page window. Then click the Web Publishing Tools topic (or you can go directly to Home Page Publishing Tools by using the Keyword: **Publishing Tools**).

Finding Prime Real Estate at AOL Hometown

If you want to create your Web page with an HTML editor other than 1-2-3 Publish or Easy Designer or by writing your own HTML, you still need to have a place online to store the Web page so other genealogists can access it. AOL Hometown is just such a place.

AOL Hometown offers three different storage plans:

▶ **2MB:** Just for being an AOL member, you automatically receive an allocation of 2MB of space free to store your Web page.

▶ **4MB:** If you create a Web page without using an AOL HTML editor and you'd like to have AOL Hometown store it, you receive an allocation of 4MB free for your particular screen name. You can also get the free 4MB if you use 1-2-3 Publish to create a page.

▶ **12MB:** If you add all your pages to AOL Hometown at once, you receive an allocation of 12MB of space free for your screen name.

You can add a Web page that you created on your own to AOL Hometown by following these steps:

1. Create a Web page in your HTML editor or text editor and then save it to your hard drive.

2. Type the Keyword: **Hometown** in the text box on the navigation bar and click the Go button. AOL takes you to the AOL Hometown home page.

3. At the top of the page, just under the AOL Hometown banner, click the Add Pages link. This brings up the Add & Manage Pages page, shown in Figure 12-8.

4. Click the Upload link to begin the process of uploading your page to AOL Hometown. The My FTP Space window appears.

5. Click the See My FTP Space link. This launches a window showing the files that are contained in your screen name's directory for your screen name, as shown in Figure 12-9.

Definition

File Transfer Protocol, or FTP, is a standard way of transferring files over the Internet. Uploading is the specific process by which you transfer a file from your computer to a remote computer, usually by using FTP. On the other hand, downloading is the specific process by which you transfer a file from a remote computer to your computer.

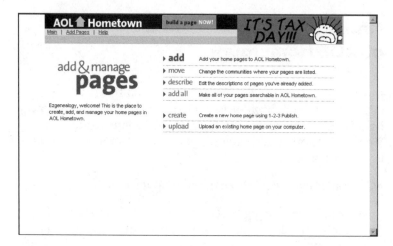

Figure 12-8. Keep up with your AOL Hometown Web pages on the Add & Manage Pages page.

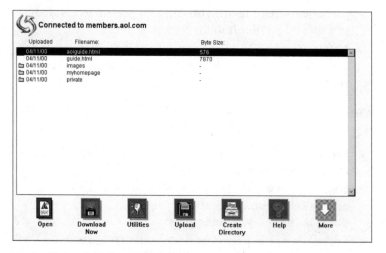

Figure 12-9. Upload files in My FTP Space.

6. To upload a file, click the Upload button. In the window that appears, type in a filename — this is the name that your file will be known as in the AOL Hometown area, which will be part of the URL for this Web page. Then indicate whether the document is a text file (ASCII) or a program/graphic file (Binary) and click the Continue button. The Upload window appears.

7. Click the Select File button to locate the file that you want to upload from your hard drive. After you find the file, click the Send button to upload it.

Your Web page is uploaded from your computer to AOL Hometown.

Find It Online

You can access your FTP area by using the Keyword: **My FTP Space.**

Learning About Other Neighborhoods

At some point, 12MB may not be enough room for all the photos and graphics that you want to place online. When this time comes, you'll have to search for additional places to store things online.

Many companies offer space for individuals to store their Web pages. Some offer free space (although in most cases you must carry company advertisements on your site), and others offer a block of space for a monthly fee. For example, Verio (Keyword: **Verio**) offers eight different Web hosting plans: four for personal accounts, and four for business accounts. The basic plan for personal accounts provides 50MB of space, and the Powered plan provides 120MB.

It's a good idea to compare different services before commiting to a provider. That way you can see the entire spectrum of what is available and find the best plan for you. To find other Web hosting providers, try entering **Web Hosting** in AOL Search.

Cross-Reference

Chapter 8 covers finding a genealogical database, Chapter 9 walks you through setting up a family file by using Family Tree Maker and Personal Ancestral File (PAF), and Chapter 11 covers creating reports in Family Tree Maker and PAF.

Tip

Make a practice of removing information about any living people from any research findings you plan to share online.

Getting Help from Others

When you create a genealogical Web page, your genealogy database software may be able to do some of the work for you; then you can forget about trying to write the HTML for your Web page yourself. Over the past couple of years, exporting reports and information to the Web has become a standard feature of genealogical database software.

To give you an idea of what is involved in using genealogical databases to generate Web pages, we examine exporting information from a Personal Ancestral File (PAF) database and a Family Tree Maker database.

Hitting the Web with PAF 4.0

Exporting information to the Web through Personal Ancestral File (PAF) centers around the Create Web Page feature. This feature allows you to create Web pages focusing on ancestors, descendants, or selected individuals. Follow these steps to export information through PAF:

1. Make a copy of your database that does not contain information about living individuals. You can do this by choosing File➪Export, and then under the Include column, remove the check marks from the Full Information on Living and Names on Living check boxes, shown in Figure 12-10. Then click the Export button.

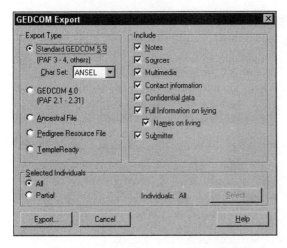

Figure 12-10. The information on the living check boxes appears in the right column under Include.

2. Create a new Family File by choosing File⇨New from the menu bar. Enter a name for the file and then click Save. When the new Family File appears, import the file that you exported in Step 1 by choosing File⇨Import.

3. Now that you have a private file, select the check box for the individual that you want to be the subject of the Web page.

4. Choose Tools⇨Create Web Page to open the Create Web Page dialog box, shown in Figure 12-11.

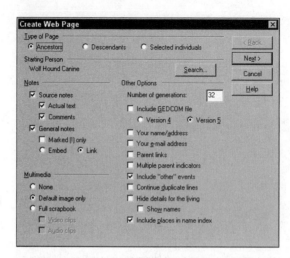

Figure 12-11. The Create Web Page dialog box in PAF 4.0.

5. Select the check boxes for any optional items that you want the Web page to display and then click the Next button. Another page appears, with some blanks to fill in.

6. Edit the description, page title, and introduction sections as necessary. You can also select a background color for your page by clicking the Select button under Background.

7. Click the Finish button to create your Web page. Figure 12-12 shows an example Web page.

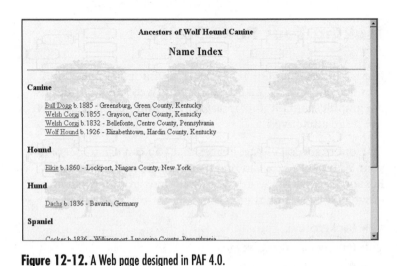

Figure 12-12. A Web page designed in PAF 4.0.

Tip

For detailed information about creating Web pages with Family Tree Maker, check out *Family Tree Maker For Dummies* from IDG Books Worldwide, Inc.

Posting Web Pages with Family Tree Maker

Creating Web pages with Family Tree Maker is a bit more involved than using PAF. Unfortunately, you can't just upload Web pages from Family Tree Maker to AOL Hometown or some other Web hosting service. Instead, you have to post your Web page on the Family Tree Maker User Home Pages site. Posting a Web page with Family Tree Maker requires four involved steps:

1. Privatize your Family File.
2. Register with Family Tree Maker Online.
3. Create a User Home Page on Family Tree Maker Online.
4. Upload trees and reports that you generate in Family Tree Maker to your User Home Page.

Each of these steps requires several substeps, the detail of which is beyond the scope of this book.

Making Your Page Pretty

Tip

Including a few photos or graphics can make your Web page more interesting.

Cross-Reference

For more on HTML, see the "Just What is HTML?" section, earlier in this chapter.

Caution

It's not a good idea to use photos of living persons on your Web site unless you have their expressed permission to do so.

Caution

Having lots of photos and graphics on your Web pages can slow down the speed at which they download to individual computers.

Just like reading a book that is all text, visitors may get bored if they see nothing but plain text on your Web site. Consider using graphics and photographs to make your genealogical Web site more attractive.

AOL offers several clipart images that you can use to decorate your Web pages. You can find these images in the Web Art Resources area (Keyword: **Web Art**). Here are some examples of what you can find there:

▶ Backgrounds

▶ Banners and text images

▶ Bars and bullets

▶ Buttons and icons

You can also learn about creating Web art through the area's Web Art Creation message board, graphic arts chats and classes, and Web art tutorials.

If you have any photographs that have been scanned and saved as `.jpg` or `.gif` images, you can post them on your Web page. By using the `<IMG SRC = " ">` tag, you can tell browsers where to go to pick up those images/photographs.

For privacy reasons, make sure that you are just as careful about using pictures of living individuals as you are using information about them. Living relatives may not want their pictures placed online, so it's a good idea to get their permission before doing so. You should also make sure that you're not infringing on any copyrights by using photographs and graphics. For more information on copyrights, see the Copyrights In the Arts area (Keyword: **Copyright**).

You need to be careful about the size of photos and other graphics that you add to your Web pages. Adding really large images or lots of images can make your Web page load very slowly. Visitors are likely to get impatient waiting for your page to download and lose interest before they've even seen what genealogical information you have to offer.

Summary

Now you know a little about what HTML is, how to use it to create a Web page, and how to save some time by using an HTML editor. We also looked at some options for storing your pages and examined ways to create Web pages by using your genealogical software. And we briefly covered using graphics and photos on your Web pages. In the next chapter, we discuss how to communicate directly with other researchers by sending out family newsletters and forming group projects.

CHAPTER

13

BECOMING THE FAMILY
PUBLISHER

Quick Look

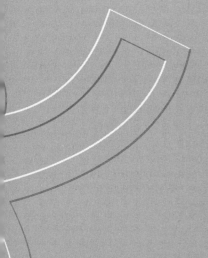

Chapter 13

Becoming the Family Publisher

Communication is one of the cornerstones of genealogical research. Researching your many ancestors would be a daunting task without the help of other genealogists. And even after you find other geneologists who share your research interests, how do you keep them interested in researching and corresponding with you? One way is to start an online newsletter about your collaborative research. In this chapter, we discuss planning a newsletter, finding people to contribute to it, deciding how to distribute it, and how newsletters can fuel research groups.

Starting a Family Newsletter

Publishing a newsletter can be time-consuming, depending on the number of subscribers you have and what your audience's expectations are. And yet, it can also be a rewarding endeavor. Knowing that you're keeping others informed of new findings and projects related to a family that you're researching can be exhilarating.

Planning is the key to ensuring the success of your newsletter. The following few sections discuss some areas to keep in mind when planning a newsletter.

Focus of the Newsletter

First and foremost, you need to determine the focus of the newsletter. Will your newsletter cover just the descendants of a particular individual? Or will it cover anyone with that surname or a variation of that surname? You can focus on many different topics, but make sure that you set some boundaries so that your readers know what kind of information they can expect to find in each issue. Also make sure that all writers and contributors know these parameters so they know what to focus on in their articles.

Tip

Identifying the focus of your newsletter and setting some parameters can make your job editing articles a lot easier.

You should also decide what specific types of content you want in the newsletter. Here are some things you may want to include:

Tip

Most genealogy newsletters contain a combination of some or all of these elements.

- ▶ Articles on the origin of a surname
- ▶ Historical timelines
- ▶ Queries
- ▶ Reviews or lists of recent and relevant books and publications
- ▶ Web site reviews
- ▶ Software reviews
- ▶ How-to and methodology articles
- ▶ Social histories (such as what was life like at the time of a certain ancestor)
- ▶ Genealogy of a specific family line
- ▶ Most genealogy newsletters contain a combination of some or all of these elements.

Delivery Frequency

How often you publish your newsletter has a great impact on its success. If you distribute the newsletter too frequently, you may have trouble finding enough content to support it. Researchers may also lose interest if they receive the newsletter too often. On the other hand, if long stretches of time pass between issues or if issues are delivered in inconsistent patterns, researchers may forget that the newsletter exists. You may want to start out with a longer publication schedule and then shorten it as interest and content grow. We recommend that you begin by publishing your newsletter either biannually or quarterly and then increase to bimonthly or monthly as interest and content grow.

Time Commitment

Finding others to help write or edit your newsletter can shorten your time commitment.

Consider how much time you're willing to devote to the newsletter, as well as how much of a time commitment you expect from others. If the newsletter ends up taking too much of your time, you're likely to cut corners, which affects quality. When the quality begins to suffer, readers' interest wanes, too. If you don't have the time to do the entire newsletter yourself, then try to find a volunteer who can assist you.

Cost of Delivery

It's free to e-mail small newsletters on AOL.

In addition to the cost of your time, every publication — online or traditional — has monetary costs associated with it. Prior to starting your newsletter, decide how much you're willing to contribute to keep the publication going.

Here are some of the expenses you may encounter:

▶ Your Internet service provider may charge you for maintaining a large mailing list (if that's the route you pursue) or for the space for an extensive newsletter archive.

▶ You may need to pay writers for articles, particularly if you're publishing a general subject newsletter.

After you project the actual cost to produce your newsletter, decide how to make up for any shortfall between the amount you're willing to spend and the actual cost. You may want to consider subscriptions, donations, or advertising to make up any cost difference.

What Do You Expect to Get Out of It?

One final consideration when you're planning your newsletter is what do you expect to get out of it? Establishing your expectations at the beginning can help you weigh the importance of meeting your expectations against the time and monetary costs to produce the newsletter. If the newsletter does not meet your expectations, chances are you'll quickly lose interest in it, and it may stress your relationship with other researchers. If you think this may be the case, it's a good idea to hold off on producing a newsletter.

Finding People to Write Articles and Columns

Producing content for a newsletter is one of the great challenges you'll face. Although you may have enough of your own material to fill several issues, eventually you may have to find other authors to contribute articles.

Finding authors and contributors is more of an art than a science. Sometimes you luck out and find a very dedicated group, and other times you search endlessly for someone to provide quality content. Here are some places to look for people to write for your newsletter:

▶ **Mailing lists:** Look for people who send messages to mailing lists that are related to the topic of your newsletter.

▶ **Web sites:** Find individuals who maintain Web sites relating to your topic.

▶ **Research groups:** Is a member of your research group (if you belong to one) interested in writing?

▶ **Book authors:** Do you know anyone who has published a family history? That person may be willing to contribute some anecdotes to keep your newsletter interesting.

Tip

For more ideas on how to start a newsletter and what things to include, check out the How Do I . . .? page in the Reunions section of the Genealogy Forum. You can get to it directly by going to www.genealogyforum.com/gfaol/reunion/HowTo.htm.

Note

You don't have to use an author who lives in your hometown or neighborhood. The beauty of the online community (and the genealogical community, for that matter) is that you can pass files back and forth without ever having met your coworkers face-to-face.

If all else fails, you can always advertise for authors in the venues in the preceding list. Just be sure that you articulate exactly what you're looking for so potential authors know whether their talents match your expectations.

Avoiding Newsletter Burnout

No matter how successful your newsletter is, you're bound to face burnout at one time or another. Constantly trying to dig up new content can really wear on you after a while.

One way you can prevent burnout is to look for volunteers who are willing to write columns in each issue of the newsletter and have a writing style you like. Regular columns take up space in your newsletter and hopefully provide quality information that requires little editing on your part. Having regular columnists does have some drawbacks, however. Your regular columnists may burn out, depending on the frequency of your newsletter. And, over time, they may lack imagination. Although dependable columnists may start out on a roll, they may eventually run out of ideas. Repeating the same information issue after issue doesn't really help your readers.

Another way you can avoid burning out is to use a group of writers in cycles. For example, if you have six authors and a newsletter that comes out monthly, you can ask three authors to write an article every two months. This approach keeps your content fresh, and authors aren't as pressured to come up with new material and meet deadlines.

Which Shall It Be: The Web or E-Mail?

After you decide on the content of your newsletter, as well as consider some of the logistics (such as time commitments, costs, and your author pool), you need to decide how you want the newsletter delivered. This can be a tough decision. The two main methods of delivering newsletters online are via e-mail and on Web sites. Each online delivery method has its own pros and cons, and in some cases, you may even want to use both methods.

E-Mail Newsletters

E-mail is the least time-consuming method of distributing on-line newsletters. E-mail newsletters are especially attractive if you're delivering them to a small group of people, because you can simply add new e-mail addresses to the addresses you already have. However, when your subscription level reaches 50 people or more, e-mailing your newsletter and keeping up with all the e-mail address changes, subscriptions, and cancellations can be tedious. A solution to this is to use an automated mailing list. Figure 13-1 shows a weekly e-mail newsletter that uses an automated mailing list for distribution.

Tip

You may want to create an archive of your e-mail newsletters on a Web site so that anyone who misses an issue can catch up.

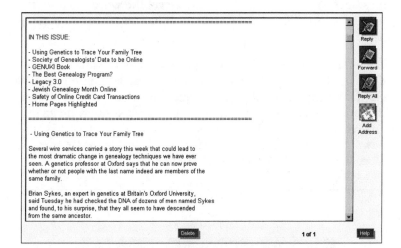

Figure 13-1. Eastman's Online Genealogy Newsletter, an example of an e-mail newsletter.

An automated mailing list allows individuals to subscribe or cancel their subscriptions by replying directly to the mailing list software; this means that you don't have to deal with all the administrative tasks related to the e-mail addresses. When you want to send out a newsletter, you simply post a message to the mailing list, and it's automatically delivered to all the subscribers. You can set up a mailing list to broadcast only the messages that you send out, rather than let everyone post to the list (unless, of course, you want everyone to have access to post to

Find It Online

One popular service is Listbot, which offers a fee-based plan and a free mailing list plan. You can find more information about this service at
www.listbot.com.

the group). If you don't want to buy the hardware and software to host a mailing list, you can have a company host it for you. Some of these companies charge a flat fee, whereas others provide free mailing list service as long as they can add advertisments to your newsletter.

Web-based Newsletters

Tip

Some people use HTML mail, which is a hybrid of the e-mail and Web-based newsletter. With HTML mail, you code an e-mail message into HTML so that e-mail programs interpret the message and display it as a browser would. The catch here is that your subscribers' e-mail programs must be able to display HTML, so make sure that that's the case before using this type of strategy.

The second online option is to post your newsletter on a Web site and have subscribers stop by to read it. If you have a large subscriber base, you can save money by using Web site delivery rather than an automated mailing list. Instead of sending out messages to every subscriber, you can get the word out about new issues by posting a message to an existing surname mailing list.

Creating Web-based newsletters gives you the flexibility to dress up the look and feel of your newsletter with photographs, background colors, icons, and links to other Web sites that are mentioned in the newsletter. You can also create an archive of past issues that is available on the front page of your newsletter, much like the archive that is available for George Morgan's "Along Those Lines . . ." column (see Figure 13-2).

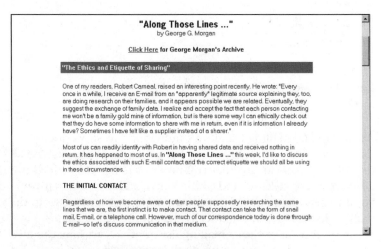

Figure 13-2. "Along Those Lines . . .," a Web-based column.

One drawback to Web-based newsletters is that subscribers have to make the effort to go to the Web site to read them (which some people forget to do). You also have to make sure that you have enough space to store back issues, as well as current issues that have lots of photographs and other graphics.

Enhancing Your News with Group Projects

Newsletters can be a great vehicle not only for informing people but also for getting them to coordinate their research as a group. You can advertise the creation of a research group in your newsletter and solicit involvement from your subscribers. Then, to increase awareness of the project, include periodic updates in your newsletter about the progress of the group.

AOL has an area that is perfect for both your group projects and your online newsletter. It has resources that help guide and organize projects, as well as facilitate communication among the group members. The Groups@AOL area, shown in Figure 13-3, allows families, friends, and other groups to share resources and communicate with one another. Your Groups@AOL forum is a secure area that is open only by invitation.

Tip

If all the subscribers to your newsletter are part of a Groups@AOL group, you can use the Send Group Email function to deliver your e-mail.

Note

Only an AOL member can start a group using the Groups@AOL service, but you can invite non-AOL members to participate in your Groups@AOL forum. Anyone invited to join a group can join as long as he or she has an Internet connection.

Find It Online

You can get to Groups@AOL by using the Keyword: **Groups**.

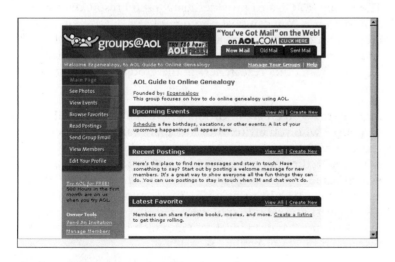

Figure 13-3. A group area at Groups@AOL.

To form a group follow these steps:

1. Go to Groups@AOL by using the Keyword: **Groups**.
2. Click the Create Groups Now button. This launches the Creating a Group Step 1 page.
3. Fill in the fields on this page, including the name and description of the group. Select a time zone and select the check box agreeing to the group guidelines.
4. When you're finished entering information, click the Submit Information button to go to the Step 2 page.
5. Select a category for the group (family, friends, activity group) and a title for the group. Click the Submit Information button when you're done. This brings up the Step 3 page.
6. Select a style for the group and click the Submit Information button. This takes you to the Step 4 page.
7. Complete the member profile by typing your first and last name, indicating whether to make information public or private, and selecting a image to represent yourself. Click the Submit Information button when you have completed the form. This brings up the Group Completion page.
8. You can invite other members to join the group or visit your new group by clicking links on this page.

The Groups@AOL area provides many useful resources for research groups. You can post photographs or digitized images, create a list of events (such as chats, research trips, meetings, and so on), create a list of favorite books or Web sites, read postings from other researchers in the group, and send group e-mails.

A group that you create in Groups@AOL can be accessed only by people who you invite. Your members can be connected through AOL or any Internet service provider, but if they are not on AOL, they need to get a free AOL Instant Messenger screen name to sign in. Invited members can then reach your group on the Web by using a URL that you provide. This URL also appears at the bottom of every Group e-mail. This feature makes Groups@AOL an ideal area in which to coordinate your research projects and online newsletter.

Summary

In this chapter, we discuss how you can communicate with other researchers who share similar interests. You can create an online newsletter, delivering it by e-mail or the Web, and even form research groups built around your newsletter. In the next chapter, we talk about how you can use resources to plan a reunion with your relatives and fellow researchers.

Quick Look

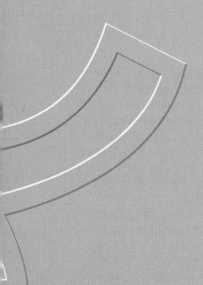

Chapter 14

Planning Your Reunion

Have you ever had the pleasure of attending a family reunion? After you begin meeting other researchers and family members online, you will undoubtedly be invited to attend at least a few. And you may even be invited to help plan some. When the time comes that you wish to plan a reunion or participate in the planning process, this chapter may come in handy.

Reunions are gatherings of people who have something in common, such as a familial relationship or the same graduating class. They can be a lot of fun — not to mention that they can give your research a wonderful boost. After all, they provide you with the opportunity to meet people with whom you've been corresponding and to trade information first-hand.

There are a couple of types of reunions:

▶ Family

▶ Special groups (includes school, military units, team, camp, and other organizations)

Of course, in this chapter, we focus on family reunions because these are of particular interest to you as a genealogist. However, most of the principles of planning a family reunion hold true for other types of reunions as well.

The Family Reunion Center

The Genealogy Forum on AOL has a resource center set up just for reunions, which is called the Family Reunion Center (see Figure 14-1). The topics covered by the center include

Figure 14-1. The Genealogy Forum's Family Reunion Center.

▶ **About This Area:** This section describes how the Family Reunion Center works and explains where the ideas and feedback come from — you and other AOL members like you.

Continued

Definition

A reunion is a gathering of people who have something in common, such as a family connection.

Note

Type the Keywords: **Family**, **Families**, **Reunion**, **Reunions**, or **Family Reunions** to go to the Families Forum window, which leads you to the Genealogy/Family History area by Ancestry.com.

14

Planning Your Reunion

The Family Reunion Center *(continued)*

▶ **How Do I . . . ?:** Here you can find links to resources that help you plan a reunion, find missing relatives, form a family association, and publish family histories and newsletters.

▶ **Family Associations:** This is a listing of some family associations, and there's an explanation about how to get your family association listed at this site.

▶ **Family Newsletters:** Here's a list of some online family newsletters; you can also find out how to get your own family newsletter added.

▶ **Schedule of Online Family Reunions:** As you've probably already guessed, this is a schedule of reunion-type chats on AOL. The chats are open to all AOL members, but you may not find them interesting unless you share a common bond with the other participants.

▶ **Schedule of Family Reunions:** This is a schedule of upcoming family reunions of the traditional variety. You can use the list to locate reunions of interest to you — reunions for family lines you're researching but about which you haven't had online contact with anyone else. There's also information about how to get your family reunion added to the list. Lists like this are a good way to try to find long-lost relatives.

▶ **Submit Your Own Family Reunion Data:** This is an online form you can complete to submit information about your family reunion to the Genealogy Forum.

Here's how to find the Family Reunion Center:

1. Type the Keyword: **Roots** in the text box on the navigation bar and click the Go button to bring up the Genealogy Forum.

2. Click the Reunions button, and the Family Reunion Center window pops up.

If, after reading through the resources at the Family Reunion Center, you still want more information, you can always conduct a search of the Genealogy Forum by using the word *reunion.* You'll get a list of articles that discuss various aspects of family reunions.

Is Yours a Family Association?

A family association is a group that is formally organized around a particular family line — the members are interested in researching and sharing information only about that line. Typically, a family association is a traditional organization — meaning that it exists in the offline world and may have a board of directors and formal membership. Many family associations have created quite an online presence that facilitates communication, encourages global memberships, and boasts Web pages, message boards, and mailing lists.

When it comes to planning a reunion, you may discover a couple of advantages to being part of a family association.

▶ **You have a ready source of help.** You can turn to the members of the association for help planning and preparing for the big event. You can recruit people for various committees in order to distribute the workload. This extra help keeps you from becoming overwhelmed with work on the reunion.

▶ **You have a ready source of money.** You have funds that you can use to pay for certain aspects of the reunion. This is not to say that your family association will necessarily be able to pay all of the charges related to the reunion. You may still need to charge attendees a little to offset the costs between actual expenses and what the family association can pay.

Before you decide to start your own family association and recruit other researchers you meet online, first check to see if a family association already exists for the family line in which you're interested. If one does exist, you can save yourself time and energy by joining and becoming involved in the existing association.

You can check to see if other associations are already in place a couple of different ways. You can check the list of family associations kept at the Genealogy Forum on AOL, look up the surname for the family line at a comprehensive genealogical index, or you can run a search on the name at a genealogically focused search engine.

Definition

A family association is a group that is formally organized to research a particular family line.

Note

It's not unusual for reunion attendees to be charged a few bucks to help cover some of the costs of the reunion (such as food and entertainment). The overall amount will vary depending on when and where the reunion is being held, as well as how much money reunion-planners are able to gather from other sources.

14

Planning Your Reunion

Tip

Whenever you conduct research online, be as thorough as possible. When checking to see if a family association already exists, try checking by using AOL's Genealogy Forum and by conducting a search using at least one genealogy search engine.

To check the Family Associations list (see Figure 14-2) at the Genealogy Forum, follow these steps:

1. Type Keyword: **Roots** in the text box on the navigation bar and click the Go button.

2. After the Genealogy Forum window appears, click the Reunions button.

3. After the Family Reunion Center pops up, scroll down the page and click the Family Associations link.

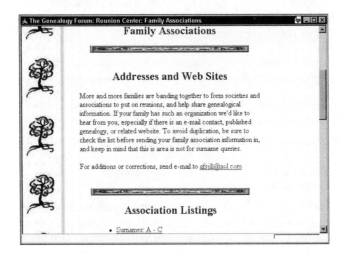

Figure 14-2. You can look through a list of family associations at the Family Reunion Center.

To look for information at a comprehensive genealogical index, follow these steps:

1. Type **sitefinder.genealogytoolbox.com** in the text box on the navigation bar and click the Go button.

2. The Genealogy SiteFinder page appears, listing various search options. Click the People link and then click the letter of the alphabet that begins the surname you're researching. For example, if you're looking for associations organized around the surname Sanders, click S.

3. Scroll through the alphabetical list of links that appears to see if any resources for that surname are listed. The list shows several resources, so be sure to look particularly for family associations.

4. If you find a family association for the line you're researching, click it to visit the Web page for that organization to find out how to join.

To search a genealogically focused search engine, follow these steps:

1. Type **www.genealogy.com/ifftop.html** in the text box on the navigation bar and click Go.

2. The Genealogy.com Internet FamilyFinder page appears, showing search fields for first name, middle initial, and last name. Typing the first name is optional, but you're required to enter the last name for which you're trying to locate a family association.

3. Deselect the check boxes for the GenealogyLibrary.com and Commercial Genealogy CDs search options. The GenealogyLibrary is a subscription-based service, and the other option brings up results about CDs you can purchase.

4. Click the Search button.

5. Scroll through the results that appear to see if any family associations are focused on your ancestor or family line. If you find one or more existing associations, click the appropriate link or links to find out more information.

If you don't find an existing family association after looking around using these three methods, then you may consider starting one of your own. Of course, you'll need to recruit other members for the association, but that shouldn't be difficult if you've made a lot of online contacts.

Here are a few tips to help you find ways to organize your budding association just by visiting existing family association Web sites:

▶ Find out whether to hold monthly chats (instead or in addition to association meetings).

Tip

If you want to limit the results of your search, you can use your mouse to click and remove the check box next to the GenealogyLibrary.com option and the Commercial Genealogy CDs option.

Tip

Starting a family association may seem daunting at first, but the key to success is utilizing your online contacts. E-mail all of the other online researchers you've corresponded with to gauge interest in creating a family association and to begin getting feedback on how you should organize the group.

14

Planning Your Reunion

> ▶ Discover whether to charge annual dues to cover any costs associated with the group and to find out how much members typically pay in dues.

> ▶ Find out whether to form a library or archive to store information submitted by members. You can also find out how other associations have organized their libraries and archives, thus getting a head start organizing your Web site's structure.

After you get some of the preliminary parameters out of the way, you can start discussing whether, when, and where to hold a reunion for all family association members.

Find It Online

Type the term **family reunions** in the text box on the navigation bar and click the Search button to see matches, including links to sites with more information about upcoming family reunions and some sites that focus on planning a reunion.

Definition

An online reunion is generally a chat session devoted to a particular surname or family line.

Cross-Reference

For more information about chats, check out Chapter 3.

Planning and Executing the Big Day

You want to plan a reunion that's fun and runs smoothly, right? Well, there are a lot of things to consider in your planning. Let's take a look at them.

Type of Reunion

When we talk about the type of reunion, we're really talking about two different things: the medium of the event, and the size or extent.

> ▶ **The medium of the event:** You have a couple of choices about how the attendees of your reunion will meet and greet each other. You can choose a traditional reunion where people gather in a physical location and spend some amount of time together, or you can opt for an online event where Internet-users can meet in a particular chat room or discussion forum and exchange information. Figure 14-3 shows a schedule of online reunions. To find this schedule, check out the sidebar earlier in this chapter called "The Genealogy Forum's Family Reunion Center."

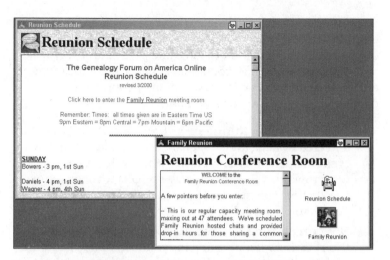

Figure 14-3. A schedule of online family reunions to be held in the Family Reunion chat room on the Genealogy Forum on AOL.

▶ **The size or extent:** You need to decide how large you want the reunion to be. Will you invite only the descendants of your parents? Only the descendants of another ancestor a couple of generations back? Or even more extended family? If your reunion is a family association-sponsored event, then the group will probably determine the invitation list — the main two choices for an association-sponsored reunion are typically to either include members only or every known descendant of the focal person. If your family is really large and spread out all over the world, you might consider having several smaller, regional reunions, and then sharing photos and information about each online.

Forming a Committee

Whether you need to form a committee depends on the type of reunion you plan to have (considering both the medium and the size factors). If you're having an online chat or a traditional reunion with less than 30 people, then you can probably handle the planning yourself. But if you're having a traditional reunion to which more than 30 people are coming, you should consider forming a committee to help plan and carry out everything. And if you're part of a family association, chances are you'll have a committee of some sort anyway.

Your reunion committee needs to have a person in charge — a chairperson. And the number of committee members is highly subjective — you may want to have one person for every major area of planning (such as communications, accommodations, finances, and activities). When recruiting people to serve on the committee, keep these things in mind:

> ▶ **Did the person volunteer to help out?** If the person volunteered to help, then the chances are good that this is an event the person is excited about and will enthusiastically work toward. If the person was a reluctant volunteer or was drafted, you may find yourself having to motivate that person to do his or her part.

> ▶ **How much time can the person commit to planning the reunion?** If a person joins your committee but works full-time, has young children at home, and is involved in several other activities, he or she may not have a lot of time to devote to planning the reunion. This doesn't mean the person can't help out — it just means that you need to work together to gauge his or her level of involvement. Find tasks for that person to handle that won't drive him or her over the edge.

> ▶ **What are the person's special talents?** We all have areas in which we excel — some people are good at writing or have great organizational skills, while others have a knack for figures or decorations. Try to identify what people are good at and place them in positions to use those talents.

> ▶ **Is the person's personality compatible with the chairperson's?** If someone who is interested in helping out has any negative history with another committee member, think twice before assigning him or her an essential role. Whenever possible, you should avoid creating an environment in which contention thrives or that fosters resentment among members. This will cost you time, money, and patience in the long run. Consider politely taking a rain check from one or both of the parties.

After you've selected people to serve on the reunion committee, be sure to take advantage of their skills and to do so wisely. Identify a list of tasks that must be completed prior to, during, and after the reunion; then start dividing those tasks up among the committee members.

Tip

Work with committee members who have busy lives of their own to see what they're able to handle without too much stress. Ask them to do tasks that they can do while doing something else, such as addressing invitations or collecting RSVPs.

Corresponding with Others

Your correspondence-related activities can be broken down into two categories: tracking down invitees and actually corresponding.

Tracking Down Invitees

You can't determine who to invite to the reunion until you decide the type, as well as the size and extent, of the reunion. You need to know in advance how extensive the reunion will be before you begin looking for contact information for family members in each branch of your family tree. Here's how you can break things down:

> ▶ If your reunion will be held for descendants of your parents, then you need to make a list of your parents, your siblings and their spouses, and your siblings' descendants (children, grandchildren, and so forth).

> ▶ If your reunion is more for extended family than for immediate family, you need to develop a guest list using any resource you can:
>
> • Pull names and addresses of potential guests out of your genealogical database
>
> • Contact other family researchers to get names and addresses
>
> • Enlist other family members to spread the word about the reunion through newsletters and Web pages

Actually Corresponding

At several stages in the reunion process, you may need to send correspondence to invitees, committee members, the general public, and possibly family association members. These are the classifications of correspondence you'll use:

> ▶ **Invitations:** This one is self-explanatory. Invitations are the means by which you invite people to come to the reunion.

> ▶ **Reminders:** You may find yourself needing to send postcards or other brief reminders for various reasons. In particular, you'll send reminders to those people who haven't responded to your initial invitation. You may also want to send reminders regarding hotel reservations, special needs, and/or particular activities for which people need to bring certain supplies.

Tip

The strategy of using family members to help put together a list of invitees can also help you track down relatives whose names you know but whom you've lost track of over the years — those who have moved around or simply lost contact.

14

Planning Your Reunion

Be sure to allow a realistic amount of time to organize a reunion and begin planning as soon as possible. Many resorts that are wonderful for reunions have long waiting lists (a year or more), so you can't expect to begin planning an August event in July of the same year.

Instructions can include anything from driving directions to the event from various local hotels to information about reserving hotel and car-rental accommodations. You should also provide a list of planned activities and a schedule of events.

▶ **Notices:** While you may not send notices to every person invited to or involved with the reunion, you should post them in areas or media that many people see. As long as you'll be online soliciting feedback about the time and place to hold the reunion and tracking down long-lost relatives to invite, why not post notices in newsletters, on Web pages, and on e-mail mailing lists to get the word out?

▶ **Instructions:** We can think of three times during the reunion planning and executing phases that you absolutely have to give potential attendees instructions, but there are probably other times as well.

- In the invitation packet, you should include any instructions for making reservations to attend the reunion. You need to get a realistic count of the number of people who plan to attend so you can make proper arrangements regarding food and entertainment.

- Once you've determined where the reunion is going to be held, you need to send invitees instructions about making hotel and car-rental reservations, and directions to the location from major towns or interstates.

- At the beginning of the reunion, you should include a packet that contains a schedule of events, any useful information attendees need to know if they plan to participate in structured activities (such as the type of clothing they should wear to the tug of war you organized). If you have arranged a special meeting place for those who want to join in the fun, you should include this information as well. Don't forget to include what we call housekeeping announcements (where guests can find restrooms and refreshments, in particular).

▶ **Thank-you notes:** After the reunion has come and gone, you need to send thank-you notes to anyone who helped to make it a success (beyond those who just showed up and had a great time). You should expres your written gratitude to committee members, hosts, activity organizers, entertainers, and caterers.

▶ **Follow-up:** You may have materials that are compiled at the reunion that you'll need to distribute after it ends, as well as any announcements about future reunions or family activities.

Scheduling Your Reunion

In many ways, the time of year that you hold your family re-union depends on the place where you choose to hold it and the kinds of activities you want to plan. The availability of a par-ticular location directly impacts your reunion — for example, if you want to have your reunion at a dude ranch in Montana where great-grandpa once worked, you'll have to arrange your reunion schedule around the dude ranch's availability. This is one good reason to set realistic expectations of when to hold your reunion and why you should begin planning it as soon as you see there's interest in having one. Don't wait until July of this year to begin planning an August event!

Just as you should consider the availability of a location, you need to keep in mind activities and how they may affect your timing. If you hope to go boating, hiking, water-skiing, or bicy-cling, you need to hold the reunion in an area that's warm year-round or you need to plan it for spring, summer, or early fall. If you want to do some snow-skiing or ice skating on the family pond, then you probably have a winter reunion in mind.

Planning a Three-Day Gathering

You need to decide how long your reunion is going to last. Many people plan their family reunion over a weekend. Attendees arrive and meet informally on a Friday night, and then have structured activities all day Saturday and Sunday morning. Having the reunion last more than just one day enables those who can't arrive for a main activity to still come and enjoy meeting others, and this schedule allows travel time on Sunday afternoon for those who have to be back at work on Monday morning.

If most of the people you're inviting live within a couple of hours of each other, you might consider having a one-day or meet-for-a-meal type reunion. You can meet for a lun-cheon and then spend the afternoon and early evening together before everyone heads home.

Tip

When you have a general season in mind, you should get some feedback from those who are helping you plan the reunion — and those who plan to attend — to find out their schedules during specific dates and their interests (besides family history).

Note

The amount of time it may take to plan and execute a reunion varies from person to person, and event to event. For example, Matthew's fam-ily holds a one-day reunion every July that takes only a few weeks to plan. The only constraint on their plans is the time by which they must reserve a pavilion in a particular park. On the other hand, one branch of April's family holds a big reunion periodically for all of the descendants of one of her great-great-grandfathers. This reunion, because of the sheer size and length (it usually lasts three days over a week-end), takes anywhere from three to five years to plan.

After you've determined the date(s) and duration for your reunion, you need to put it on your calendar and set interim dates for meeting task deadlines. If you're working with a committee, you can indicate who is responsible for the particular task, as well.

Here's how to use My Calendar on AOL to keep your plans in line:

1. Click the My Calendar icon on the Welcome screen.

2. When you use My Calendar for the first time, you need to enter your Time Zone and U.S. Zip Code. (If you live outside of the United States, leave the Zip Code field blank.)

3. Click Save.

   My Calendar pops up, as shown in Figure 14-4.

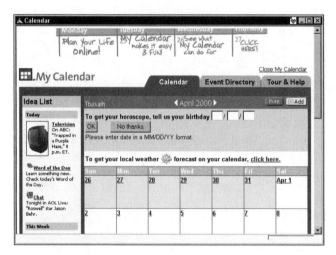

Figure 14-4. AOL's My Calendar feature.

You can choose to view My Calendar by day, week, or month. It also has an Event Directory that shows you activities in your area at particular times, including book releases, movies, chat events, music releases, concerts, cultural events, special interest events, family festivals and events, sporting events, finance matters, television schedules, holidays, tradeshows, and seminars.

Use My Calendar on AOL to help keep your plans on schedule.

The Tour & Help tab explains everything about My Calendar. It shows you how to add appointments to your calendar and how to change the view, as well as how to use the Idea List and Events Directory.

Think about asking the Chamber of Commerce nearest the reunion's site to give you some maps and information about the area, as well as asking local retailers to donate items, which you can include in bags of goodies that you give each attendee.

Figuring Out the Finances

You knew eventually this subject would come up, right? Money! Unless you have a rich relative who plans to foot the entire reunion bill, you're going to have to think about funding for your event. If you're part of a family association that is sponsoring the reunion, some of the costs may be covered by an allocation from the organization. But you'll most likely still have part of the expenses to cover. Here are just some of the things that add up when you're planning a reunion:

▶ Buying supplies for correspondence and postage

▶ Printing services (posters, hand-outs, materials to mail)

▶ Posting notices in newsletters, magazines, and Web pages

▶ Renting or buying equipment

▶ Making deposits on rented space and/or equipment

▶ Purchasing all of the food to prepare or having the event catered

▶ Paying for entertainment

▶ Covering transportation costs of a shuttle van

So how will you pay for these things? Most likely, you'll need to charge a registration fee or ask for donations from attendees. The registration fee is the most secure way to go because you're assured to get money from those who attend. Asking for a donation may sound nice, but may not yield as much as you need (depending on the generosity of your relatives). You may also choose to raise a little money holding an auction — ask each person attending to bring an item to donate to the auction. While this can be a fun activity and raise some money, it probably won't elicit enough in funding to pay all of your expenses.

After you determine how you plan to pay for the reunion, you and your reunion committee need to sit down and prepare a budget. Identify everything you can think of that's going to cost money and estimate how much you'll bring in through registration fees (or whatever means you choose for raising money). You may have to make some adjustments when you see the differences between your anticipated income and costs.

Note

It never hurts to contact genealogical companies to see if they are willing to donate prizes for raffles or items to auction at your family reunion.

Note

Make sure that you inquire about special needs on the reservation form that invitees must return to you. This way you can better plan for those needs. In particular, you'll need to make sure that the location is accessible by disabled and elderly persons, and that you have food to address dietary concerns (allergies and special diets).

Note

No matter what kind of place you pick for your reunion, if you're expecting people from out of town, you need to help them make arrangements for a hotel or motel room. Call a couple of local establishments and block some rooms for your reunion attendees. Most hotels and motels will hold a block of rooms for you, and they may give your group a discounted rate. You also need to consider whether any of your relatives will be flying in or taking the train, and in need of a rental car. Identify local car-rental places for them to call and make arrangements.

Finding Accommodations

The matter of finding accommodations is another one that is closely related to the type of reunion you're planning and your scheduling concerns. If you're reunion is a one-day or meet-for-a-meal deal, then you can probably find a place to hold it rather easily and inexpensively — a park, someone's house, a local church, or even a restaurant. But if you're planning an event that will last for a couple of days, you need to start looking for a place to hold it several months (if not at least a year) in advance. Here are some places to consider:

▶ **Someone's home:** Using someone's home is a cozy solution if you have a relative who is willing and has enough room at his or her house (inside the house or out in the yard if the weather is agreeable). Having the reunion at a home is cost-effective, but unless the property is relatively large, we don't recommend it for reunions that last more than one day.

▶ **A park or a church:** If you're having a one-day reunion, a park or a church is a wonderful and inexpensive way to go (which one you choose will probably depend on the time of year and potential weather). You can plan a picnic lunch (potluck or catered) and then spend the afternoon exchanging family stories and going over all your genealogical data. Then, those who want to do so can go to dinner together before everyone heads home.

▶ **A hotel/motel or resort:** While choosing a hotel or resort may cost you a considerable amount of money (deposit, renting a meeting room, and food and refreshments), it's a nice solution if you expect a lot of people to come to the reunion. A hotel, motel, or resort is particularly convenient for out-of-town attendees because they can book a room in the same hotel or motel. And if you choose a resort location, you're bound to be have plenty of activities — so you may not have to plan as many on your own.

▶ **A campground:** We've heard of a lot of people who say this is the way to go for a family reunion. But you need to make sure that the campground is near a lodge, hotel, or motel for those relatives who are not campers; otherwise you're inhibiting the total number of potential attendees. A campground is more cost-effective than a hotel or motel, and of course nature-related activities of all sorts are nearby.

▶ **A cruise:** Depending on the number of attendees you get and the kind of deal you arrange with the cruise line or travel agent, taking a cruise is probably the most expensive option. However, it could be an exciting and fun one! The ship will most likely have some standard activities so you may not need to plan as much.

The key when it comes to accommodations is to make things as easy as possible for your guests — send them all the information they need to make their room and transportation arrangements, as well as maps so they can find the reunion easily.

Caution

If you plan to combine camping with your family reunion, don't forget to work out alternate accommodations for attendees for whom camping isn't an option.

Traveling for Your Cause

If you're planning to attend a reunion that requires you to travel any distance, or if you have people coming some distance to attend a reunion you're planning, you can use AOL to help make travel arrangements.

Click the Travel button on the Welcome menu to get to the AOL Travel area (shown in Figure 14-5). From here, you can make plane reservations, locate a hotel and make room reservations, and make arrangements for a rental car.

If you plan to drive to the reunion in your own car, you can also use the Maps & Directions at AOL Travel or type Keyword: **Directions**. Click the Maps & Directions link in the AOL Travel window, complete the fields in the resulting Web page, and then click Get Directions. AOL and MapQuest.com work together to generate a map and/or driving directions for you.

Figure 14-5. You can make flight, hotel, and car reservations in the AOL Travel area.

Caution

Whenever large quantities of food are added into the equation, the possibility of food-related incidents goes up. You should choose a caterer who is familiar with the standards enforced by the board of health. If you and other attendees are handling the food arrangements yourselves, make sure you have adequate refrigeration for food and avoid serving food that spoils easily.

Tip

You should make sure that the location is accessible by disabled and elderly persons, and that you have food to address dietary concerns (allergies, vegetarian needs, and other special diets).

Don't Forget about Food

We have yet to attend a family reunion that didn't have at least one meal. In fact, we're pretty sure that the term reunion implies food at some point. Here are some options:

▶ If most of your guests are coming from nearby, you can always opt for the old potluck meal. Ask each person or family to bring an item or two that feeds a certain number of people (the number will depend on how many attendees you expect, but a good potluck rule is one dish that feeds 12–15 people per family of 4).

▶ Depending on where you're having your reunion, you may prefer to have the meal(s) catered. While this costs more than potluck, you're better assured that you'll have enough food to go around.

When planning the menu, remember to take into consideration special dietary concerns. You don't necessarily have to prepare an entire meal to address one person's food restrictions, but you should make sure you have something available for everyone. Among all of the dishes, have at least a few items that meet each these general but special diets — vegetarian, low-sodium, low-fat, and peanut-free. If you know some of your guests have specific dietary restrictions based on religion, make sure you have something they can eat, too. And be sure to have some non-alcoholic, sugar-free, and caffeine-free drinks available.

Coming Up with Activities

This is a fun part of planning and carrying out your reunion so you shouldn't have any problems finding others who will help you. While you surely want to allow some time to exchange genealogical information, you need to have some other activities planned, too. Here are just a few ideas:

▶ An opening address or welcome session

▶ A talent contest

▶ A dance (you could go with theme dancing — country or line, ballroom, or disco depending on the age and abilities of the crowd)

▶ An awards ceremony (give certificates to guests who meet certain criteria — came the farthest, oldest, youngest, one with most children, and so forth)

- ▶ A church service
- ▶ A family recipe book put together at the reunion
- ▶ A scrapbook created during the reunion; each person designs a page using photos they bring
- ▶ Competitions (horseshoes, sack races, chess, card games, etc.)
- ▶ Icebreakers
- ▶ A video that chronicles the reunion
- ▶ A family quilt pieced together at the reunion
- ▶ Karaoke night or a sing-along

If you plan to give prizes for any of the activities or if you need supplies, be sure to account for them in your budget and assign someone the responsibility of gathering or purchasing everything.

And although these things aren't really activities, here are some other items to consider:

- ▶ Having everyone wear a nametag
- ▶ Keeping a guest book that each attendee can sign
- ▶ Putting up decorations including family charts and copies of old photographs
- ▶ Having a professional photographer on hand to take pictures of everyone

Picking Your Relatives' Brains

As a genealogist, a reunion presents you with an incredible opportunity to pick your relatives' brains. You want to make sure you plan both at least one activity that is centered on family history and also some free time during which people can sit around and visit, exchanging stories and information. Be sure to print out some reports and charts from your genealogical database to bring along. You can then have others fill in any blanks for which they know something. You might also want to take along copies of old photos — you can use them to help jog memories or to share with others who have not had the opportunity to see your shared ancestors. And you can exchange contact information so you can keep in touch after the reunion.

Find It Online

Ready to post information about your upcoming reunion or looking for ideas? Check out Family-Reunion.com (family-reunion.com) and FamilyReunion.com (www.familyreunion.com). Both sites have a variety of resources to help you.

Find It Online

Looking for books about family reunions? Search for the term family reunion at Shop@AOLSearch.

Afterwards

In all your planning for the big day, don't forget to make arrangements for after the reunion. Depending on where you hold the reunion, you may need a clean-up committee. Don't forget to thank all of those volunteers who made the day a success. If you decide to collect evaluations to assess how the whole event was received, be sure to gather the data together and make it available to others. And be sure to follow up on anything that needs following up — distributing copies of charts and information that people brought to share, sending out a list of attendees and their addresses so people can keep in touch, and sending out announcements about the next reunion (whether it's next year or several years down the road).

Looking For a Little Help?

If you're looking for some help planning and organizing a family reunion, Family Reunion Organizer software from FormalSoft, Inc. might be just the thing for you. It has a variety of features that help your plans go smoothly.

You can use this software to print out invitations, nametags, mailing labels, a list of invitees and their addresses, a schedule, an assignment list, an expense log, reminders, certificates, a registration form, a shopping list, an evaluation, and thank-you notes.

You can download a demonstration version of this software at family-reunion.com/organizer/demo.htm.

Summary

Here it is — the end of the chapter and the end of this book! In this final chapter, we've explained planning family reunions and how to find some resources to help. While attending family reunions can be fun and a boost to your genealogical research, planning them affords you the opportunity to get more involved with your living relatives — to learn more about them and work with some of them toward a common goal that is genealogy-related yet social at the same time. We think you'll find that reunions can be rewarding on so many levels. And they are a perfect culmination for our topic here because they enable you to meet other researchers in person whom you've met through the Internet with the help of AOL and this book.

Glossary

A

Ahnentafel

A numbering system based on a mathematical relationship between parents and their children.

ancestor

A person from whom you are descended.

attachment

An electronic file that you send attached to an e-mail message.

B

bloodline research

Research that focuses on the researcher's direct (bloodline) ancestors.

buddy

A person with whom you correspond frequently by using AOL's Buddy List feature.

Buddy List

A list of buddies with whom you correspond frequently by using AOL's Buddy List feature. You can use a Buddy List to see which of your buddies are currently online.

C

census

An accounting of the people inhabiting a particular area at a given time; the United States government conducts the federal census every ten years.

census schedule

A record of individuals collected during a census.

chat room

A real-time forum to which you can connect and carry on an electronic discussion with others.

civil registration

A record created during a landmark of a person's life, including birth, marriage, divorce, and death; also called a *vital record.*

clipart

Small graphics that are frequently used in publications to decorate text.

commercial software

A program that is generally available through traditional retail channels, including in stores.

comprehensive genealogical index

A categorized list of Internet resources of interest and value to genealogists and family historians.

compression

Using a special program to make the files on your computer more compact so you have more room on your hard drive.

D

demo program

Short for *demonstration program,* a free, trial copy of software meant to allow you to test-drive the program.

descendant

A person who descended from a particular ancestor.

descendant chart

A chart that shows all the descendants of an individual including siblings of those descendants.

digitization

The process of producing an electronic copy of an object for storage on a hard drive or other magnetic medium.

digitized record

A digital representation of an original record such as a manuscript or photograph.

download

The process of pulling files off the Internet and onto your computer.

drop-in-hour

An open discussion time in the AOL chat rooms.

E

e-mail (electronic mail)

A basic building block of online communication that allows you to send a message over the Internet to a single individual or multiple people at once.

emoticon

A little face made out of characters on your computer's keyboard — such as the sideways smiley face :-).

enumeration

The act of recording individuals into the census records (called *schedules*).

enumerator

A person who goes from house to house conducting the census.

e-zine

An electronic magazine that you can access on the Web.

F

family association

An organization whose goals and membership criteria focus on researching a particular branch of a family with a certain surname (or people with that name in a specific geographic area).

family group sheet

A reporting form that contains the following information on each person in the nuclear family: full name, dates and places for birth, marriage, and death (as well as baptism and burial in many cases), and the full name of the person's spouse (if married).

family research

Research that looks at the lives of entire families — not only the researcher's direct ancestors, but also the collateral (indirect) branches of the family tree.

family tree

A representation of an individual's ancestry.

FAQ

Acronym for *Frequently Asked Questions.*

forum

An area on AOL where people with similar interests can exchange information and find resources pertaining to a specific topic.

freeware

Computer software that you can download from the Internet or get on disk and use for free.

Frequently Asked Questions

A section of a Web site that identifies the questions that are asked most frequently at that site, along with the appropriate answers to those questions.

G

GEDCOM

Stands for GEnealogical Data COMmunication; this text-file format gives genealogists who use two different genealogical software packages a common file format so they can share their family information more easily.

genealogical database

A computer program in which you enter, store, and use information about people.

genealogical search engine

A program that indexes the text at genealogical Web sites, and then allows you to search the index for particular keywords.

Genealogy Forum

An area on AOL where you can go for all sorts of genealogical help and discussions (Keyword: **Roots**).

Genealogy/Family History area

An AOL forum developed by Ancestry.com.

global search

A search of an entire Web site or resource for a particular word or term.

H

Helm Online Family Tree Research Cycle

A five-phase research model that explains the ongoing process of genealogical research.

historical research

Researching your genealogy to find out how historical events affected your ancestors.

HTML

Stands for HyperText Markup Language, a code in which text documents are written so Web browsers can read and interpret those documents.

HTML editor

A program that helps you write HTML by inserting the tags for you.

hyperlink

On-screen text that you can click to jump to another area in AOL, a Web site, or another Internet resource; also called a *link*.

I

immigration

The process by which a person moves from his or her native country to another in which he or she takes up residence.

immigration record

A record of a person's entry into a country of which he or she is not a native resident or naturalized citizen.

Internet

A collection of computer networks that are connected with *backbones* (high-speed data lines).

Internet service provider

An organization that gives people access to the Internet; also called an *ISP*.

K

keyword

A word that acts as a shortcut to an area within AOL (or to a Web site of one of AOL's partners).

L

land record

A document that shows the transfer of property from one person/entity to another; typically, land records include the original purchase of government land, applications for land patents, surveys, claims, sales of land, and grants of bounty lands for service in the military.

lineage

A group of people who descend from a common ancestor or progenitor.

link

On-screen text that you can click to jump to another area in AOL, a Web site, or another Internet resource; also called a *hyperlink*.

location research

To research details about the places your family members lived.

lurk

To monitor a mailing list for a little while without participating in order to learn the group's online customs, culture, and format for posting.

M

mailing list

An e-mail exchange forum consisting of people who share a common interest.

message board

A Web site where you can post questions to which others can respond at their convenience.

military record

A record reflecting military service —
including muster records, service records,
pension records, military census records,
unit rosters, cemetery records, regimental
histories, and casualty lists.

Modified Register system

The official numbering system used by the
National Genealogical Society for its
publications; also referred to as the National
Genealogical Society Quarterly (NGSQ)
system or Record system.

N

naturalization

The process by which a person becomes a
citizen or subject of a particular country
where he or she was not born.

naturalization record

A record proving a person is a naturalized
citizen of a specific country.

netiquette

Internet etiquette — good manners or
consideration of others as expressed on the
Internet.

newsletter

A letter-like publication that contains news
of interest to members of a particular
group of subscribers (for example,
branches of a particular family).

numbering system

A way of assigning a unique number to
each individual who appears in a report.

O

one-name study

A Web site that collects and stores any and
all information about a given surname,
regardless of the locations in which people
with that surname lived.

online

Getting access to the Internet; finding
information available through the Internet.

online database

A data storage file or program that is
accessible through the Internet.

online reunion

Generally a chat-session devoted to a
particular surname or family line.

P

pedigree chart

A chart that shows the direct ancestors of
an individual; also commonly referred to as
a family tree or an ancestor chart.

primary source

A source that is created or compiled at or
shortly after the time when an event
occurs; primary sources include
documents, photographs, tape recordings,
film, and oral accounts (if conducted right
after an event occurred).

progenitor

The farthest-back ancestor about whom
you have information in a family line.

R

Register system

The official numbering system used in the New England Historical and Genealogical Register, a publication of the New England Historic Genealogical Society.

report

A standard way of viewing genealogical data; often also called a chart.

research cycle

An idea of how to approach researching your family history.

research plan

A means for assessing what genealogical information you lack and ideas of where to look for it.

reunion

A gathering of people who have something in common.

S

secondary source

A record, a document, or another account that was created some time after the original event or by someone who was not actually present at the event.

shareware

Software marketed directly by its creator that you can test prior to purchasing it.

Soundex

An indexing system that groups together (under a particular code) those names that sound alike but are spelled differently. The code includes the letter that the name begins with, followed by three numbers determined by a formula.

source citation

Reference information about the resource you used to get a particular piece of information; documentation of your findings.

surname

A person's last name; generally, it's the family name passed down from one's father or taken from one's spouse.

surname research

To research all individuals of a certain surname regardless of their relationship to the researcher or where they were located geographically.

T

Tiny Tafel

A numbering system that is generated by genealogical software, which summarizes the facts (names, dates, and places of people you're researching) in your database.

template

A Web-based form in which you simply plug in information to create a Web page.

tertiary source

A work that points you to primary and secondary sources.

transcribed record

A record that has been copied (usually by a volunteer or researcher) from an original record. Transcribed records are often available on the Internet.

U

utility

A small program that performs specific, limited functions instead of trying to do multiple functions.

V

vital record

A record that is created during a landmark of a person's life, including birth, marriage, divorce, and death; also called a *civil registration*.

W

Web

Short term for the *World Wide Web*.

Web browser

Software that you use to see HTML documents on the Internet.

Web page

A document created in HTML, made available on the Internet, and accessible through the use of a *Web browser.*

Web site

One or more Web pages created by a person or organization; also called a *site*.

World Wide Web

A system for viewing and using documents on the Internet.

Index

Symbols & Numbers

A

Continued

Continued

Continued

NOTES

NOTES

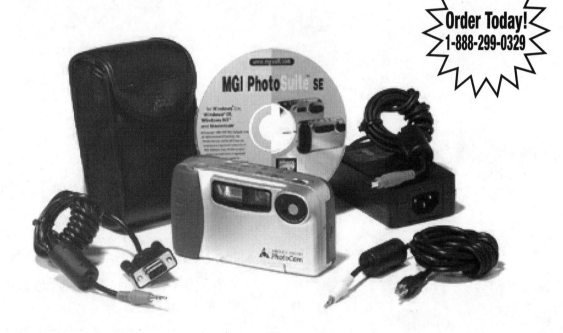

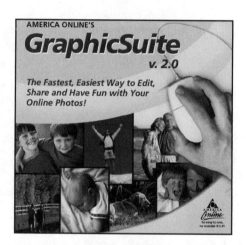

Share LIVE Videos with Friends and Family!

- Interact with friends over the Internet within minutes of installation
- Capture still images and short video clips
- Optimized for video conferencing
- Use it as a web cam, create time-lapse movies, e-mail images and more!
- Easy install

Intel PC Camera Pack

The Intel® PC Camera Pack is a high-quality camera plus our most popular software. There are lots of ways to be creative with the intel PC Camera Pack. Make video phone calls over your Internet connection or phone lines. Add excitement to your e-mail with video or snapshots recorded with your Intel PC Camera. Or, take a break with fun PC Camera games that put you in the middle of the action. You'll appreciate the many features that make this PC Camera an incredible value – and a lot of fun.

Single Camera $79.95 (s&h $7.95)
#0014369N00011838

Camera 2-pack $99.95
after $50 mfg. mail-in rebate (s&h $8.95)
#0014374N00012500

**Order Today!
1-888-299-0329**

AMERICA *Online*

*So easy to use,
no wonder it's #1*

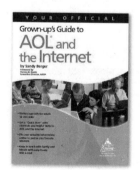

Your Official AOL Press Book Collection

Your Official America Online® Guide to Internet Living

America Online puts the world at your fingertips. But where do you go to plan your summer vacation? Or get a deal on your next automobile? Or find recipes for dinner tonight? This guide will show you the way. Packed with detailed directory information, it takes you to the best online address-es – from banking and job-hunting to hobbies and games – and shows you how AOL and the Internet can make your life easier every day.
$24.95 (s&h $4.95)   #0014384N00011906

Order Today!
1-888-299-0329

Your Official America Online® Guide to Creating Cool® Web Pages
2nd Edition

Find out just how easy it is to build your own personal Web page. As an AOL member, you're entitled to a FREE Web page. Web pages are a great way to post family news, promote your career, share personal inter-ests, and let your kids express themselves. And with AOL, creating Web pages is a cinch. This easy-to-understand guide explains how to use the AOL Web design tools – and shows you step-by-step how to put together a great-looking page with all the bells and whistles. And, once your page is done, you'll get the scoop on setting up a Web address in AOL Hometown – and spreading the word about your page.
$19.95 (s&h $4.95)   #0014385N00011904

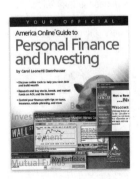

Your Official America Online® Guide to Personal Finance and Investing

America Online and the Internet are packed with personal finance tools. This indispensable guide shows you where they are and explains step-by-step how to make the most of them. Whether you want to set up a college fund, save for a home, or put money aside for your retirement, this guide shows you how AOL can help you make the right financial decisions and achieve your goals.
$19.95 (s&h $4.95)   #0014386N00011905

AMERICA Online®

*So easy to use,
no wonder it's #1*